Behind Fences
A Prison Chaplain's Story

BY NELSON AND ESTHER ZEISET

BEHIND FENCES
A PRISON CHAPLAIN'S STORY

by Nelson and Esther Zeiset
nzeiset@comcast.net

Copyright © 2021

Library of Congress Number: 2021938568

International Standard Book Number: 978-1-60126-737-5

ᴍasthof ᴘress
219 Mill Road | Morgantown, PA 19543-9516
www.Masthof.com

TABLE OF CONTENTS

INTRODUCTION

Even before my husband reached his teens, he aspired to go to prison. Other boys his age may have dreamed of becoming firemen or race car drivers, cattle ranchers, or big shots in some uppity corporation. Not Nelson. He wanted to go to prison, not as a career criminal, but as one who would come alongside those who were.

It was an odd ambition for a twelve-year-old, and several years passed before he would recognize it as a call from God. The conviction grew and took an unshakeable hold, yet Nelson held the calling to himself. To do otherwise would have seemed presumptuous in his traditional Mennonite culture. Yet from the time I met him, when he was a mere sixteen years old, and I was all of eighteen, it was apparent that God's plan held unique purposes for Nelson. And now, distanced by decades since our story began, its unlikeliness takes my breath away.

How is it that God would call a twelve-year-old boy from the isolated confines of Lancaster County, Pennsylvania, to a shadowy world behind prison fences, inhabited by criminals of all manner? Why would He entrust Nelson with the message of hope and redemption through Jesus for thousands of men who had lost their way?

Indeed, that is a question for every follower of Jesus. What is the specific purpose to which God has called you? Why has He placed you here, at this time in history, and for what purpose has He uniquely gifted you? Mark Twain is credited with saying, "The two most important days in your life are the day you were born and the day you find out why."

You had nothing to do with the day of your birth. It happened, and you had no say in the matter, but nonetheless, the date has tremendous importance for you. The "why" is infinitely more monumental. It is your life calling. It is what gives purpose and meaning to your existence.

First and foremost, God calls us to salvation. Although we are separated from Him by our sin and incapable of attaining to His standards, He provided a way back to Himself through Jesus. When we confess and repent of our sins, God is merciful and gracious to forgive (1 John 1:9).

The secondary calling is to live out our devotion to Jesus in our spheres of influence. You may be a truck driver, an electrician, a nurse, or an engineer. Maybe you're a busy stay-at-home mom. You could be a laborer—or maybe you've scrambled the heights of the corporate ladder. Secular work is intertwined with ministry. Nelson served in full-time prison "ministry" for thirty-three years, yet his calling was no more "spiritual" than yours.

When we pursue God's purposes, we *are* in ministry. Every one of us.

• • • • •

The process of writing about God's workings in our lives took much longer than I anticipated, and it has been both maddeningly frustrating and a joyous journey. The trials came in the form of carving out time, wrestling with words, and entering the frighteningly foreign world of publishing. The joys came in recalling God's hand at each milepost along the way. It is for that reason, I believe, that God repeatedly told the Israelites to remember. Remember His mighty works. Remember His strong arm. Remember His marvelous deeds. Remember His mercies.

This project stirred a profusion of remembrances. People, events, and conversations long forgotten resurfaced, and happenings that seemed inconsequential in the moment took on lasting significance. I'm so thankful for Nelson's faithful notes (albeit pitifully vague in spots) and for my own journals (decidedly more detailed, yet woefully sporadic). Those written records filled in where Nelson and I lacked memory and corrected my storytelling when memories proved faulty.

Exact conversations from years ago, of course, cannot be recalled, so I utilized dialogue to carry the story along in a manner that best represents them. I wrote the bulk of the narrative in Nelson's first-person voice, but occasionally you will see an italicized segment that tells the story from my point of view.

Writing one's life story can be risky business. Others may hold differing perspectives and interpretations of events I wrote about. I aimed for accuracy and truth in every instance, and where I failed, I ask your gracious forbearance.

Names of inmates and identifying characteristics were changed to protect their identities. In a few instances, however, I used actual first and last names because the details of their crimes are on public record. I refer to inmates in the masculine sense because Nelson interacted only with male inmates.

Writing this story renewed our appreciation for the many people who nurtured and supported us along the way. For our parents, who taught us of a loving God. For pastors and teachers who, from our earliest memories, urged us to pursue God and His purposes. For friends, whose encouragement overshadowed the naysayers. For those who gave generously from their hard-earned paychecks so that Nelson could "volunteer." For those who offered services such as mechanical, home maintenance, or babysitting when we lacked the know-how, time, and energy. For those who, like "John the Plumber" (as our children knew him), pledged daily intercession. And for the core group of Christian brothers at Mahanoy State Correctional Institution who assured us frequently that we held the prize for the "most prayed-for family anywhere."

We are humbled as we contemplate God's mandate for ministry. During the writing process, a Facebook meme occasionally showed up in my feed that said, "When God called you, He already factored in stupidity."

That is the truth.

Abraham lied. Moses lashed out in anger. Jonah ran away. Elijah pouted. Job argued against God. Peter spoke and acted impulsively. Thomas doubted. God certainly knew the depths of their deficiencies, yet He tasked them with a specific calling. When God called Nelson to prison ministry and me to a supportive role, He knew us in and out—and yet He called. How astounding that He would entrust mere mortals to propagate the greatest message ever told—the Good News that mankind can be reconciled to God through Jesus Christ!

This writing project strengthened our faith in a sovereign God, for in remembering, we see His hand moving in astounding ways. And if He worked so wondrously in the past, then we can surely trust Him with whatever will come in the future.

We pray that this book will motivate you to contemplate God's purposes for your life, and that you will follow His specific call. Wherever you are on your journey—whether only a few steps in, or nearer to the end—step back to view and to remember God's marvelous workings. May your faith abound in remembering His faithfulness.

-Esther Zeiset

CHAPTER ONE

The Call

Stale air hung in the crowded foyer at Martindale Mennonite Church on a Sunday night in November of 1973 where a crush of people waited to be seated in the sanctuary. An usher wove among them, lugging an armload of wooden folding chairs. He stopped abruptly by my dad and leaned in to whisper.

Dad nodded and motioned for us boys to follow him down the stairs, across the full length of the basement, and up another set of stairs. Dad gripped the railing and heaved himself up each step until we reached the landing that brought us to the front of the sanctuary, right into the "amen corner," an overflow area normally reserved for solemn-faced ministers. I felt hundreds of eyes fasten on our parade. My father, bearing the result of a birth injury, hobbled with a distinct rise and fall of each labored step until we reached a pew where an usher rested his hand. He nodded a silent greeting as we slid past him and settled onto the bench.

Wedged shoulder-to-shoulder on the pew, I tugged at the sleeve of my suit coat, so hot and stuffy and conspicuous. So far I had been unable to convince Dad to let me wear a dress shirt and sweater vest to church like other seventh-grade boys.

My older brother, Nevin, seemed unwilling to join my persuasive efforts. "I don't know what the big deal is about wearing a suit coat," he'd said a few weeks earlier. "Not unless . . ." He stopped mid-sentence and eyed me with a widening grin. "Do you like a girl or something?"

Girls weren't so bad. But these outdated suits—where did my mother get them, anyway?

1

"A suit coat shows proper respect for God's house," said Dad.

So that was that.

Dad's sense of respect also outlawed talking in church. Nevin and I, and even three-year-old Marlin, had learned a long time ago that so much as a whisper swiftly netted Dad's stern look and a firm pinch on the knee.

There was no margin for misbehavior on that November night at Martindale church. Not there, where the amen benches sat at a right angle to those in the main sanctuary, making our every move visible to the crowd. Not there, hemmed in among old men and ministers in their dark Sunday suits, and so near the pulpit that it seemed we might be in the holy of holies.

"We need to go early if we want a good seat," Dad had said at Sunday dinner. "You know how Martin Weber draws crowds."

Good seat all right, I thought. Smack dab in the preachers' amen corner.

Ushers hurried about, shoehorning people onto the pews and setting folding chairs in the center aisle to accommodate the growing crowd. Mothers shushed their crying babies. Just when it seemed the reverential pre-service hush would collapse under restless anticipation, a chorister stepped to the podium and announced a song selection. I glanced at my watch, my parents' gift to me for my twelfth birthday. It was still eight minutes until the service would begin, but the packed-out crowd warranted an earlier start and gave occasion for we Mennonites to engage in the a cappella singing we relished.

Lusty four-part harmony swelled as the song leader beat out the timing with his right arm—down, left, right, a dramatic upswing, and down again. I sang along with the familiar hymn, although not too loudly, for I suddenly felt self-conscious of my inability to mimic the deep bass behind me.

Across the main aisle, in the women's section, a few gray-haired women fanned themselves. I scanned the sea of faces, looking for Mother and my three sisters. They had probably been seated in the back somewhere. Here and there, some younger families sat together, but most of the congregation still practiced an established tradition of separated seating—boys with their fathers, babies and girls with their mothers.

Martindale Mennonite Church nestled itself among cornfields between Hinkletown and Terre Hill, Pennsylvania, and was one of eight congregations in the Weaverland District of the Lancaster Mennonite Conference. Bishops J. Paul Graybill and John E. Hollinger fought an uphill battle against progressive trends that encroached on more progressive congregations in the conference's twenty-seven districts. In the Weaverland District, however, ordained ministers and deacons still wore distinctive Mennonite attire—a white shirt peeking from a clerical-type collar of a "plain suit." Neckties were forbidden. Ministers' wives wore cape dresses that incorporated an additional bodice for modesty's sake and large head coverings.

My family often attended Sunday evening services at neighboring churches, and the size of the crowd at Martindale that November night confirmed that many other families did the same. Martin Weber, an evangelist and prison chaplain, preached fiery sermons and captivated his audience by peppering his sermons with stories about his work behind bars. More than a decade earlier, he and his wife, Anna, uprooted their family from Lancaster County and moved to southern Alabama. There he volunteered at Atmore State Prison Farm and was subsequently hired as a state prison chaplain.

When Martin stepped behind the pulpit that night, I was stunned by his height and his authoritative bearing. Sitting there on the amen bench, I got an unobstructed view of his full profile, from the top of his graying shock of hair to the tips of his shiny black shoes.

I'd stood behind a pulpit once, while tagging along with Grandma Beyer, a janitor at Hammer Creek Mennonite Church. While Grandma dusted and swept, I wandered into the auditorium, meandered among the empty pews, and hesitantly climbed the wooden steps to the pulpit, that sacred place from which preachers delivered God's message. I stretched up on my tiptoes, looked out over the vacant pews, and wondered how a preacher might feel when he stands to address a congregation.

Martin Weber didn't seem the least bit scared or nervous. He held his Bible aloft in one hand and read a passage in a sure, strong voice. Then he lowered it onto the pulpit and spoke confidently of the power of God to transform hardened criminals into men seeking after God.

"I've met a lot of tough men in prison, but none as tough as Bill,"

Martin said. "He told me he didn't want to hear about God's love, and he threatened to kill me if I ever came by his cell door again!" Martin paused and scanned the audience. He turned to sweep his gaze across the mass of dark suits in the amen corner, and for just a second, fixed his eyes on me. I held my breath until he continued. "And I believed him! Bill was in jail for murder. He was the meanest, most hateful man I ever met, and I knew he would kill me if he had even the slightest chance!"

Chills ran up my back.

Martin picked up the story, telling how he went to the solitary confinement unit again the next week, just as he did every week, carrying his Bible and talking to men about Jesus. He felt Bill's eyes on him as he neared the man's cell. They flashed with wild rage. Suddenly Bill lunged toward his cell door, and just as quickly, he stopped as though frozen in place. "Beyond a shadow of a doubt," Martin declared, "I believe God himself stopped Bill. He would have killed me that day if he could have reached me!"

I leaned forward on the pew, listening to Martin's sermon with rapt attention. He went on to describe a prison cell—a concrete block room behind heavy metal bars, and barely big enough to contain a bed, a toilet, and a washbowl. I tried to conjure up a mental image of the cramped room but shook it aside as Martin explained how he established New Life Foundation in 1970 to provide training for volunteer chaplain assistants. It was patterned after other Mennonite church-sponsored Voluntary Service (VS) programs that served as alternatives to military service. Although the draft had ended, church leaders still encouraged young adults to voluntarily give a year or more of their time to extend practical service to a community in the name of Christ.

My heart pounded in my ears. I sat stock still, bewildered by a rousing of emotion similar to what I'd sensed a few months earlier from this moment.

"We're having revival meeting at church soon," Dad had said to Nevin and me, "and you boys are getting to an age when you might hear God speaking to you. I hope you will listen when He calls you."

God's call had been unmistakable at that revival service. Struck with the reality of my sinfulness and recognizing my need for a Savior, I had responded to Evangelist Frank Zeager's altar call and cried unashamedly when he led me through the sinner's prayer. Nevin also accepted Christ that night.

Dad's happiness matched my own. "You boys made the best decision of your lives tonight," he said. "Take time, every day, to read God's Word and to hear from Him."

Dad practiced what he preached. I often heard him shuffle into his study in the middle of the night to read scripture and pray before leaving for work. Whether at midnight or four o'clock in the morning, Dad always started his day with God.

Now, listening to Martin Weber, I wondered whether God was speaking to my pounding heart as He had on the night of my conversion. Was He calling me to prison ministry? How could it be that God would lead a twelve-year-old Mennonite boy wearing a stuffy, outdated suit coat into such a venture?

I lay in bed that night, deep in thought and unsure of what stirred within me. It would be several years before I spoke of my calling to anyone, but from that November night in 1973, I held the stirring close to my own heart and planned my life in preparation for God's further direction.

Initially I may have held some childish ambition, perhaps like a child wanting to be a policeman or a fireman. But the call never left me. It never waned, and only intensified at family reunions when I edged close to my great-uncle, Earl Wissler, to hear stories about his ministry at Lancaster County Prison.

When I was barely into my teens, I eagerly joined a group from church who traveled two hours to hold a service at Jim Thorpe Jail, a cavernous and foreboding stone building in Pennsylvania's coal region. And later still, I relished opportunities to talk with Willis Burkholder, who succeeded Earl Wissler at the Lancaster prison, and spoke passionately of his work among inmates. Each experience and conversation solidified my conviction that God was calling me to prison ministry.

But how, and when?

First and foremost, God calls us to salvation. We all sin against Him and can never attain to His standards, but the good news is that He has provided a way back to Himself through Jesus. When we confess and repent of our sins, He is merciful and gracious to forgive (1 John 1:9).

Secondly, He has a call, or specific life purpose, for each of His children. No matter your age or profession—a student, a mother of toddlers, a plumber, a construction worker, a dentist, a retiree—God uniquely equips you to bless others and to honor Him through your call. How will you pursue your call today?

CHAPTER TWO

Lancaster County Boy

It would have taken an event of monumental significance like, say, the bubonic plague, to keep my family from going to church. On Sunday mornings, we went to our home congregation at Churchtown Mennonite Church, and in the evenings, to services within the Martindale District or in a neighboring Mennonite district. Church was the hub of our lives. "As long as church doors are open, it is our privilege to go," Dad said.

In November, 1970, my father was ordained as deacon at Churchtown, one of the smaller congregations within the Martindale District. His unpaid role was considered a life-long charge of responsibility for the financial aspects of the church and its members.

At home, finances seemed to be chronically tight. Nevin was the oldest in our family, and I was born nineteen months later, on September 7, 1961. Arlene, Elaine, and Joanne arrived in successive two-year intervals, and Marlin brought up the tail end, making a neat count of three boys and three girls in the Ellis and Lois Zeiset family.

Sometimes I overheard my parents talking about how to stretch Dad's paycheck to pay for his frequent chiropractor visits and to buy Wolverine shoes, the higher end of men's shoes offered at Weaver's Store in Fivepointville. At the time, my parents believed polio had caused my father's pronounced limp. His leg muscles contracted tightly so that he walked on his tiptoes and dragged his feet. Chiropractic treatments and a sturdy pair of shoes provided a measure of comfort, but in a short time, his shoe tips wore through. Mom, eyeing his tattered shoes and appraising her children's growth spurts, would pinch her face with worry and say, "If we keep spending money like we are, we'll end up in the poorhouse!"

It would be several years before my parents learned that Dad had cerebral palsy, the result of an injury at birth. On December 14, 1937, my grandmother, Charlotte Zeiset, struggled to deliver her first-born—premature twins, as it turned out. Clayton, her husband of almost a year, summoned the doctor from a Christmas party, and he arrived with alcohol on his breath and intentions of getting back to the festivities sooner rather than later. Clayton's protests against the doctor's impatient use of forceps went unheeded.

The damage showed itself when Dad was in elementary school, and his condition steadily deteriorated over the years.

"You may as well plan to be in a wheelchair by the time you're forty," a doctor told Dad.

His twin brother, Earl, fared much worse. Stiff and contorted limbs prevented him from sitting or walking, and his neck bent at an angle that shoved his face upward, his mouth perpetually open to emit garbled sounds understood by only his family. In spite of his severe disability (or maybe because of it), Earl endeared himself to his parents and twelve younger siblings who doted on him for the extent of his thirty-seven years.

Dad, like Earl, inherited his mother's good humor, and in spite of ongoing deterioration, he refused to give in to self-pity. "There's nothing I can do to change it. It's just the way it is," he said. But he fought against his doctor's prediction of becoming wheelchair-bound at a young age.

There were times I wished my dad could play ball with me like other fathers did. Or hike, or take a bike ride. But Dad had something few of my friends' fathers had. He drove a green and white Marmon cab-over truck to haul farm equipment for EZ Manufacturing into neighboring states, and when I climbed into the cab to make delivery runs with Dad, I felt like I was on top of the world.

My mother was born on January 12, 1937, the fourth of Russell and Mary Beyer's nine children. Her parents still grieved the loss of their one-year-old son, John, who had died of pneumonia the previous March. Grief visited again in 1946, when Arlene, also one year old, died of measles.[1]

From early childhood, sorrow seemed to stalk Grandpa Beyer. He was six years old in October, 1913, when his father died of a heart attack and left behind a destitute wife and seven young children. In those days before Social Security and welfare programs, my great-grandmother had no choice but to give up her children to foster care.[2]

Grandpa ended up at Millersville Children's Home. Other children found foster and adoptive homes, but no one seemed interested in my grandfather. In time he would learn that his red hair, the cause of much teasing from the children, was also the reason prospective parents rejected him. No one wanted a "carrot top." Nearly two long years passed before Henry and Anna Mary Benner took Russell into their Christian home on January 1, 1916. He remained with them until his marriage to Mary Wissler in 1930.[3]

Grandpa Beyer's solemnity governed his family, and my mother grew up in a household much more subdued than the Zeiset family, which thrived on noisy bantering and mischievous teasing.

My parents held the conservative Mennonite tenets of their upbringing in high regard, but taught us that salvation is found, not in tradition, but in Jesus alone. I will always be grateful for their authentic faith, for they were the same people at home as at church.

Early in 1974, Martin Weber came back into our area again. I willingly shrugged into my suit coat, if that's what it took, and climbed into the family station wagon to go hear him preach. He spoke of a need for inmates to have their own Bibles. My heart hammered in my chest. I had been feeding my savings account at Blue Ball Bank from my Grit paper route earnings—

---

[1] Anna W. (Beyer) Gehman, *Russell R. Beyer Family History* (2000), p. 16.

[2] Ibid., p. 7.

[3] Ibid., p. 11.

for what, I wasn't sure—a car maybe, or a house. But that would be years from now. I could do something now!

I couldn't wait to ask Dad for permission to draw from my savings to send a Bible to an inmate. The details of how I got an inmate's address from Martin Weber are lost to history, but I remember that Nevin and I pooled our money for Johnny's Bible, and we wrote him a letter, telling him about our family and about our paper routes.

In May 1974, we received a letter postmarked from Atmore, Alabama, and addressed to "Masters Nevin and Nelson Zeiset." *Masters*? I had never heard the term, but thought it sounded rather dignified, and eagerly slit open the envelope to read Johnny's two-page letter.

"I will cherish this Bible as long as I live. Your names I will write in the very front," Johnny wrote. He seemed especially pleased that his name had been engraved in gold on the front cover. His letter urged us to listen to our parents and to keep going to church so that we would not end up in prison as he had. Then he assured us of his prayers and signed off as "your brother in Christ."

I immediately dashed a letter back to Johnny along with my school photo and told him of trips in the truck with my father. In subsequent letters, I wrote about my seventh-grade class at Gehmans Mennonite School, about riding our pony, and how I broke my arm in a bike accident—the stuff of a preteen boy awakening to the reality of a world beyond Lancaster County.

Until I was eleven years old, we lived on the west side of Martindale, an upcropping of houses punctuated by three stop signs. The town crammed a lot of industry along its few streets: Eby's General Store, Ray's Plumbing, a hardware store, a sewing factory, the volunteer fire station, and a farm machinery dealership. Our rented two-story house stood a short distance from the cavernous hole at Burkholder's Quarry, where clacking stone crushers disgorged limestone dust that seriously vexed my mother's housekeeping ideals.

Nevin and I spent hours building dams and catching minnows in a small stream within a stone's throw of our house. A greater adventure lay across the road and beyond a meadow dotted with cow poop. There the Conestoga Creek rippled and beckoned a motley barefoot gang of neighborhood boys on lazy summer afternoons.

We boys were only vaguely aware of our cultural differences, and were quite content to let our fathers and preachers work them out. We had fish to catch. Marvin and Ammon wore straw hats and suspenders and easily lapsed into speaking Pennsylvania Dutch, forgetting or maybe not caring that Nevin and I couldn't understand much of what they said. They were of the Groffdale Mennonite Conference, also named "Joe Wengers" after their church founder, and drove horse-drawn black buggies. The women wore net head coverings and long dresses bunched at the waist with pleats or gathers. Wenger men often wore plaid shirts on weekdays, but on Sundays they wore white shirts and black suits to their church services in the white frame building up the street.

I grew up in a conservative streak of the Lancaster Conference Mennonite Church. Even in the summertime, we boys wore long pants, and my sisters wore dresses. Unlike the Wengers, our family drove a car, and our church held Sunday School. We also had a radio. Dad got an earful of static along with the news from Philadelphia's KYW station, and Mom preferred listening to Christian music on WDAC. On Saturday mornings, we kids crowded around the radio to hear Ranger Bill episodes. For thirty minutes we had Mom's approval to exchange cleaning chores for breathtaking suspense as the Warrior of the Woodlands battled raging forest fires, floods, rattlesnakes, and mountain lions.

Radio waves also featured weekday preachers that one had to be careful about, said some of the preachers that I listened to on Sunday mornings. They warned that those radio preachers were liable to put odd thoughts into your head and whack your theology off-kilter.

Leslie, an older neighbor boy who came from a more progressive Mennonite family, sometimes joined us at the creek. I figured his family may have listened to those radio preachers. They probably had television, too. Maybe that's where he learned that Richard M. Nixon was nominated the Republican Party's candidate for the presidency. When Leslie dumped that bit of trivia on me, I was both awed at his worldly wisdom and a bit mystified as to why it should matter.

It apparently mattered to an older girl who rode on my school bus, for she wrote Nixon's name on a foggy bus window with her finger. I was puzzled. Her family belonged to the Weaverland Conference Church, also known as Horning Mennonites, and nicknamed "Black Bumper" because of their practice of painting their cars black—chrome accessories and all. Her church, like mine, steered clear of politics. I might have expected such political leanings from "town kids," a term we ascribed to worldly kids who used bad language, wore shorts, and listened to rock and roll.

There weren't many town kids in my neighborhood. Of twenty-seven classmates in my second-grade class at Hinkletown Elementary School (a public school which has since become a Mennonite school), at least twenty-one were of some strain of Mennonite upbringing, and nearly half of them from the conservative Wenger group. Martindale was a safe, isolated, and insular community.

In 1972, when I was eleven years old, we built a house on a lot purchased from Mennonite Bishop J. Paul Graybill along Weaverland Road, near Goodville. Here too, most of our neighbors were farmers of the Wenger group or of a conservative branch of Mennonite.

From his jail cell in Alabama, Johnny could not have fathomed my life. We were worlds apart geographically and philosophically and separated by age and background, yet Johnny and I wrote regularly. He told of accompanying Chaplain Weber to area churches where he shared his testimony, and he urged Nevin and me to do our best in school and to memorize scripture. I stashed his letters into a shoe box and tucked it under my bed. After eighteen months of writing, Johnny's letters suddenly stopped. Years later, I learned he drowned in a prison farm pond accident just prior to his release.

By the time I reached ninth grade I had a growing sense that God might be calling me, not only to prison ministry, but perhaps to be a preacher. I purposed to prepare by going to Rosedale Bible Institute (RBI), a Mennonite school in central Ohio. I was fourteen or fifteen, so it would be several years before I could attend, but I obtained a school catalog and spent hours poring over course selections and reading the school handbook. There I learned that the school encouraged students to have a vital devotional experience by spending an hour a day in the Word. I adopted the practice for myself and incorporated a Bible memory program, figuring there was no better time than the present to become familiar with the scriptures.

I knew, however, that my parents could not afford to send me to Rosedale, so I squirreled away my money. About that time, Nevin turned seventeen and started looking around for a car.

"You don't need to buy your own if you're satisfied to drive my vehicles," Dad told him.

But Nevin had his eye on a green 1975 Dodge Dart Sport with a Slant-6 engine.

I decided that buying a car was a waste of money and determined to make myself happy with Dad's car. I would save up for Bible School instead. Although I took some teasing for it, I didn't buy my own car until several years after I was married.

Classes at Gehmans Mennonite School extended only through ninth grade. From there some of my classmates transferred to Mennonite high schools, and a few went to public school. Others, like me, left school and got full-time jobs. My parents subscribed to the conservative Mennonite philosophy that cast a suspicious eye at the worldly influence public high school might have on us.

My father had recently quit trucking and established EZ Bulk Foods which sold nuts, dried fruit, and baking products at several farmers' markets. Dad needed my help, so while my peers wrestled with trigonometry and chemistry, I gained work experience in various facets of the business.

In September 1977, soon after my sixteenth birthday, I talked Nevin into joining the Singing Servants Chorus with me. It was one of several Mennonite choruses in or near Lancaster County that simultaneously provided a social outlet and an opportunity for ministering through programs at churches. There were no auditions. The only requirements were an interest in singing and a commitment to active participation in programs.

Every Friday night my brother and I carpooled with others from our area and drove north into neighboring Lebanon County to Krall Mennonite Church where about fifty people gathered for chorus practice. They were mostly from Mennonite and Church of the Brethren backgrounds and primarily in their teens and early twenties.

One evening I leaned against a church pew talking with several new friends in the minutes before practice started. That's when I saw her—a tall, slender brunette wearing a red and white polka-dotted dress. She breezed in and seated herself in the alto section, but she may as well have walloped me up the side of the head, because the impact could not have been greater.

I made it my business to learn all I could about Esther Allgyer, and liked what I saw and heard. Several weeks later, in preparation for our first program, the chorus directors arranged the members on risers, me on the third step, and Esther directly on my left. Surely God was on my side!

In the spring of 1978, the chorus director announced the forming of the first Singing Servant Gospel Team. The fourteen-member team would travel to Atmore, Alabama, to sing at the prison where Martin Weber served as chaplain and at churches along the way. I eagerly volunteered for the opportunity to see firsthand the ministry that occupied my thoughts. An additional bonus was that Esther also signed up, and because of extra practice sessions, I saw a lot of her.

We sang at churches every day of the week-long tour in June. As we approached Atmore, Alabama, I scoped out the area from the van window, contemplating God's plans. Would I someday make this area my home, I wondered. Would I live in this community and minister at the prison?

After a program at Freemanville Mennonite Church, just outside of Atmore, I was thrilled to learn that my overnight hosts were Mary Jane and Calvin Schrock, Martin Weber's daughter and son-in-law. I'm sure I peppered them with endless questions about Martin's prison ministry.

The next day the Gospel Team drove to G. K. Fountain Prison where Chaplain Weber served. My excitement ran high. At last I could see the prison that I'd only imagined for nearly five years. We were escorted through a side gate and into the small white concrete-block chapel. It seemed that in no time the program ended and we were ushered out again, with little opportunity to talk with inmates or to see the rest of the prison.

My disappointment was tempered only by opportunities to spend time with Esther that week. Increasingly, I hoped she had at least as much inter-est in me as I had in her.

> **No matter your age, prepare for God's call for your life. Identify His unique purposes for you. Think about it. Pray about it. Learn about it. What steps can you take—today—to fulfill His plan?**

CHAPTER THREE
Love in Bloom

ESTHER'S STORY:

At one of the first *Singing Servants Chorus* practices in the fall of 1977, a girlfriend and I whispered about the boys seated across the aisle. "What do you think?" she asked.

I shrugged. "I'm not seeing many possibilities."

Nelson wasn't on my radar until several months later when the directors arranged our placement on the risers, and I stood beside him. Several times that evening, he tapped my shoe with his to indicate I should sing louder. "Beautiful!" he said. I couldn't decide whether he was flattering or obnoxious.

In January 1978, during free time on a weekend chorus tour to Maryland, I saw a group of girls gathered around Nelson. As I approached, a girl exclaimed, "You've got to be more than sixteen years old!"

Nelson grinned, shook his head, and pulled his driver's license from his wallet. "See for yourself," he said.

Several girls crowded in close to examine his license. "Nuh-uh!" one laughed. "This is your old license!"

"Check the date," Nelson said.

The girls huddled close and passed the document among themselves. I got the distinct impression they were disappointed that Nelson was several years their junior. Truth be told, I had a similar tinge of disappointment but soon discovered I could enjoy a platonic relationship with him. I told myself that, given our age difference, no one—not me, not him, nor anyone else—would read anything into the friendship.

I was fascinated by Nelson's ability to veer from teasing and bantering into philosophical and theological discussions. He knew what he believed and why he believed it. He knew where he was going in life. But, I kept telling myself, he was only like a little brother and nothing more.

Halfway through the summer Gospel Team tour to Alabama my friend, Shirley, told me Nelson was interested in me.

"You can't be serious!" I protested. "He's only sixteen! I'm nineteen!"

"Does that matter?" she asked.

"Well, it might. Anyway, I can't believe he likes me."

"And I can't believe you don't see it," Shirley said. "He's so obvious about it!"

Over time, I allowed myself to see what Shirley saw and realized I had suppressed my growing interest in Nelson. That's when things got awkward. (Nelson will argue that was when I started playing hard to get.)

Whatever.

I knew the rule in Nelson's family was that he couldn't date until he was seventeen, and I anticipated that he would ask me out by his birthday on the first weekend in September 1978. But the weekend came and went. He didn't ask for a date, and gave no indication of doing so anytime soon. I was utterly confused!

It seemed Nelson waited for a yunge avichkeit—*my parents' Dutch expression, literally meaning a "young eternity"—to ask me out. In reality, he dilly-dallied only two weeks beyond his birthday, but it seemed like forever. (In time Nelson explained his delay: He didn't want to appear too eager, too over-the-top, and because he wanted to exercise some self-discipline.)*

Forty-some years later, I still fail to comprehend his reasoning, but again, whatever.

I wasn't surprised that Nelson showed up for our first date in his parents' green 1977 Dodge van to take me to youth meetings at Meckville Mennonite Church. I knew that he chose to save for Bible School rather than sink his money into a car. Vestiges of the muscle car era persisted into my teens, but I never understood my girlfriends' infatuation with loud mufflers and wide tires. It just wasn't in my DNA. I knew what I wanted in a man, and his choice of wheels had little to do with it. Still, Nelson and I were both glad when his parents bought a 1978 Dodge Colt later that fall, and it became "Nelson's car."

I soon realized I dated a very principled man. Because of his age, Nelson thought we should date only once a week for a full year. And at every date, he left my house at precisely seventeen minutes after eleven o'clock to meet his midnight curfew. He carried this kind of structure into other areas of his life, notably that of planning for his educational future.

Rosedale Bible Institute required students to have a high school diploma, but I had quit school after ninth grade. In what would have been my senior year I began working to obtain my GED but was not permitted to take my test until my class graduated. I applied to RBI anyway, and they graciously accepted me for the April/May term in 1979. I earned my GED diploma later that summer.

Early in my time at Rosedale I realized how little I knew of God and the Bible and purposed to utilize the extravagance of resources in the school library. It held so many books, and I had so little time! I shunned the opportunity for playing volleyball in the evenings and sequestered myself in the library. My lack of evening social interaction stemmed from two additional factors: First, I wasn't good at sports, and second, I relished the quiet library setting both for reading books and for writing daily letters to Esther.

I finished my term at Rosedale with a thirst for more Bible knowledge. Determined to go back, I picked up three jobs to earn additional money—two days a week for Dad's market business, four days at Blue Ball Garage, and two nights at Terre Hill Concrete plant. I set aside every penny.

Later in 1979 and 1980, I returned to Rosedale for two more terms and also attended a term at Sharon Mennonite Bible School, in western

Pennsylvania. I threw aside my tightwad tendencies only at gas pumps so I could make frequent trips home to see the girl I had fallen in love with.

While Nelson studied at RBI, he and I alternated in making the four-hundred-mile trip to see each other. Early in 1980, my parents invited me to join them and my younger sister, Nancy, on a trip to Florida in their motorhome. To sweeten the deal, Dad promised we'd swing up to Rosedale to see Nelson before going home.

Dad's lure drew me in. But first came the trip to Florida.

At Disney World, Dad and I nearly spilled our weak stomachs in an IMAX theater, and grew even sicker when Mom begged to ride on the Space Mountain roller coaster.

Then we were off to Sarasota, the wintering place of Amish and Mennonites, where I snapped photos of Uncle Isaac, dressed in black broadfall pants and suspenders, and Aunt Leah, wearing a long dress with a matching apron. Both of them held beards of Spanish moss to their chins and giggled like school children.

Further into the trip, at a Long John Silver's restaurant by the side of a Florida highway, Nancy and I were mortified that our parents—otherwise well-adjusted, respectable middle-aged folks—cozied up in the booth to steal a kiss.

At long last, the Florida trip drew to an end and we turned northward. But Dad wanted to make one last stop. His dream of building a grandfather clock lured him to a clock factory in Fairhope, Alabama, on the east side of Mobile Bay. "I'll make it short and sweet," he said with a grin. "And then we'll head to Ohio so you can see your sweetie."

He and Mom were enchanted with the factory. I was bored and impatient to get on the road. After an hour or so, I wandered outside to the motorhome and paged through the road atlas, tracing our route north. With a start I realized that we would drive by Atmore, Alabama, home of Chaplain Weber's New Life Foundation, and the object of Nelson's interest. I didn't know what to make of Nelson's attention to the prison ministry, nor what it would mean for us.

Finally, Dad got behind the driver's wheel, and we began the northward trek on Interstate 65. Nancy climbed into the bunk above the cab, and I retreated to the back of the motorhome, away from my parents' chatter and alone with my thoughts as we bounced—b-bump, b-bump, b-bump—across bridges spanning lonely Alabama swamplands. I read road signs, watching for the Atmore exit, and silently praying for guidance. My heart pounded in my ears as we passed the nondescript exit. There wasn't much to see. Just some spin-dly pine trees and a country road that stretched to nowhere in either direction. "God," I prayed, "is this area in Your plan for me?"

I would not choose this for myself.

My plans for the future were simple, if not naive. I envisioned a loving husband (would it be Nelson?) who worked an eight-to-five job and came home cheered by my gourmet meals in a perfectly neat home behind a white picket fence. We would have darling children, all of them well-behaved and neatly scrubbed, of course, and life would be all sunshine and roses.

Nelson's plans seemed unsettled, tenuous, and outside the norm. How would this work?

Tears streamed down my cheeks as I continued praying. "God, I want to follow as You lead! Show me! What is Your will? Where do You want me? Is it here, in Atmore? Oh, if only You would write it in the clouds, Lord!"

My own will stormed about on that drive through southern Ala-bama, yet my heart desired full surrender to God's will. The miles dragged on and the internal battle raged strong. If only I could make some sense of God's plan for my life!

By the end of my time at Rosedale, Esther and I had been dating for eighteen months, and we had talked of my sense of call to ministry on sev-eral occasions. When she visited me in the spring of 1980, I felt an urgency to be clear about my intentions. Although we had not yet discussed mar-riage, the path seemed clear to me. I wanted to marry her but needed to be sure she understood the call to ministry I felt God had placed on me. I knew we could not continue dating if she were not in agreement. It nearly tore me up to even think of that possibility.

Rosedale had strict measures in place regarding the amount of time dating couples could spend together while on campus, but I followed their protocol and obtained permission for us to have a private conversation in the balcony above the chapel. Taking her hand, I wasted little time in getting to the point, but my heart and mind and words were in such a jumbled mess that it all came out pell-mell and I said something like, "If you can't see yourself being a pastor's wife, or if you can't see yourself going to Alabama for VS, then we probably need to end our relationship."

Then I held my breath and waited for her response. I could only hope and pray she wouldn't shatter my quaking heart into a million pieces.

Nelson didn't have to tell me about God's call to ministry on his life. It was written all over him! How many other sixteen- or seventeen-year-old boys taught an older men's Sunday School class, or got an invitation to speak at another church's prayer meeting, or organized door-to-door evangelism efforts at church? From the time I met him, I knew he would someday be a pastor. Others sensed it too and said so, sometimes with a tinge of mockery, sometimes in teasing, and sometimes half-joking, yet all serious. It was as though they didn't quite know what to do with God's call for ministry on a teenage boy.

In the Mennonite church—at least in our type at that time— preaching and pastoring were not goals to aspire to. Only a proud and presumptuous man would declare his call to ministry. When a congregation needed a pastor, they looked among themselves and nominated candidates who were put through extensive interviews to examine doctrine, finances, and relationships. Next came an ordination service in which solemn-faced candidates chose "the lot," a practice patterned after the account in the first chapter of Acts, when Matthias was chosen to take the place of Judas.

In a somber and suspenseful ordination service, books were lined up on the pulpit, one for each of the candidates. Only one book held a slip of paper, the charge to ministry. At the conclusion of a sermon, the candidates each chose a book and the ministerial charge was given to whomever possessed the slip of paper. Thus, the call to ministry was affirmed by the congregation and confirmed by God.

My father, Melvin Allgyer, was ordained as pastor at Schubert Mennonite Church (Berks County, PA) in 1973 when I was fourteen years old. His call did not surprise me in the least. From my earliest memories, my parents were involved in many areas of church life. Dad served capably as song leader, Sunday School teacher, and Vacation Bible School superintendent. When he and Mom were youth group leaders, they towed us kids along, giving me the opportunity to see Dad mentor young men in the tumultuous 1960s. My parents befriended a number of Mennonite couples on the fringes of the church as well as non-Mennonite friends. I listened with fascination as Dad engaged in lively conversations about faith with Catholic friends and shared the Gospel with a neighbor who argued he could escape the Rapture in a homemade spaceship that would miraculously take form on command.

When Dad was ordained, I had a front row seat to watch as he juggled the complexities of pastoring while holding down a full-time job and raising a family of six children. I knew something about the sacrifices necessary to prepare sermons, to deal with parishioners' emergencies and expectations, and of obligations to attend a slew of meetings. It was ministry. It was our life. It did not seem a hardship to potentially be married to a pastor. I understood something of that life.

But I was not sure what a VS term with New Life Foundation in Atmore, Alabama, would look like. I wasn't opposed to it, but I didn't know when or how it would happen. Nelson and I didn't talk directly about marriage. He was only eighteen. Would he leave for a year of VS while we were dating? Or did he intend for us to go as a married couple?

From the time Nelson led me into the balcony room over Rosedale's chapel, I sensed he carried a burdensome weight. Then came his questions. Could I imagine myself being a pastor's wife someday? Could I envision moving to Alabama?

I answered quickly, but not without forethought. Yes! Yes! A thousand times yes!

I restrained myself from such an exuberant verbal response. I knew this was not a marriage proposal, but simply a heartfelt need for clarification of where our relationship stood, and whether I would back Nelson up on what he felt was God's call for him.

I would.

Without hesitation.

What sacrifices will you need to make in order to follow through on God's purpose for your life? How might it affect your family members?

CHAPTER FOUR

Sorting Out the Call

On a moonlit night in June 1980, I proposed to my sweetheart, and she accepted without second thoughts. Esther was a month past her twenty-first birthday, and I was two months from turning nineteen, but we were buoyed by youthful optimism and excitement to dive into marriage and adult life. Many of our friends married young and we forged ahead too, eagerly counting the days until our Valentine's Day wedding.

I awoke on February 14, 1981, to a dusting of snow that melted quickly in unseasonably warm temperatures. This was the day I would publicly pledge my love to my sweetheart! We would vow a lifetime of trust and honor and walk the journey of life together, wherever God would lead us.

After a traditional wedding ceremony at Martindale Mennonite Church (a cappella singing, a small bride's bouquet, and an hour-long sermon) and a reception at New Holland Fire Hall, we meandered south toward Florida for our honeymoon.

At some point in planning our trip, I had asked Esther how she would feel about taking a wide swing westward to Atmore, Alabama, so I might try to visit the prison there. She readily agreed to give up part of a day from our twelve-day honeymoon.

My new bride and I took a leisurely four days to reach the Deep South. "Ahhh," I said as we climbed from the car at an Alabama Welcome Center along Interstate 85. "Warm sunshine! This is Alabama, Dearie!"

She gripped my hand tighter and flashed a smile. Inside the building, a cheerful attendant with a strong southern drawl welcomed us to Alabama with a cold glass of freshly-squeezed orange juice. As we stood there drinking it, a peculiar sense of belonging flooded me. I could make this place home, I thought.

The next morning, at a Days Inn in Evergreen, Alabama, I pulled a scrap of paper from my suitcase and dialed Calvin and Mary Jane Schrock's phone. I hoped they would remember me from the Gospel Team tour nearly three years earlier and that they could connect me with Mary Jane's father, Chaplain Martin Weber. They did—on both counts. The Schrocks and Webers extended the best of southern hospitality to us in the next hours. While Esther visited with Mary Jane, I rode to the prison with Martin Weber, awed at how everything had come together so seamlessly.

Since 1973, I had maintained contact with the New Life Foundation and supported it financially as I was able. In return, I received the ministry's newsletter, sometimes with a hand-scrawled note from Martin Weber or his associates.

In 1979, at my request, Chaplain Weber had provided the name of a death row inmate, and Chuck and I wrote for more than two years. Chuck told me his parents both died when he was fourteen years old and that he married young. He and his wife got in trouble with the law only a month after they got married. "They say we killed a man but Jesus knows we didn't," he wrote.

In time, Chuck's wife got off death row but his own appeal for resentencing dragged on and on. Then his wife split up with him, and Chuck sank into depression. Soon his letters consisted only of lengthy pleas for money and postage stamps. I mailed him thirty-some stamps, and shortly thereafter, he sent a six-page letter begging for more. My stamps, plus more, had been used to mail fifty letters to an impressive list of Christian leaders that included Billy Graham and Rex Humbard. Now Chuck wrote that all but one ignored his plea for money. "Tell me where the real Christian love is!" he challenged.

The demands increased. In his following letters, Chuck instructed me to send him a ten-dollar money order every month, but instead of using my own name and return address, I was to use his brother's. "I'm not running no con game to get money. I really do need the money," he wrote.

I didn't know what to make of Chuck's letters. I did not send him the money orders, nor the "name of a good Christian girl" to whom he could write to ease his loneliness. Like Billy Graham, I ignored Chuck's requests.

In Alabama, I hoped to talk with Chuck face to face. But as Chaplain Weber walked me through the prison gates and into his chapel office, he explained the visit was not possible because the prison was on lockdown stemming from an incident a day earlier.

Four inmates had climbed onto the roof under cover of thick morning fog, Martin said, and crawled to the edge by the fence. A tower guard spotted them before they jumped to their freedom.

As punishment, the warden sent them to work in the field under supervision of Sergeant Frank, a tough shotgun-toting officer. At lunchtime, instead of taking the prisoners to the mess hall as was customary, he handed bag lunches to them. Tensions mounted. One of the inmates threatened to run, and the other three inmates echoed the threat.

"You know I'll have to shoot if you run," Sergeant Frank warned.

"You ain't got the nerve. 'Sides, you couldn't shoot us all if you tried!" one inmate taunted.

The words were barely out of his mouth before one of the men took off running. The other three scattered. Sergeant Frank fired after them, taking one man down, and shouting for the others to stop. They surrendered.

"But one man's dead," Martin finished with a heavy sigh. The chaplain talked of deep despair within prison walls and of his desire to reach more inmates with the hope of the Gospel. "There's a great harvest within the walls of this prison," Martin gestured beyond his chapel office. "We need young men like you to help with the work."

I left the Atmore area with an even stronger sense of call to ministry with New Life Foundation. Esther and I talked about it as we drove into Florida to spend a delightful week as the new Mr. and Mrs.

All too soon it was time to take my bride back to Pennsylvania where we rented half a farmhouse near New Holland for $175.00 a month, including electricity.

We plunged into a variety of church activities and settled into our jobs, Esther at Shady Maple grocery store, and me at Paul B. Zimmerman's, a hardware store owned by a Horning Mennonite man and his six sons.

We frequently talked about moving to Atmore, Alabama, for a yearlong VS term. To further explore that possibility, I organized a trip to participate in a week of New Life Foundation's revivals in February, 1982. Esther was the only woman in the group. We towed our car behind the van so Esther and I could take a week-long anniversary vacation in Florida after the prison crusade ended.

New Life's primary work focused on G. K. Fountain Prison in Atmore, but had recently begun work in the Montgomery area, at both Frank Lee Youth Center and at Julia Tutwiler Prison, a female institution. I spent most of my time at Frank Lee, an all-male facility, with Chaplain John Mark Yoder. Esther attended several of the services, one of which was on our first wedding anniversary. She also visited Tutwiler Prison and participated in an evening service. Sometime during that week, we met with Martin Weber to further discuss the possibility of joining the New Life team.

At week's end Esther and I split from the group and headed to Florida, with plenty of driving time to process our impressions of New Life's work and our future with the organization. Shortly after we got back home, however, I sensed some resistance from Esther about making definite plans to move to Alabama. She felt pressured and frustrated by my pushing. I finally decided that if God wanted us in Alabama, He would need to speak to her about it. I promised to back off. "All I ask is that you pray about it and listen to what God may be saying," I told her.

And I waited.

I had been praying about moving to Alabama, for several years already, and I continued to pray. I tried to listen to God, but I wasn't hearing from Him. There were other voices and distractions. Adjustments in our first year of marriage were more difficult than I'd anticipated. My new job turned out differently from what I had been promised. There were new people, new expectations, and new pro-

cedures. At church there were new practices and new ways of doing things. At home, well . . . there was so much to learn.

My first lesson smacked me square in the face even before I unpacked our honeymoon suitcases. Two days before our wedding, I had purchased ten pounds of ground beef on sale, and in my pre-wedding haste, threw it all into the freezer. All clumped in one big bag. The act was part and parcel of my "it-will-all-work-out somehow" mentality.

But it wasn't working out.

I grunted and sweated and chipped away at the frozen clump with the tip of a new knife until the knife broke—and so did I. Nelson found me crying in the kitchen. When he got over the shock of my stupidity, he took me in his arms, soothed my ego, stoked my confidence, and helped me prepare dinner with an over-sized clump of frozen ground beef.

Although I'd moved only thirty-some miles from Berks to Lancaster County, it seemed worlds apart. Lancaster County in general, and New Holland in particular, is a mecca of the Plain Community, housing innumerable splits and splinters of Anabaptists. At the outset, I felt like I was going back to my Amish roots; I had Amish relatives and knew their Pennsylvania Dutch language well enough to carry a halting, though adequate conversation.

But I didn't know them as well as I thought. One afternoon, while driving through New Holland, I pointed at an Amish man riding a scooter along Main Street. "Look at that!" I said.

The man's straw hat bobbed as he pushed off on one leg, coasted a short distance, and pushed again. His purple shirt ballooned around the restraints of his black suspenders.

"What?" Nelson asked.

"He's riding a scooter!"

"Yeah . . . you never saw an Amish man riding a scooter?"

"Only for kicks and giggles. Never for transportation!"

I gaped after the man in astonishment as we passed by him. Nelson laughed. "Welcome to Lancaster County!"

This was a different world from the one I grew up in. On our drive to church on Sunday mornings we wove among buggies and bikes, and I often asked, "Tell me again, are those Wenger or Pike Mennonites?"

Nelson pointed out the subtle differences. "Pikers" drove windowless buggies and the women wore larger black bonnets than the Wengers did. About the time I thought I had it sorted out, Nelson threw more trivia into the mix, pointing out a group of Thirty-fivers.

"Huh? What's a Thirty-fiver?"

"Thirty-five families left the Wenger Church. It's a nickname. Officially they're called Reidenbach Mennonites."

Oh. I felt like a tourist on a different planet.

I was not quite two years old in 1961 when my parents, Melvin and Nancy Allgyer, moved to Lenhartsville, a small farming community north of Reading, in Berks County. My parents were twenty-five years old, married five years, and already had four children. Two more would follow.

Anna was born eleven months after my parents' wedding, and the rest of us arrived at the party in quick succession. Mike was a mere thirteen months old when I was born on May 19, 1959. Nineteen months later Mel Jr. came, then Jim, and nearly three years later, Nancy. Like Nelson's family, we were a family of three boys and three girls. We six Allgyer children were born within nine years. I never heard my mother complain about how close we were in age—more a testament to her positive outlook and can-do attitude, I think, than to our behavior.

I'm not sure why my parents made a sixty-mile move from Lancaster County to Lenhartsville. Was it because of their break from the Amish church and the resulting life-long shunning, or was it simply a location where they could purchase a dairy farm at an affordable price?

Our closest neighbors lived at least a quarter mile away, on the west side of our farm, but still close enough for the elderly Mrs. Hein-

ley to watch our goings-on through binoculars from her haymow, information she let slip to my mother in an unguarded moment several years after we moved into the neighborhood. Maybe she spied on us out of sheer nosiness. Maybe she found us six kids entertaining. Maybe she was driven by curiosity, wanting to learn about these Mennonites who had moved into an area largely populated by Lutherans of German stock.

We lived fifteen miles across winding back roads from Fredericksville Mennonite Church. My parents had come to faith in Christ only a year or two earlier, but they jumped into congregational life and willingly served wherever they were needed. Like Nelson's family, our life centered around church.

Late in the winter of 1970, Lancaster Countian evangelist Glen Sell held revival meetings at Fredericksville. The Holy Spirit convicted me of my sinfulness, but Satan countered persuasively. Nope, I decided, people wouldn't believe that a ten-year-old girl could understand salvation, and besides, neither of my older siblings had yet accepted Christ. If I made the decision before they did, they might call me a "goody two shoes." As I recall, my sister, Anna, responded on the last verse of the last invitational hymn, on the last night of the meetings. I sat rooted to the pew. If I went forward now, I might be called a copycat.

These were ridiculous arguments, all of them, but that's how Satan works. I felt miserable in the next months—terrified that I would miss out if Jesus returned, yet too stubborn to bare my tormented thoughts to my parents.

In August, Glen Sell came to our church again. When he issued an invitation, I couldn't get down the aisle fast enough to confess my sinful state and accept Jesus as my Lord.

In the next days I felt giddy with the lifting of the weight of sin, and when the pastor asked for testimonies at the next Sunday's service, I jumped up before giving a thought to it. "Jesus, Jesus!" I exclaimed as though shouting His lovely name from the rooftop. But suddenly I *felt like a million eyes were boring into me and I blurted, "He's . . . He's just so wonderful!"*

I blushed a thousand shades of red but never felt so good in doing it.

The day after my baptism, I wore a head covering to school. Only one other Mennonite family attended Hamburg Elementary School, so unlike Nelson, I had lots of friends among "town kids" and they fired questions at me.

"What's that hat for on your head?"

"Will you wear it all the time?"

"Do you like wearing it?"

I didn't mind the questions. I had heard my parents graciously answer such questions from perfect strangers—except for the one time that Dad deviated. In all fairness, the question was different. We were on a family trip to Plimoth Plantation in Massachusetts and had already gotten more than our fair share of stares. One little boy had pointed at us and yelled, "Mommy, look at the pilgrims!"

A little later a man approached Dad and said, "Excuse me, mind if I ask a question?" We all expected a question about my mother's "hat" but instead he asked, "Do you pronounce it 'A-mish' (with a long a) or 'A-mish' (with a short a)?"

"Neither," said Dad, his eyes sparkling with merriment. "It's pronounced 'Men-no-nite.'"

We kids thought our dad was the funniest man around.

In the fall of 1970, my parents sold the farm and dairy herd, and we moved to Bernville, in western Berks County, where Mennonites were better known. Still, I did not have the wide options for Christian education as I might have had in Lancaster County. I went to a public high school and interacted with many non-Mennonites.

I was in for a huge culture shock then, when Nelson and I married and moved to Lancaster County, forty-five minutes from my parents and siblings. In those days of expensive long-distance calls from the black rotary dial phone that hung on my kitchen wall, I missed my family. But the geographical distance was not the only distance. Something else stood between us, but I wasn't sure what, or why.

From where I stand now, it makes more sense. At our suggestion, my father preached our wedding sermon from Psalm 127:1: "Except the Lord build the house, they labor in vain that build it." Then he wandered to Proverbs 30:19 and seemed to be as mystified as the writer about four of life's complexities. "The way of a man with a maiden" seemed especially puzzling. My father spoke of how a woman will leave the security of her parental home for a man who she didn't even know existed only a few short years earlier.

I thought Dad was a bit overly sentimental. But perhaps the change hit him harder than I knew. Most parents feel a loss when their daughter transfers her love and loyalty to a young upstart. I understand that better now than I did then.

My parents' Amish upbringing placed little value on education and put a premium on a strong work ethic. Work, marry, and have children. In that order. And work, work, work. It was how they had grown up. It was what they subscribed to.

But Bible College and VS were new ideas for my parents, ideas that they had seen tried with little success. They were youth group advisors during the 1960s when young Mennonite men, citing religious objection to war, chose alternative programs like 1-W and Pax Service. Loosed from the moorings of family and church, too many young adults succumbed to the sexual revolution and drug culture. In addition, my parents carried their friends' heartbreak over a son's crumbling marriage, troubles that began while in VS. In my parents' minds, college and VS programs were suspect as avenues for infusing adventure into life while simultaneously delaying responsibility.

I knew my husband's heart and trusted it. My parents had not yet seen his heart so clearly, nor the consistency of a solid job history, patch-worked as it was while he paid his way through Bible college. And now, shortly after snagging a job at the hardware store, he spoke of leaving it for a year of voluntary service where we would each receive only $35.00 per month to cover incidental expenses.

My parents were not alone in their reservations. Later, when we chose to go into VS, one of Nelson's relatives emphatically declined contributing to our financial support by saying, "I'm not gonna pay for your year-long vacation!"

I felt torn between two philosophies, between supporting my husband's call and craving my parents' approval. Perhaps a further complication was learning how to work with Nelson's and my own personality differences. I am a people-pleaser and tend toward caution and operating within a safe framework of expectations and norms. Nelson is a leader, a visionary not easily inhibited by status quo and others' opinions. I am content to sit back and see how the way winds. Nelson is the type who builds the way, straight and level, no meandering. Further, he believes that if the way is to be built, there is no reason to delay its building.

Given time and mutual understanding, those seemingly incongruent philosophies can complement and balance quite nicely.

We were not there yet.

How do your unique personality traits lend to God's purposes? How do they hinder? If you are married, how do you work out those differences to mutually come to agreement of His call for you both?

CHAPTER FIVE

Pursuing the Call in Alabama

In spite of my best intentions, I fear I pressured Esther. I felt sure of God's plans for us and found it hard to be patient. After about six months, Esther told me she'd come to peace about moving to Alabama. I wanted to turn somersaults!

We felt it important to have our parents' blessings. Mine were favorable to the idea, and after snagging a somewhat reluctant blessing from Esther's parents, we applied to New Life Foundation. In October 1982, we received word of acceptance.

Three months later, early on the Monday morning of January 3, 1983, we left Lancaster County's farming community for southern Alabama. My parents drove their van and trailer stuffed with our possessions, and we followed in our 1976 Toyota Corolla. The seventeen-hour trip gave us plenty of time to reflect on how God had prepared the way before us.

I'm not sure what motivated me to agree to move to Alabama. God didn't favor me by writing His directive in the clouds, nor by giving me a dream or vision. But He did envelop me with a peace about moving a thousand miles away, and I shared Nelson's excitement about the move.

And then I learned I was pregnant.

God's timing didn't seem to make much sense. How would we furnish a nursery and pay maternity expenses on VS wages of only $35.00 per month? Who would help me through the mysteries of pregnancy and delivery or teach me to change diapers and burp the

*baby? Questions aside, we were ecstatic. And God already had the
details worked out.*

*A few days before leaving Pennsylvania, we went to People's
Bank in Lebanon to pick up a freshly-cut profit-sharing check from
Martin's Farm Market, my first employer. I had worked there for
more than five years and knew of the generous benefits. Still, we were
stunned at the amount—$8,215.01—equivalent to about eight
months' wages!*

*Equally stunning was a check I pulled from our mailbox a few
weeks before my pregnancy due date. Unknown to us, Singing Servants Chorus had raised funds that, combined with other gifts from
friends and relatives, completely covered my maternity and hospital
costs. God also arranged for grandparent substitutes in Joseph and
Martha Horst, our pastor and wife at Byrnville Mennonite Church.
That wasn't all. Their daughters, Noreen and Norma, became like
sisters to me and aunts to our son. That Christmas the Horsts, knowing how lonely our holidays would be, included us in their family
celebrations. After we moved back to Pennsylvania, our friendship
continued to span a thousand miles and nearly four decades.*

But we didn't know all of that yet.

*We moved into a mobile house trailer on a wooded lot owned by
New Life Foundation, and previously occupied by Elvin and Charlotte Ranck. But now, nearing the end of their VS term, the Rancks
graciously vacated it so we could have the privacy of our own home for
the entire length of our stay in Alabama. They moved next door to the
sprawling brick house known as "The Bridge," where Ken and Mary
Ann Burkholder served as houseparents. In earlier years, New Life had
operated a boys' home in the building; now it housed several families
and single men, some of whom had come to volunteer with New Life
for just a few months. A few, like us, intended to stay for a year.*

Within forty-five minutes of arriving at our Alabama home late on
Tuesday afternoon, my father and I joined a vanload of male staff going to

the evening service at the prison. I hadn't anticipated jumping into the work so suddenly, but it was an opportunity for my father to see the prison before he and Mom headed back home.

The next days were filled with unpacking, getting acquainted with the community, and going through New Life's orientation. The ministry was undergoing significant changes. After eighteen years of prison chaplaincy, Martin Weber had recently handed his responsibilities to Sam Mast, a pastor from South Carolina. This freed Chaplain Weber to devote his time and energies in developing We Care, a crime prevention program.[4] The two ministries would merge into one and be named the We Care Program by the end of 1983.[5]

During our first week in Alabama, about eighty volunteers arrived from twelve states to help with the annual week-long Atmore prison revival. They fanned out into the four Atmore prison camps to share the Gospel with more than 1,600 men.

This was my second year of joining New Life's revival effort. I rode the spiritual high that accompanies the activity of the week: earnest prayer with fellow volunteers, conversations with inmates, gathering into the crowded chapel each evening for spirited preaching and dynamic music, and leading inmates to Christ at the altar. But this time I didn't leave with the wave of volunteers at the end of the week. Now the entire year stretched out in front of me for ministering in the prisons.

I spent most of my time at G. K. Fountain Correctional Facility, a medium-custody prison on 8,200 acres, opened in 1955.[6] Its concrete one-story block building sprawled across flat and treeless terrain like a massive spider, baking beneath the harsh Alabama sun. The complex had long ago been coated with lifeless white paint, but was now as dirtied, chipped, and faded as the lives of the nearly eight hundred men confined behind a perimeter of fences topped with barbed wire. At the main entrance of the prison,

---

4   *New Life Newsletter*, Nov. 1982, p. 3.
5   http://www.wecareprogram.org/PDF/Information-Timeline1980.pdf
6   http://www.doc.state.al.us/facility?loc=17

in the shadow of an octagonal guard tower, high walls darkened a deep-set massive barred gate.

Inside, a main corridor stretched past administrative offices, the lock-up unit, and the mess hall. Narrow hallways bisected the main walkway at regular intervals and led to the housing units. The smaller dormitories held about sixty men; larger ones housed around one hundred fifty. Each unit had a common bathroom of maybe twelve toilets, all in plain view of fellow inmates, the guards, and anyone else who happened through the area. In the dayroom across the hall, a single TV shared by all inmates on that unit blared day and night. Brawls over channel choices erupted frequently and easily spilled into the dorms.

The stench of days-old sweat hung in the stale air of the dormitories and mingled with a haze of cigarette smoke. Bunk beds spaced a leg's length apart lined the perimeter of the large room, and two rows of single beds crowded into the center. Metal lockers that held inmates' personal belongings were wedged between beds, and offered more substantial seating than did the thin bed mattresses topping creaky, sagging coil springs.

Inmates did not have a choice in bed assignments. No one would have chosen the beds in the center of the dorm. Foot traffic around them was constant and left occupants feeling especially exposed and vulnerable. A top bunk held a bit of an advantage because of the outdoor view granted through the narrow panel of windows near the ceiling. Lower bunk beds were favored because sheets could be hung around them to create a private escape.

"Lock everything up in your personal locker!" guards warned new inmates at orientation. "Even a dirty pair of underwear left on your bed is sure to get stolen!" That was not an exaggeration. Anything not glued down, screwed down, or locked down would likely disappear.

Fifteen or so guards assigned to each shift usually congregated in the hallway and seldom entered the dorms except at count times. During non-working hours, several hundred prisoners from six dorms roamed about freely and aimlessly. Fights broke out over the slightest provocation, often stemming from illegal gambling that occurred in huddled groups out of the guards' sight. Prison commissary cigarettes, a luxury few could afford, substituted for cash. For personal use, most men rolled their own cigarettes with loose tobacco, or if they had the means, paid someone to roll them. Rumor had it that some men brazenly ripped pages from Bibles to use for cigarette papers.

Frequently someone yelled out, "Hot rail!" and the term ricocheted throughout the dorm, warning of a guard's approach. Inmates sprang into action, attempting an air of nonchalance as they hastily stuffed betting cards and weed into hiding places and yanked privacy sheets from beds. As the guard strode through the dorm with a mass of keys jangling on his hip, everyone assumed a perfect look of innocence.

I entered the dorms armed only with a New Testament tucked into my back pocket and looked for men disengaged from activity. "How's it going today?" I'd ask.

Some ignored me. A few cursed at me and ordered me to leave them alone. Some talked—maybe to escape boredom, to amuse themselves, or perhaps to argue about some point in scripture with the "preacher man." Some tried to con me out of something: my pen, my belt, my shoes, my watch, whatever they laid their eyes on. "C'mon, man," they said. "You're a Christian, ain't ya? Christians are supposed to share."

Sometimes inmates asked serious questions about spiritual matters and how they applied to the tangled mess of their lives. It was no easy task to maintain conversation over slamming locker doors, yelling and cursing, constant movement of men, and the occasional jeers about the preacher on the block. The dorm blocks, however, seemed to be the most effective place for ministry. It was their "house," and for many men, the place where they were most inclined to open up. A handful of inmates regularly hung out in the air-conditioned chapel, but the masses remained on their sweltering blocks. I would have preferred the chapel myself, but it seemed that the Spirit goaded me onto the blocks. Maybe God wired me for my time in Alabama; I would rather sweat than shiver.

One day I entered a dorm and immediately sensed tension, as thick and murky as an Alabama bayou. An inmate stepped in front of me and cautioned in a low voice, "You might not want to be in here right now."

I followed his eye drift to a knot of inmates milling about. In the center of the frenzy, I caught a glimpse of an inmate whose white tee shirt was red with a widening ribbon of fresh blood from a stab wound.

Another time, while talking with an inmate in the main hallway, a knife skated by my feet. A few seconds later a prisoner raced by me, pursued by an officer with nightstick in hand.

Chaplain Weber knew such incidents were all a part of a day's work in prison. In orientation notes given to chapel volunteers he wrote, "Look the other way when you see drugs, knives, or suspicious activity."

Prison officials also insisted on a blind eye from the chaplains. "The preachers aren't here to snitch on you," officers told incoming inmates. Getting involved would not only have taken time from the task given to us, but more importantly, it would have eroded the trust we sought to build with inmates. Years later, I would find that Pennsylvania prison policy viewed this security philosophy as naive and reckless.

Rampant violence plagued Alabama prisons during my time there, and even the chapel area was not exempt from the potential of violence. Just prior to my arrival at New Life, a chaplain discovered a gun in the prison chapel, taped securely beneath a pew. Chilling speculations about its owner and intent died down quickly when staff realized the weapon, looking amazingly real and menacing, was only made of cardboard.[7]

Many inmates possessed homemade knives called "shanks." Near the end of my year with New Life Foundation, an officer showed me a large trunk filled with confiscated weapons, and allowed me to take a few as a souvenir of sorts. Inmates' creativity and desperation showed themselves in the variety and abundance of weapons.

I chose a twelve-inch knife, possibly made from a bed rail that had been ground to a sharp point on the concrete floor. The other end was bound with gauze and wrapped tightly with tape to create a firm hand grip. Another weapon was made of a pitchfork tine, most likely stolen from the farm. A thick elastic bandage, held in place with a length of brown shoe-

---

[7] *New Life Newsletter,* Jan. 1983, p. 4.

string, girdled its blunt end. The smallest knife, less than an inch in width, probably originated from a kitchen utensil. It was sharpened to a deadly point, wrapped with a molten material (possibly several toothbrushes), and molded to fit securely in a man's hand.

Beyond the back fence of G. K. Fountain's facility, the "trusty barracks" housed men who had earned clearance for work on the prison farm. A mile or so farther across the open fields, a cluster of trailers formed the Work Release Center where Elvin Ranck provided chaplaincy services. As his VS term came to a close, Elvin asked me to assume his responsibilities. Every Monday night I dropped Ken Burkholder off at "Trusty," drove a little farther up the road, and bounced in a long gravel lane to Work Release.

The mindset of Work Release inmates differed from that of men in the main prison, distracted as they were by their outside jobs and upcoming release dates. I visited among the trailers but found few men who were interested in talking or attending the services held three nights each week.

Soon after I started there, the scheduled chapel speaker didn't show up, and I scrambled to come up with an impromptu Bible lesson. I had no time to do more than shoot a desperate prayer heavenward for guidance and inspiration. I don't remember what I shared, but felt pleased that the men seemed especially attentive and engaged.

A week or so later another speaker stood me up. "Okay, I got this," I thought smugly, and promptly launched into a total crash-and-burn scenario. I picked myself up from the dust of humiliation to learn two valuable lessons. First, I could never trust in my own ability to present the Gospel, and secondly, I would do well to heed the apostle Paul's advice: "Preach the word; be ready in season and out of season" (2 Timothy 4:2; ESV). From then on, I made sure to have a mini sermon prepared. Another realization was that prison ministry has few success stories, and not nearly enough to keep me going. Only a clear call to this work would see me through.

In addition to responsibilities at the Fountain and Work Release Center, I also spent two mornings a week at nearby Holman Prison, a maximum-security facility that housed all of the state's death row inmates. It had a reputation for being one of the most violent prisons in the nation.

Concrete block cells housed solitary prisoners in rooms barely the size of my bathroom at home. A washbowl, open toilet, and a narrow bed were crammed into the space, allowing just a few feet in which a prisoner might pace thousands of times a day. Floor-to-ceiling steel bars spanned the front of the cells. If an inmate could afford a TV, it was hung on the wall across the narrow hallway. The less fortunate sometimes jammed themselves in contorted positions against the bars of their cell doors to catch a glimpse of their neighbor's screen. TV remote controls were banned (its components could be used for devious purposes), so prison inmates devised telescoping instruments made of rolled-up newspapers, which they used to adjust the volume or change channels.

With lots of time and little to occupy it, many inmates were only too happy to talk with New Life staff and to accept literature, books, and Bible Study courses offered to them.

Several weeks after I arrived at New Life, John Evans, a thirty-three-year-old Holman death row inmate, lost an appeal for a new sentence hearing. Plans began for his execution. It would be the first in Alabama in eighteen years.

John Evans met his crime partner, Wayne Ritter, in an Indiana prison. Shortly after his 1976 parole, Evans and Ritter paired up for a two-month-long crime spree across seven states that included nine kidnappings, more than thirty armed robberies, two extortion schemes, and the murder of a Mobile, Alabama, pawn shop owner.

When the criminals were captured, Evans gave a cold-hearted detailed confession, but was denied a guilty plea. At his trial he callously said that he would kill again under the same circumstances, and further threatened the jury that if they did not sentence him to death, he would escape and murder each of them. After less than fifteen minutes of deliberation, they found Evans guilty, and he was sent to Holman Prison to await his execution.

Around 1979, John Evans became a Christian. Chaplain Weber and New Life Foundation's chaplains mentored him in his faith.

Now, as Evans' execution date loomed, his case was forefront in the minds of many inmates, particularly those on death row. The ominous electric chair known as "Big Yellow Mama" for its bright yellow color, dominated many conversations.

"What do you think about the death penalty?" inmates frequently asked of New Life's staff.

This was no time for flippant or evasive answers. New Life personnel debated and examined the question from all angles. It seemed that the first verses in Romans 13 offered the best response: while we couldn't personally endorse the taking of any life, God granted authority to the government to deal out justice.

A twist surfaced in the John Evans sensation when he granted permission to We Care, Chaplain Weber's crime prevention program, to share his life story through the film "Dead Wrong," which premiered on CBS TV in 1984.[8] He also requested that Chaplain Weber escort him to the electric chair. When the media learned of these developments, they hounded Chaplain Weber and New Life staff.

On April 22, 1983, the morning of John's execution, a media circus and throng of protesters gathered outside Holman Prison. Guards worked twelve-hour shifts, and additional sheriffs were called in to assist. Tensions ran high on all sides.

Minutes before John Evans was to die, Chaplain Weber led him to the yellow electric chair. The warden pulled the switch that sent 1,900 volts of electricity into the condemned man.

But he did not die.

A guard refastened the electrode to John's left leg. Spark and flame accompanied a thirty-second jolt of electricity. The doctor examined Evans for the second time. Again, he found a heartbeat.

John's lawyer begged for clemency to Governor George Wallace through an open telephone line, but the governor declined interference. A third charge was administered. Fourteen long minutes after the first charge, John Evans was declared dead.[9]

Martin Weber took it hard. We all did.

---

[8] http://www.wecareprogram.org/PDF/Information-Timeline1980.pdf

[9] *The New York Times*, April 23, 1983, "Alabama Executes Killer, 7th in U.S. to Die Since '76," http:// www.nytimes.com/1983/04/23/us/alabama-executes-killer-7th-in-us-to-die-since-76.html

But no one had time to catch their breath. Three days after Evans' execution, Charles Campbell, a fifty-one-year-old man who had served thirty-two years behind bars, was released on parole from G .K. Fountain. Although Charles had not yet made a decision for Christ to reign in his heart and life, he had developed close friendships with many of the New Life Foundation staff. Charles had nowhere else to go upon his release, so Chaplain Weber invited him to temporarily move into "The Bridge."[10]

Staff spent countless hours with him, helping him to adjust to life "on the streets." It appeared evident that the Spirit's conviction weighed heavily on him, but something held him back. Charles left "The Bridge" and struck out to do life his own way.

New Life lost contact with Charles, and then we learned of his arrest for a crime spree involving theft and kidnapping across state lines. For all of his adult life he had been told when to get up, when and what to eat, when to go to bed, when to line up, when to shut up. He had little say regarding his tightly structured life. In the absence of that prescribed framework, Charles found life on the streets incredibly more difficult than he'd ever imagined. On top of that, increasing health issues dogged him. With no money to pay for medical help, he resorted to crime, and netted a life sentence in the federal prison system where he would be taken care of for the rest of his life.

Charles spent his last years in Pennsylvania's Lewisburg State Penitentiary, a two-hour drive from Lancaster. Martin Weber and some former New Life staffers such as Ken Burkholder, Aaron Martin, and Marvin Reed visited him frequently and wrote letters. Through their love and witness, Charles eventually came to Christ, and in turn, he shared a vibrant faith with others in prison. Upon his death in 2014, his body was released to Marvin Reed, who arranged for burial at Lichty Mennonite Church, near East Earl, Pennsylvania.

---

[10] *New Life Newsletter*, May 1983, p. 2.

My time at New Life was filled in a variety of fulfilling ways. Like other women at "The Bridge," I helped to grade inmates' Bible Study courses. Occasionally I helped to prepare food for visitors staying at "The Bridge," and Nelson and I served a two-week stint of houseparenting while Ken and Mary Ann Burkholder visited family in Pennsylvania. We also attempted gardening, but found that our northern methods were largely ineffective in Alabama's hot and dry climate.

In an effort to learn about criminal culture, Nelson brought testimonial books home from the prison. They were heart-stopping stories of criminal escapades, imprisonment, and an eventual transforming conversion to Jesus Christ. I read one such book during a week when Nelson and the neighboring men from "The Bridge" were upstate for a week of revivals. Reading provided medicine for my lonely and homesick soul, and I curled up on the couch late into the night, losing myself in the story of Tex Watson, one of Charles Manson's accomplices.

Watson described the night that they set out to kill someone, just for kicks. They had agreed on mass murder at a particular house, but reconsidered at the sight of a collection of family photos hanging on the living room wall. They moved on to another target with less familial connection.

I lay there in a cold sweat, breathless at this world's madness, and turned my eyes to the wall above our couch. There they were—photos of my parents, Nelson's parents, both of our families, and our wedding picture. I hoped the smiling images clearly spoke for close family ties, sufficiently so to scare off serial killers lurking in the darkness outside our trailer. It was a long time before I picked up another prison testimonial book—and never again at night when I was at home alone!

In the months prior to our son's birth, I volunteered at a county nursing home in Atmore. Although in a decidedly more sedated and safer environment, my assignment was similar to Nelson's in that I was to provide conversation and companionship to residents. The work was far too ambiguous for my more reserved temperament. I *didn't know how to maintain small talk with vacant-eyed dementia patients, and in spite of my supervisor's urging to do so, I disliked waking them up from peaceful slumber. I took to hiding out in the bathroom for long minutes, praying for courage to go out there to strike up meaningful conversations. I never learned to enjoy that job. Now I might do better at it, but not then, when insecurities bound me. Eventually I came to peace with my failure, concluding that I simply was not gifted for such a task.*

During our year in Alabama, we were blessed with quite a few visitors from home. Among the first were my parents and sister, Nancy, who spent three enjoyable days with us in May. From that time, we noted a marked difference in our relationship with my parents, and they became some of Nelson's best prison ministry cheerleaders.

Nelson's family visited in June and others followed later, each helping to fend off the homesickness that loitered by my doorstep. In spite of that ache, I grew to love the Atmore area and the friends we made, and was gratified to see Nelson embrace his role at the prison with enthusiasm.

Early on the morning of July 26, 1983, I checked into Greenlawn Hospital in Atmore, a facility so small that I was the only patient on the maternity ward. Half an hour after our arrival, my doctor entered the delivery room, rubbing sleep from his eyes, and just in time to deliver our baby, Joel Andrew.

A male nurse examined our firstborn and handed him to me. "I'm giving him an Apgar score of nine," he said.

I caught my breath. "Is something wrong? Why not a ten?"

He smiled and shook his head. "Nope, only Bo Derek gets a ten."

I didn't know much about the actress, but allowed the nurse his opinion. In regards to our newborn son, however, he was perfect—a solid ten, for sure.

Later that summer, I was assigned to supervise the chapel at G. K. Fountain Prison while the Nation of Islam group held their service. I'm not

sure how the task fell to me that afternoon. Even now, I'm astounded that we volunteer chaplains were entrusted with the supervision of the chapel, but it was probably an indication of the trust that prison officials placed in Chaplain Weber and New Life's staff.

On that sweltering Sunday afternoon, the chaplain's office door burst open and an inmate rushed in, his eyes wide with excitement. "Did you hear about the escape at Holman Prison? A bunch of guys took off!"

Details filtered in over the next few days through a combination of prison rumors and news reports. A group of inmates had somehow obtained a wire cutter. While one inmate employed a ruse to distract the tower guard, his friends cut through the fence. A fellow inmate, serving a life sentence without parole, was running laps in the recreation yard and watched with growing interest as the first inmate slipped through the fence. Another followed, then another . . . and another . . . and another . . . until he counted ten men in white prison uniforms escape through the double fence, dash across an open field, and disappear into a stand of pine trees. He expected to hear shouts from the guard tower. Or gunshots.

But nothing happened.

Apparently, the escaping inmates had gone undetected! Making a split-second decision, he ran for his own freedom, following the escapees through the cut fence. But luck had run out. His movement caught the guards' attention, and suddenly shouts and a barrage of shots split the air.

Officials combed the wooded area between the prison and Interstate 65 and found a getaway car stashed with civilian clothing and food. Within forty-five minutes, nine escapees were rounded up. A massive manhunt located another the next day.[11]

I think at least several days passed before the last fugitive was located, and by then, Esther and I were headed to Pennsylvania for a few weeks to show off our newborn son.

---

[11] Rod Griffith, August 29, 1983, "Eleven Maximum Security Inmates in Alabama's Toughest Prison Ran," http://www.upi.com/Archives/1983/08/29/Eleven-maximum-security-inmates-in-Alabamas-toughest-prison-ran/5480430977600/

The trip back to Pennsylvania wasn't as we expected. It didn't feel like home anymore. We realized our hearts had taken root in Alabama where Nelson found fulfillment in prison ministry. We had established some deep friendships at Byrnville Mennonite Church and among New Life personnel. The mild weather and the beautiful white sand beaches of Pensacola, only an hour's drive away, were added bonuses.

Our year-long VS term drew to a close, and New Life Foundation offered Nelson a full-time paid staff position. We prayed and deliberated about what God would want us to do.

Our pastor friend, Joe Horst, grinned. "You got that southern sand in your shoes," he said. "It's hard to shake that out."

Indeed, it was hard, but in the end, we didn't sense peace about staying. So, we stretched our year-long commitment to thirteen months and reluctantly left behind the community and the experiences that had shaped us.

Our time in Alabama left an indelible impact. Time would reveal its extent.

Does your call hinge on "success stories," or will you pursue it even when obstacles and hardships surface? No doubt about it—your call will be tested. God isn't as concerned about your success as He is in your faithfulness. Continue on in the work He has given you, and along the way, look for His faithfulness and for confirmations of your call. Anticipate surprises along the way and allow the pursuit of the call to shape you in ways beyond your wildest imagination.

CHAPTER SIX

Persistent, Insistent Call

B ack to Pennsylvania we went. Back to Lancaster County. Back to my former job in the paint department at Paul B. Zimmerman's hardware store.

No sooner had we settled into a rented house in February of 1984, and I started feeling restless. Again. The feeling slipped in like an uninvited guest, camping in the living room, and lacking the sense to leave at nightfall. Staying interminably. Taking over the house. Try as I might, I couldn't get rid of this troublesome visitor.

Since 1973, I'd focused on serving a year in VS. I should have felt fulfilled, but now that experience seemed to only act as a catalyst for something more. Where did God want to take me? Saint Augustine, a Christian theologian of the first century, said, "Thou hast made us for thyself, O Lord, and our heart is restless until it finds its rest in thee."

Even as Esther and I sought God about the source and solution for our restlessness we began settling into a prescribed pattern of living: we had begun our family, and I earned a decent wage on my job. Next on the American Dream checklist was purchasing our own property.

Less than seven months after our move from Alabama, we bought a five-acre farmette in northern Lancaster County, outside of Schoeneck, a town whose German name means "pretty corner." The property cost $65,000, and we secured the mortgage at only twelve percent interest, a bargain over earlier rates that had skyrocketed as high as eighteen percent.

Our property was a dream come true—plenty of space for our children to roam freely, and acreage to raise a few chickens and sheep. Granted, the house desperately needed a facelift, and the garden and fields had been neglected, but it was ours to whip into shape, starting with the orchard of fifty-some fruit trees.

I spent countless hours in that orchard, mowing weeds taller than myself with an old-fashioned scythe. A distant relative with orchard experience offered advice on pruning and spraying, and later admitted to biting his tongue to withhold what he really wanted to tell us: to cut those misshapen trees down and start over! Two years later he shook his head in amazement at the progress we had made in coaxing apples, peaches, and cherries from our tired orchard.

We spent a month of Saturdays forking piles of manure from the chicken pens and barn stalls and hauled it to the garden in an attempt to loosen the unyielding red clay soil. That done, we pick-axed holes beside the stone driveway to plant two dozen arborvitae for a privacy hedge.

Backbreaking work aside, we were proud of our accomplishments. Yet our to-do list seemed endless. The barn and chicken house desperately needed fresh paint, and the house needed a new roof and sewer system. Our dream was fast becoming a nightmare. Too often I felt torn between maintaining the property and pursuing the call to ministry that was taking shape in my heart and mind.

Around the same time that we bought the property, I became involved with Jubilee Ministries, an organization formed within the Lebanon County District of Mennonite churches. Esther's family had attended Schubert Mennonite Church, one of the congregations in the district. In 1973, when she was fourteen and eagerly awaiting her next birthday so she could begin attending youth group functions, revival broke out among the district youth. She heard from the sidelines of the group's new spiritual fervor and their exploration of opportunities for evangelism, including that of holding Bible studies at Lebanon County Prison. From that movement, Jubilee Ministries was born.

When we moved back from Alabama in 1984, Jubilee had a full-time director and three part-time paid chaplains. I approached Jubilee's director, Donald Martin, about the possibility of volunteering with the organization.

He put me to work interviewing new inmates two mornings every week. I was to gather information about their religious affiliations, thereby opening a door for them to talk about the gnarl of personal issues in their lives. Landing in prison was a wake-up call for many who were desperate for hope and help.

Soon my schedule at the prison also included Tuesday evening Bible studies. My employer at Paul B. Zimmerman's store graciously adjusted my work schedule to accommodate my ministry. Still, I didn't feel settled. Esther and I continued to seek God about our persistent restlessness and the sense that God was nudging me on to something more. At times self-doubt crept in, and I wondered whether the idea of full-time ministry was of God or just some egotistical hair-brained notion of my own.

Although I couldn't see God's movements, He nonetheless moved in ways that even now make me shake my head in wonder. Moses, the Old Testament leader who was chronically discouraged by the Israelites' complaints, doubted God's provisions.

"Is the Lord's hand shortened?" God demanded of Moses in Numbers 11:23. He might well have asked the question of me.

At the hardware store in late summer of 1984, while cutting a key for a customer, I noticed a young man standing at the end of the aisle, patiently waiting his turn in line. He was a regular customer with whom I'd spoken a few times, and I knew him to be a fellow believer who took his faith seriously. I guessed he might be a few years older than me, but rumor had it that he had already become a successful businessman.

I didn't know how successful.

More than three decades later, he reflected on the events that brought us together in 1984. He had been blessed financially, thanks to business innovations, but his unexpected upturn weighed on him and his wife.

"We sought God for ways to bless others as He had blessed us," my friend said. "One day, while driving my brand-new truck into Ephrata, I prayed that God would grant wisdom in using the money for the furtherance of the Gospel. I remember exactly where I was, at the top of the hill overlooking the town near the Brossman Center, and just like that, the name Nelson Zeiset came to my mind."

Shortly thereafter, he sought me out at Paul B. Zimmerman's hardware store. We made small talk for a minute before he asked, "Are you still interested in getting back into prison ministry?"

Sensing this wasn't a casual question, I heard myself telling him of my restlessness and prayers for God's direction.

He nodded thoughtfully. "Perhaps this is the answer to our prayers. If you are interested, my wife and I would consider supporting you."

Interested? I couldn't believe my ears! "Of course I'm interested!" I felt like shouting.

"Let's get together and discuss it sometime, along with our wives," he said.

I told him I'd get back to him soon. After he left, I found it difficult to keep my mind on my work and could hardly wait to get home to tell Esther. "You're not gonna believe this! I think he's talking about more than just a few hours of support. Maybe a couple of days!"

The businessman seemed as eager as me to talk, and soon the four of us sat at their kitchen table to discuss his proposal. He would pay me to work at a prison for twenty-nine hours a week, with just three stipulations: that I would find a prison to work in, that I would find a ministry through which to channel the money, and that he would remain anonymous.

My mind went into overdrive. Prior to our leaving We Care, Martin Weber said that if I ever wished to get involved in prison ministry elsewhere, he would do whatever he could to help. That time had come.

Camp Hill State Prison, located near Harrisburg, was the closest facility. I obtained the name of the administrative chaplain, a Chaplain Frederick Widmann, and called Chaplain Weber, who listened with interest and promised to call Camp Hill on my behalf.

In the meantime, I approached Jubilee Ministries' board of directors. The idea of expanding into the state prison system was new to them, but they discussed the opportunity at several meetings and agreed to hire me if the businessman would indeed come through with the funds.

Once again, my boss at the hardware store consented to whittling my hours. The final hurdle was getting into the Camp Hill Prison. After a series of phone calls with both Chaplain Weber and Chaplain Widmann, I arranged to meet Chaplain Widmann at the prison chapel. Everything, it seemed, hinged on the Sunday afternoon meeting at Camp Hill.

An odd combination of excitement and trepidation settled over me as I merged onto the westbound lane of the Pennsylvania Turnpike and headed toward Harrisburg. Would the chaplain be friendly? Would he welcome me to work in his institution? And could I actually carry out the work that God seemed to be laying out for me?

Restlessness may be an indicator that God is moving you on to some new endeavor. Can you trust His leading?

Many people contributed to Nelson's call. His employer adjusted his work schedule. A successful businessman provided financially. Martin Weber recommended Nelson to the Camp Hill chaplain. Each was moved to cooperatively join with Nelson in his pursuit of God's call. How can you assist in someone's calling?

CHAPTER SEVEN

At Camp Hill Prison

December's waning sun peeked from behind low clouds on that Sunday afternoon as I walked across the parking lot at Camp Hill Prison. At the main entrance a massive iron gate stood between two imposing brick guard towers. A connecting catwalk topped the gate. Razor wire, looped like a giant barbed Slinky, flashed on the high chain-link fence that encompassed the fifty-two-acre prison grounds. Inside the perimeter, red brick buildings scattered across large grassy areas. Compared to the single dirtied white building at Fountain Prison in Alabama, Camp Hill looked more like a college campus than a prison.

Up on the catwalk, an officer held a shotgun by his side and scrutinized me as I approached the front gate. I lengthened my stride, hoping to look more confident than I felt. I could only guess that check-in was at the squat building beside the gate where a sign in thick block lettering proclaimed ABSOLUTELY NO WEAPONS ALLOWED BEYOND THIS POINT.

Through a bank of multi-paned windows, I saw a guard sitting behind the desk. He looked up at me, annoyance written on his face. Slowly he pushed himself up and ambled to the door to unlock it. "Yeah? Whaddaya want?" he growled.

"I have an appointment with Chaplain Widmann," I said.

He grunted, motioned me inside, and locked the door behind me. His keys jangled noisily. I followed him to a desk where he drew a thick finger across a book, searching the entries. "Yup," he said in a slow, bored drone, "clip this ID tag somewhere above your waist and keep it on for the duration of your visit."

He motioned me to follow him and slowly sauntered across the room to unlock another door opening into the prison compound. Then, gesturing with the large brass key in hand, he said, "There's the chapel, across the walkway and the grass. The chaplain will meet you there."

Hardly believing prison policy would allow me to walk inside the compound without escort, yet relieved to escape the guard's glum company, I followed his directions the short distance to the chapel. In the shade of the building, I surveyed it; it was a lighter colored brick than the surrounding buildings.

My heart pounded in my head. I climbed the chapel steps, squelching the impulse to mount them two at a time. Then I took a deep breath and swung open one of the glass doors.

An inmate looked up as I entered the hallway.

"I'm here to see Chaplain Widmann," I said.

He pointed to a door on the right. "There's his office."

A graying man sat behind the desk. A dark turtleneck rose to his bearded chin, and he peered at me over reading glasses. "Nelson Zeiset?" he asked.

Before I had a chance to respond, he waved me in and motioned for me to take a seat. "I'll be with you in a minute," he said, and turned back to papers spread across his desk. A crossword puzzle book and Dr. Peck's book, *The Road Less Traveled,* lay to the side.

The chaplain's chair creaked. He reached across the desk for his pipe and cradled it in his hand, then swiveled to face me again. "So . . ." His single word dropped off into nothingness while he lit his pipe, shook out the match, and looked at me over his glasses. "So, you think you want to work here, do you?"

His tone of voice told me he thought my idea was a bit loony.

Recovering from that unexpected start, I told him of my work in the Alabama prison system, of volunteering at Jubilee, and of my desire to minister to inmates at Camp Hill.

The chaplain grunted and blew smoke into the air until the office filled with a blue haze. "You'll draw a paycheck from, what did you say, ah, Jubilee Ministries?"

"And a generous donor who wants to support prison ministry." I started to tell him about it and trailed off, realizing he wasn't the least bit interested.

"You understand you would be granted volunteer status at Camp Hill? That's different from being an employee," he said.

I nodded.

The chaplain took a long draw on his pipe and shrugged. "Well, as far as I'm concerned you can be here forty hours a week, if you want."

So ended my forty-five-minute interview. On one hand, it didn't feel like much to go on. On the other, it felt like he'd handed me the world.

I walked out of the chapel as if on air and down the steps, one at a time, although I felt I could jump the four of them with a wild whoop of joy. Instead, I reigned myself in and walked back to the guardhouse where the same unhappy officer begrudgingly let me out the main gate. Up on the catwalk, the guard still cradled his shotgun and looked me over again. Then I climbed into my rusting Toyota Corolla and headed home to share the good news with my wife.

My first day as an employee of Jubilee Ministries was on Monday, March 4, 1985—a date with a directive. March fourth, I mused . . . march forth. Yes, I *would* march forth wherever God led. Where and when and how. I winced to think of the many times my impatience edged out complete submission and full obedience to God's will, yet total surrender *was* my heart's intent.

Five or more years earlier, during our engagement, Esther visited my church where the chorister led a hymn that was unfamiliar to her. I leaned over and whispered, "I want this song sung at my funeral."

I didn't want to make a scene there in church, but this caught me off guard. We were planning a wedding, not a funeral! A quick look at Nelson's grin told me he was teasing, but his eyes were serious. I pulled the hymnal away from his grasp to study the words:

My God and Father, while I stray
Far from my home, on life's rough way,

Oh, teach me from my heart to say,
"Thy will be done!"
Thy will be done! Thy will be done!
Oh, teach me from my heart to say,
"Thy will be done!"

Renew my will from day to day;
Blend it with thine, and take away,
All now that makes it hard to say,
"Thy will be done!"
Thy will be done! Thy will be done!
All now that makes it hard to say,
"Thy will be done!"

In the chorus between stanzas, Nelson's deep bass sang out the echo, "Thy will be done, thy will be done!" Funeral song or not, the lyrics expressed our shared desire for God's sovereignty in our lives. Still, I made a face at Nelson (as much as I dared to at Churchtown Mennonite Church) and finished singing with him.

My work with Jubilee took me to Lebanon County Prison every Monday and to Camp Hill State Prison the next three days. On Fridays I worked at the hardware store. If funds had been available for full-time employment with Jubilee, I would have accepted without hesitation.

Over time, however, I came to understand how providential it was that I had one day to decompress through secular work. Statistics from the Bureau of Labor indicate that correctional officers suffer high rates of injuries and illnesses due to job-related stress. Security concerns and the ever-present potential for violence contribute to a high divorce rate, depression, and burnout among staff.[12]

---

[12] Bureau of Labor Statistics, U.S. Department of Labor, *Occupational Outlook Handbook, 2016-17 Edition*, Correctional Officers. http://www.bls.gov/ooh/protective-service/correctional-officers.htm

Eventually I would recognize a predictable pattern among too many new prison employees. They started their jobs with a degree of concern for inmates, but somewhere around the second year, after they'd been played for a fool once too often, they adopted an attitude of just getting the job done. By the third year, cynicism and resentment toward inmates became all too common. Unless staff took deliberate steps to alter their thinking, they coped in subsequent years by finding and creating humor at the expense of inmates.

I was no different. I didn't see it in myself at the outset of my ministry, but over time, I became increasingly aware that the craziness and the negativity of the prison environment could create serious drag. My Friday work at the hardware store offered a welcome reprieve, even if it involved a long thirteen-hour day.

When I entered Camp Hill that first Tuesday, I carried my briefcase in hand and a great deal of nervous energy in my heart. Chaplain Widmann invited me into his office and gestured toward a chair. "I want you to meet the chaplaincy staff and join us for our morning reading," he said.

They dribbled in one by one. Chaplain Brooks seemed to carry an attitude bigger than his husky frame. I would soon learn his primary gripe was rooted in the fact that his paychecks weren't coming through, a recurring complaint from other contract chaplains at that time. He took his bitter grievance all the way to the governor's office. Not surprisingly, his contract expired that summer and was not renewed.

Mrs. Shettle, the chapel secretary, offset Chaplain Brooks' gloom with a cheerful personality and contagious laughter.

Keith and William, inmate clerks, actually did very little clerical work at Camp Hill. Their jobs consisted primarily of janitorial type work, for which they may have been paid somewhere around twenty cents an hour.

Introductions done, we all crammed into the office for the "morning reading," a practice in progressive liberal philosophies and verbiage that I endured only because I had to. After weeks of reading Dr. Peck's philosophies from *The Road Less Traveled*, we took up a book on the spiritual powers Don Juan experienced by smoking peyote while he apprenticed with an

Indian sorcerer. Later we read Mark Twain's writings. Not once did we read scripture. Not once did we pray.

Father Beeman, an unassuming and kindly Catholic chaplain, did not attend the morning readings. I don't know whether he was uninvited or uninterested. Unlike the other chaplains who spent the bulk of their days sequestered in their offices, Chaplain Beeman seemed to enjoy visiting with inmates on their blocks.

I learned that he lived in a condemned row house in Harrisburg that often got burglarized. "I guess they had a need," he'd say with a shrug. "God understands." He believed that all people had good in them; some just needed their good coaxed out more than others. His loose-ended theology extended beyond denominational lines to the degree that he went out of his way to befriend me and make me feel a part of the chaplaincy team.

After morning reading on that first day, Chaplain Widmann showed me to a small conference room in the chapel, which would become my office for the next several months. A constant stream of both inmates and staff traipsed through, and if the space was needed for another purpose, I got bumped to an upstairs balcony loft or to a chapel pew.

Chaplain Widmann led me through aspects of orientation and handed me a stack of prison manuals to read. He left the prison at noon that day, and I had to do the same because my volunteer status did not permit me to remain there without supervision.

On my third day at Camp Hill, Chaplain Widman invited me to join him in visiting the hospital and the Restricted Housing Unit (RHU), otherwise known as "Mohawk" at Camp Hill. The name was left over from the 1941-1975 era, when juvenile offenders were housed at the facility.

I fell into step with him, eager for my first look inside the prison. We approached the gate at Mohawk. He signed his name into the registry and handed me the pen to do the same. With nothing more than a cursory glance beyond the barred gate, he turned on his heels and walked away. We went through the same procedure at the hospital. He didn't talk to a single inmate. I was profoundly disappointed with the "visitation."

Mostly, I passed those first weeks alone in the conference room office, impatiently awaiting the opportunity for "real" ministry, and filling the hours by reading. Looking back now, I value that study time as preparation for interactions with inmates.

I began to question whether I was really welcome at Camp Hill. Was Chaplain Widmann only humoring me by allowing me into the prison? Did he think I was just a religious nut who would soon give up? And what of my donor, and of Jubilee? How long would they continue to pay me to do next to nothing with inmates?

Several weeks after my arrival at Camp Hill, Chaplain Widmann stuck his head into my office, and with a jerk of his thumb, said, "Let's go down to J Ward." As we walked, he explained that J Ward was the first step back into the general prison population after an inmate completed time in Mohawk.

Chaplain Widmann looked over the ward's roster and started scribbling names of men who had not yet been assigned jobs within the prison. He filled one side of his paper and turned it over, adding name after name. Finally, he stopped scribbling and handed me the paper. "Call these knuckleheads to the chapel. Talk to them, see if they want religion."

I might have winced at his choice of words, but I'd already heard much worse. More than one inmate complained that the chaplain cussed worse than a sailor, and I'd heard plenty of sneering remarks from him about my attempts to "save souls."

Well over half of the seventy-five inmates on the J Ward list arranged to come by my office. Some showed up only a time or two. Others met with me for several years.

Randy was one of the regulars. He was nineteen years old and had a bright mind, but his dreams for college were on hold until his sentence of four to eight years was completed. In one of our first conversations Randy accepted Christ. The next time I saw him, he wore a broad smile. "Man, I know this sounds cheesy, but since I became a Christian even the grass looks greener and the sky is bluer!" he said.

Randy asked a lot of questions about living a godly life in prison, especially as it related to getting along with his cellmate. He wasn't alone. Bombarded by peripheral issues related to incarceration, frustration and anger continually simmer just below the surface. All day and every day, irritations accumulate as long as a career criminal's rap sheet. An inmate assigned to the upper bunk can hardly hoist himself up without stepping onto the lower bunk, an action often interpreted as disrespect. If that isn't enough, the bed springs creak under the slightest movement, and every sneeze and snore and cough are amplified in the concrete and steel cell. There's no privacy. None. Even the toilet is in full view of the cellmate.

Broken relationships, both in and out of prison, are chronic problems among inmates. It's extremely rare to meet an inmate who grew up in a stable, two-parent home. A vast majority had both absentee fathers and negligent mothers. It's little wonder, then, that they have difficulty navigating their own relationships.

Many of my discussions with inmates veered toward sex, as they talked about abuse they had suffered in childhood, and about their own sexual experiences. They had both questions and arguments about what is right and wrong.

And, of course, inmates assailed me with questions about doctrine. I heard things like, "Man, my cellie doesn't speak in tongues and there ain't no way he can be a Christian if he doesn't believe in tongues!" or "What's with all the different religions? Aren't we all gonna end up in heaven, no matter what we believe?" The reliability of scripture, the nature of divine healing, the free will of man and the sovereignty of God . . . it was all open game, argued and defended vehemently.

Between my appointments, I had time to interact with the two chapel clerks. Keith, a wiry inmate of about thirty years old, was especially talkative. In snippets of conversation, he told me of fighting in Vietnam's jungles and how, when he got back home, he fell into the wrong crowd. He talked freely of his slide into crime, of the thrill of risk, and of the highs he got from wild police chases. "But I've changed and learned my lessons," Keith said. "When I get out of prison I'm going to work hard and make my mother proud of me."

The only problem was, his parole date was approaching and he needed a job and home plan.

I asked around for him. By the time of Keith's release from Camp Hill in February 1986, arrangements were made for a job at Paul B. Zimmerman's hardware store and housing with Esther's parents.

Troubling signs surfaced almost from the start. He grew secretive, his stories didn't line up, and his promises for reform fell flat. And then money began disappearing from the employee lunchroom at the hardware store. When Keith was caught red-handed, Esther's dad, Mel, reluctantly turned him in to his parole agent. Keith lost his job, housing with my in-laws, and the car he'd been buying from one of the Zimmerman brothers.

Esther's father blamed himself for somehow failing Keith. Some of the Zimmerman brothers blamed themselves for being too harsh with him. And I blamed myself for putting people I loved in a bad situation.

My father-in-law and I hoped to restore Keith. On our first visit we met his parents. They were leaving his apartment as we arrived, and were visibly upset. "Kudos to you if you can help that hard head! He's duped us once too often. We give up!" said his dad.

With that ringing in our ears, we knocked on Keith's door. He begged forgiveness from Mel and me, cried convincingly remorseful tears, and insisted that he was truly serious about being a Christian and getting his life straightened out.

A knock on the door interrupted our conversation. Two men tromped in, each carrying a case of beer. Their celebratory mood quickly shifted to awkwardness when they caught sight of Mel and me. Even a numbskull would have known that drinking violated the terms of Keith's parole. And only a complete idiot could have missed Keith's moves to get us out of his apartment posthaste.

I didn't hear from Keith again until another scrape with the law landed him in the Lebanon County Prison. But he didn't stay long. He and another inmate scaled the fence and escaped in a getaway car driven by his friend's nineteen-year-old girlfriend.

They got as far as Tennessee where the girlfriend called her worried mother from a phone booth. She refused to disclose her whereabouts, but did divulge the phone number of the booth from which she called. As soon as she hung up, her mother contacted the Tennessee police, who dialed the number, and a passerby answered the phone and gave the phone booth's location. Within two hours the threesome were apprehended—ironically in Lebanon, Tennessee—and Keith soon found himself back at Camp Hill.

In just a little over a year, Keith had run a wild and circuitous route. More than three decades later, I'm still discomfited by the experience. Did I so desperately want a success story that I overlooked some red flags? Was Keith sincere but not equipped for life on the streets, or was he a manipulative con artist? Was I just naive?

Some of our friends had serious misgivings. "Why do you waste your time on those guys?" they asked. "Do you really think they'll change?" A few were more blunt and said, "Lock 'em up and let 'em rot! They did the crime, now let them do the time!"

I wondered if their attitudes would change if, God forbid, their sons or daughters found themselves on the wrong side of the law.

I don't recall entertaining the notion of quitting, but the experience with Keith and other inmates made me wary. Okay, I admit it, it went further than that. I took on a truckload of cynicism and wasn't even aware that it had sneaked up on me. My Jubilee coworker, Mimi Keller, called me on it one morning at a staff meeting.

"Nelson, do you ever think about how your sins offend God?" she asked in her signature gracious but penetrating way. "Yet He loved you. If Jesus loved you after all your sin, what right do you have to not love inmates?"

I deserved that sanctified kick in the butt. I had to regard my sin as being equally atrocious as the worst criminal's, and to understand that Jesus values him every bit as much as He does me. Intellectually I knew that, but in the framework of my ministry, I processed the practicalities of the concept.

Love is unconditional; I choose to love because I believe that every person is made in the image of God, and therefore, has supreme value. Love, however, is not synonymous with trust, and the two don't automatically come in the same package. Trust is earned over time.

I tried out this concept in conversation with a Christian woman.

She reacted in shock. "That doesn't sound very Christlike."

"You have young children, right?" I asked.

She nodded and I continued, "So, I have an ex-inmate friend who just finished a sentence for child molestation. But that's in his past. He's a nice guy and really growing in his Christian faith. Would you be okay with him babysitting your kids? Or to teach their Sunday School class?"

She backed away, her face registering an inner conflict. She wanted to fully accept this brother as a "new creature in Christ," yet his history gave her pause.

As it should.

I often told inmates, "Look, brother, I love you, but that doesn't mean I trust you. You need to prove that you are trustworthy."

Daily, I needed to remind myself that each inmate, regardless of his crimes, holds ultimate worth in the sight of God. I prayed for grace to respect each one as a valuable human being and to extend love to all.

Throughout the following years of prison ministry, the depth of my love would be tested over and over again. More than I could imagine.

Our "me" society tends to live for self and overlook God's will. What adjustments do you need to make to sincerely say, "Thy will be done?"

Do you value others, even the unlovely, to the same degree that God does? How can you show love, even in those situations where trust has not yet been earned?

CHAPTER EIGHT

Kids Behind Bars

As ministry opportunities increased, I became aware of my need for more education and enrolled in an evening counseling class at Lancaster Bible College. Esther typed papers for me while I bounced between work, the prison, college, and maintenance of our property. Clearly, something had to give.

It was becoming obvious that we'd been too hasty in purchasing our farmette. I'd rushed ahead of God, pushed aside Esther's hesitation, stretched myself too thin, and diluted His purpose and plan for our lives. We put the property up for sale about a year after we moved in and prayed for a buyer.

"Aren't you afraid about your husband working in a prison?" a woman at church asked. She drew the word afraid *out into three syllables and pushed her face closer to mine, searching perhaps, for some telltale sign of fear or of mental instability. "I mean, he's walking around in that prison with hundreds of rapists and murderers and kidnappers and . . ." Her voice trailed off and she shuddered. "Esther, doesn't it scare you?"*

"All jobs hold a degree of danger," I countered, thinking of a mutual acquaintance who had fallen onto concrete from fifteen feet up on construction scaffolding. Two years later, he still used a walker. I thought of the farmer who got trampled to death by a bull, and of the one who succumbed to lethal gases in his silo. I decided against dispensing my mental litany of deadly and debilitating accidents, in-

cidents that I rehearsed and comforted myself with every time this question surfaced.

The woman nodded hesitantly and her face softened. "Still, I don't know . . . somehow working in prison seems scarier."

"Because it's unfamiliar?" I asked.

"Maybe. I pray for Nelson a lot. And for you." Her concern was genuine, and her fear for us palpable.

The conversation left me rattled enough that I researched workplace injuries and found studies that listed logging, trucking, farming, and construction work among the more dangerous jobs in the United States. But prison chaplains didn't make it onto the list. The difference, I decided, was that many job-related accidents are the result of unforeseen circumstances, whereas if harm came to Nelson at the prison, it would likely be the result of malicious and intentional violence. It would be really ugly.

Of course I thought about my husband's safety! As Nelson often said, men aren't in prison for singing too loudly in Sunday School. No question about it, he had invaded Satan's territory. Every day he fought against negativity and cynicism, and he regularly gave ear to unspeakably dark stories of abuse and violence. Profanity and vulgar language assailed him at every turn, and each time he visited the blocks, he was exposed to obscene images plastered on cell walls. My friend's question stirred me to increase my prayers, not only for Nelson's physical safety, but more so, for his spiritual well-being.

I could not allow my fear to hamper Nelson from pursuing the ministry to which we both believed God had called him. Neither could I be so naive as to believe that being in His will would provide my husband immunity to danger. I could only cover him in prayer and release him into our loving God's care.

In May 1985, two months after Nelson began volunteering at SCI Camp Hill, Chaplain Widmann invited Joel and me to attend a Sunday service and an afternoon picnic with inmate families. I had attended numerous services in both the Alabama prisons and *at Lebanon County Prison, but taking our son into prison was altogether different. "Oh . . . Joel's not even two years old yet," I protested.*

Jitters aside, the three of us went to Camp Hill for the annual event. Immediately after Chaplain Widmann's sermon, inmates scrambled to carry chairs and tables outside. Women in heels and broad-rimmed church hats proudly unpacked coolers.

"Mama brought her famous fried chicken!" one brown-uniformed inmate whooped, and another returned, "I'll betcha my mama's chicken is better than your mama's chicken!" Good-natured bantering and laughter continued as potato salads and pound cakes and sweet potato pies competed for space on the table. Summer's early arrival added to high spirits over shared food and fellowship in the welcome shade of the chapel building.

With lunch behind us and afternoon drowsiness creeping in, Joel settled onto my lap. A strapping inmate sat down at a respectful distance, two vacant chairs between us. "Ma'am, I almost hate to ask, but your little boy makes me think of my son, and I haven't seen him in four years. Would you mind if I played peek-a-boo with your little man?"

Joel shyly buried his face on my shoulder.

Sweat glistened on the man's ebony face. "I don't mean to frighten him, nor to be presumptuous, ma'am." His soft and melodic voice drew us in.

Joel lifted his head and peeked at the man. He returned with contorted expressions and exaggerated movements. Joel giggled. The inmate responded with belly laughter. Their comic exchange grew louder and drew onlookers into conversation, not unlike a pleasant family reunion. The afternoon passed quickly and the only harm that befell us was the season's first sunburn.

Four years later, prison officials banned special meals for inmates because drugs and other contraband slipped into the institution on those occasions. Children were no longer allowed into the prison, except in the family visitation area. Prior to those reforms, however, our family had several other occasions to visit my husband's workplace.

A Christmas service in 1988 was one such event. By then we had three children. Joel was five years old; Emily was nearly three, and Renee was nine months old. Their safety and my sanity both factored into my nervousness about attending the service. "What if Renee cries?" I asked.

"If she cries, the guys will melt," Nelson replied. "It will be music to their ears."

With that question settled (in Nelson's mind, at least) we prepared the kids for the visit by warning them about contact with strangers. Using language our young children could understand, we told them that there are many "bad men" in prison, some of whom have hurt children. We emphasized that they must stay by us at all times, and under no circumstances were they to go anywhere with the "bad men."

At the prison, Nelson gave us a tour of the chapel and his office, and then he hunkered down and drew Joel and Emily to himself. "Remember that some bad men might be here, so stay with Mommy, and don't go anywhere with anyone, okay?"

The children both nodded solemnly.

A few officers came in, and took up their stations in the chapel. Nelson seated us on the back pew, close to the door where he greeted incoming prisoners.

I held Renee on my lap and Emily sat on the pew beside me, pressing her small body against my side. Joel mustered the bravado of a kindergartener, and sat protectively at the end of the pew by the center aisle.

Inmates began filing in. All of them wore drab brown prison-issued shirts and pants. Their prison identification numbers were stenciled above their shirt pockets, and "D.O.C." was emblazoned in bold white lettering across their backs, declaring the men and their uniforms property of the Department of Corrections.

They kept coming, two and three men abreast, and when they noticed the kids and me, many of them broke step to wave friendly greetings. Pew after pew filled from the front of the chapel until the steady stream of inmates entered the row in front of us.

"So good to have you here, ma'am," said one with a wide smile. "And the kids, too!"

"Amen!" said his friend. "Aren't they just so cute?"

Soft chuckles and pleasant murmurs of "Mmmm, mmmm!" echoed down the row.

The chapel filled to capacity. Two hundred prisoners in brown uniforms sat shoulder to shoulder, the white D.O.C. lettering partially visible above the backs of the pews. I couldn't shake the thought that our children, who looked around quietly in wide-eyed fascination, sat among murderers and rapists and robbers and (gulp) child molesters.

The service had barely begun when Emily stood up on the pew, steadied a hand on my shoulder, and stretched up on her tiptoes to look around the chapel. Front. Back. Side to side. Her little face scrunched up in confusion. "Mommy," she whispered, "when are the bad men coming?"

I clapped my hand over her mouth, and fervently hoped that no one heard her question. "The men are all here now," I said in a shaky voice.

At that moment, the choir belted out, "Joy to the world, the Lord has come!" and I contemplated Emily's question.

Vivid imaginations crowded into my mind. Satan storms to God's throne, his finger pointed at me in condemnation. "Look at Esther! She's so bad! Her sins mark her as plain as the numbers stamped on these inmates' brown uniforms!"

I cower in shame, feeling the weight of my offenses. The hopelessness. The despair.

Jesus springs to the Father's side in my defense. "But she has accepted My atonement for her sins, and now there is no badness in her. None at all!"

The Father nods in satisfaction and waves a dismissing hand at Satan. My accuser slinks away in defeat.

*And now the choir sang, "No more let sins and sorrows grow,
nor thorns infest the ground; he comes to make his blessings flow far
as the curse is found . . ."*

Such astounding grace!

The service ended, and yes, Renee cried a bit.

*"That was music to my ears!" an inmate told me. "It's been so
long since I heard a baby cry, and if I'd known she wasn't suffering,
I could've listened to her cries all night!" His voice cracked and tears
filled his eyes.*

*As he walked away, I realized that Nelson had it all figured out.
I needn't have worried.*

**We often pray for physical safety for loved ones but tend to overlook the need for
emotional and spiritual protection. Do we need to adjust our perspective?**

**Are you still marked by sin? Jesus is our advocate to the Father; He longs to
cleanse you of your "badness." When all is confessed and repented of, Satan's
accusations are silenced. Praise God for His mercy and grace!**

CHAPTER NINE

To Prisons Within the Prison

After working at Camp Hill for a few months, Chaplain Widmann gave verbal approval for me to hold a Bible study, but several more months passed before it became a reality. In the meantime, my contact with inmates was limited to those on my call list. Too often, it seemed, something interfered and I wasn't allowed to meet with inmates: appointments got scratched because count cleared late, or men weren't allowed to leave their blocks because of a fog alert, or staff chaplains were out of the office.

Frustration and impatience gnawed at me. I suspected the administration and the chaplaincy department both anticipated I'd soon give up and move along. But they didn't know me, nor the clear call I felt to prison ministry.

By September 1985, my report to the board at Jubilee Ministries indicated a slow change toward gathering more freedom to minister at Camp Hill. Chaplain Widmann had recently added twenty more men to my regular call list. "There's so much to be done," I wrote. "The institution is overcrowded, and the chaplaincy is understaffed."

Although meeting with inmates in my office was a small step in accomplishing the goals I'd set for ministry at Camp Hill, I longed for permission to visit on the cell blocks. I had learned in Alabama that the most effective ministry begins there. While I waited for that privilege, a dream began to take root about becoming a state chaplain with full access to the entire prison. I was discovering that godly chaplains seemed to be sadly lacking in the state system.

On the morning of January 22, 1986, I went to work bleary-eyed and distracted. Esther was still fifteen days from her due date with our second child when she went into labor in the wee hours of the night, but Emily Dawn had been eager to make her debut. And fast. She arrived only a little over an hour after we got to the hospital.

> *Fast, for sure. Too fast. My doctor later told me that I came within four minutes of death from hemorrhaging. An additional doctor rushed in, they stabilized me, and the emergency passed. By sunrise I settled into my room, and drifted into much-needed sleep.*
> "I'll go to work for a few hours," Nelson said.
> *I was too tired to suggest he go home and grab a few hours of sleep.*

My head was still spinning from the eventful night, and I called the prison to say I'd be late in getting to work that morning. When I arrived, Chaplain Widmann waved me into his office. "Congrats on your million-dollar family! First a son, now a daughter!"

"Hold on!" called Mrs. Shettle from the adjacent office. "I want to hear all about the little darling!" She bustled in with a coffee cup in hand, settled into an empty chair, and peppered me with questions about Emily's weight and length. "Did I hear she has red hair? Oh, I'll bet she's a little cutie!"

"Of course, she is!" I replied.

Out in the hallway a commotion broke out. Loud voices. Bumps against the wall. Shuffling feet.

Chaplain Widmann sauntered to the door and poked his head out. "Put it in the conference room, guys." Then he turned to me and simply said, "It's yours, Nelson."

I looked up as four inmates lugged a desk past the office. Profound gratitude engulfed me. God had blessed Esther and me with a healthy baby girl that night, and now came this unexpected blessing at Camp Hill. It was a desk, only a desk, but it hinted at permanence and my place on the chaplaincy team.

Several weeks later, Chaplain Widmann stopped by my office and sat across from my desk. Settling in, he took off his glasses and tapped them on his knee. "What might Jubilee think of you giving an extra day here at Camp Hill?"

My heart swelled. For so long it seemed I was stuck on a train, sitting motionless at the station. Now, all of a sudden, the delay was over and we steamed off on a grand trip. My very own desk and work area! On top of that, Chaplain Widmann had offered to go to bat for me with Deputy Superintendent Erhard in asking for more freedom to move about the prison. And now, this invitation from out of the blue to work more hours at Camp Hill!

My coworkers at Jubilee were nearly as excited as I was about the expanded opportunity. "God isn't just opening the door at Camp Hill," said Mimi Keller. "He's swinging it wide open, as only He can do!"

The prison chaplaincy staff increased, and I shared the conference room desk with a contract chaplain for a while, until Chaplain Widmann got an idea. "There's a broom closet behind the altar. We can clean that out and turn it into an office for you."

The room was actually pretty spacious and worked out well. Shelves of cleaning supplies remained, which made for interesting decor, and the chapel separated me from the other chaplains' offices, but that was fine with me. It was much quieter at my end.

Beginning in May 1986, I stopped going to Lebanon County Prison except for occasional evening services, and I devoted my four-days-a-week schedule to Camp Hill alone. That spring, Chaplain Widmann and I had collaborated on a proposal to the prison superintendent, and a little more than a year after starting at Camp Hill, he accepted most of the proposal, including permission to hold Bible studies in the modular unit's dayroom.

The four new modular units were the state's solution to overcrowding within the prison. About three hundred men were crammed into the units, and they roamed in and out of the dayroom where I was assigned space for leading Bible studies. A single TV blared continually, adding to the noise of slamming doors and yelling. It was like Grand Central Station. Distractions aside, the Bible class, and the time it gave me to meet guys in the unit were significant steps in building relationships with more inmates.

In August 1986, Chaplain Bryant came on staff. He and I were assigned to visit the AIDS/HIV unit.

I first heard of AIDS on my car radio in 1982, shortly after the U.S. government confirmed the earliest cases of the disease. By then, more than a hundred people had died of the mysterious affliction linked to homosexual and intravenous drug-sharing communities. On talk shows, from pulpits, and at dinner tables, discussions speculated on whether AIDS/HIV was divine retribution for a sinful lifestyle.

The disease got flushed from the shadows in 1984 when Ryan White, a teenage Indiana hemophiliac, contracted AIDS through a blood transfusion. He fought a long court battle to gain admittance to his public high school and became the poster child for AIDS-related discrimination.[13]

New cases popped up with alarming regularity, yet it wasn't until 1985 that President Ronald Reagan mentioned the disease for the first time in public. That same year, Congress allocated $70 million for AIDS research.[14]

AIDS hysteria swept the country and the panic spread into prisons. At Camp Hill, a group of inmates on F Block staged an hour-long protest on January 2, 1986, refusing to return to their block until two inmates with AIDS were removed. In response, the prison established isolated housing for infected inmates.

Early on, staff suited up in protective gear, complete with gloves, gowns, and masks before entering the AIDS block. The quarantined men ate their meals from paper plates and disposable utensils because it was believed that even a dishwasher could not sanitize properly. For a while, the infected men's clothing was burned. Even after studies determined that the virus did not spread through casual contact, AIDS inmates' clothing was still separated from the general population's laundry.

---

[13] Human Resources & Services Administration, "Who Was Ryan White?" https://hab.hrsa.gov/about-ryan-white-hivaids-program/who-was-ryan-white

[14] HIV.gov, "A Timeline of HIV and AIDS," https://www.aids.gov/hiv-aids-basics/hiv-aids-101/aids-timeline/

Paranoia still ran high when Chaplain Bryant and I began visiting the AIDS unit, and I requested permission to lead a weekly Bible study on the unit. The staff chaplains seemed only too happy to hand it off to me. The AIDS inmates, social pariahs within a community of outcasts, seemed to appreciate my interaction with them.

In one of my regular reports to my church family at Faith Mennonite Fellowship I told them of this opportunity to minister to an isolated group of inmates. One of my friends caught up with me after the service, three pews between us. "I'm not gonna shake your hand anymore," he said in his booming voice. "How do I know you don't have AIDS?"

Thinking my friend was only cracking another of his jokes, I laughed and stepped into the aisle toward him. I should have recognized the fear on his face. He raised both hands in defense and backed away. "No, I'm serious," he said. "I still want to be your friend and all, but I'm not going to get close to you."

And he didn't. He no longer shook my hand or slapped me on the back in a friendly greeting. He remained adamant about maintaining a physical distance.

My friend's fear was not unlike that in much of American society.

Uneasiness sometimes sneaked up on me, too. One day, as AIDS inmates gathered around a table for Bible study, a man stumbled against a metal chair sitting catty-corner from me. He sat down and lifted his pant leg. Blood dribbled from his ankle. He dug a tissue from his pocket and dabbed at his wound throughout the Bible study. I forced myself to concentrate on leading the study while very much aware that I sat only two feet away from AIDS-tainted blood.

Unsettling paranoia sometimes haunted me, especially one winter when unexplained fatigue and occasional fevers dogged Nelson for a few weeks. "What if we're not being told the truth about how AIDS is spread?" I asked.

For the most part, peace triumphed over irrational fear. It seemed right that Nelson should work on the AIDS unit, and he assured me that he took the best precautions he knew so that he could share Jesus with gaunt-faced men stalked by certain death.

Like the AIDS/HIV Unit, the Restricted Housing Unit (RHU) held another group of isolated inmates. According to prison policy, a chaplain was to visit RHU every day. Men were generally assigned to the unit for disciplinary purposes and held anywhere from a few weeks to as long as several years, depending on the severity of their infractions. Sometimes a chaplain invited me to join him on his rounds to the RHU, otherwise known as Mohawk at Camp Hill.

The unit's back-to-back cell arrangement made it impossible for prisoners to see their neighbors, but they yelled out to each other. Some hollered just to stave off boredom, and others kicked against their metal cell bars endlessly for the sole pleasure of annoying others. A cacophony of flushing toilets, water running in sinks, moans and curses, shouted threats and obscenities—each one louder than the other—ricocheted off concrete walls in a mind-numbing din.

I understood why the chaplains made short work of their obligatory visits. Mohawk's chaos made it hard to think, let alone carry on conversation.

From my time in Alabama, I knew something of the vast mission field in RHU, and the missed opportunities for ministry bothered me. Eventually I began visiting the unit on my own, a rare privilege granted to a volunteer. Finally, I was free to go through the unit at my own pace and began building relationships that opened a door for spiritual conversations.

The especially incorrigible RHU prisoners were held in basement cells beneath glaring lights that shone around the clock. The men frequently made allegations of abuse from guards, and they claimed that when they were moved to the basement cells, they "fell" down the stairs, courtesy of a guard's shove from behind. Being handcuffed behind their backs, there was no way to break the fall. They insisted the abuse only intensified when an inmate dared to lodge a grievance against their attackers.

One afternoon Chaplain Beeman invited me to ride with him to visit an inmate in a Harrisburg hospital. He filled me in on the details as we drove across town. An RHU inmate had been out in the "dog run" for exercise. "I don't know why, but he refused to get handcuffed to go back to Mohawk, so the officer called for backup. They beat the inmate up so badly that he will probably lose sight in one eye." The chaplain shook his head. "It's senseless. There will be a payday for this."

Occasionally officers lost their jobs over such incidents, but too often, it seemed, staff won exoneration on counter-charges of fabrication.

Early in 1987, I leaned against an inmate's barred cell in the RHU, straining to hear him above the background noise. A prisoner in the next cell began yelling at me. I tuned him out and continued my discussion with the inmate in front of me. The shouts grew more obnoxious and vulgar, until from the corner of my eye, I saw sudden movement on the right. I jumped back instinctively, but not quick enough to avoid the contents of a cup flung at me. It splashed onto my head and dripped to my shoulders. I looked up in surprise, just in time to see him throw a second cupful. Brown liquid splashed onto my chest. Stepping beyond further attack, I cautiously reached into my hair. Plenty of stories floated around of inmates throwing human excrement at staff.

I don't know what motivated the attack—attention, amusement, or anger—but I was relieved to identify the mess in my hair as soup and the chest missile as coffee. I spent the rest of the day walking around the prison with matted hair and a brown stain on my shirt.

When I reported the incident to the sergeant, he asked whether I wanted to write up the inmate. A write-up results in a hearing and discipline for the inmate. Not wanting to cause trouble for anyone, I let the matter go. But Chaplain Widmann did not. He told me I could no longer visit Mohawk on my own; to do so "would reward the inmate," he said. I didn't see the logic there, but I had to go with his dictates for several months until he relented.

Later, a new deputy superintendent suspended my RHU visiting privilege for a time because he felt it was too much of a liability to have a volunteer mingling in Mohawk.

More and more, I thought about becoming a state chaplain to maximize the calling I had for prison ministry. But two obstacles blocked that path. First, I would need a Bible degree. The state required all chaplains to hold, at minimum, a bachelor's degree. I had been picking up college classes here and there, but at the rate I was going, it would be decades before gradu-ation. I would have to figure out another way.

Second, I needed ministerial credentials, a bona fide backing of a church body. My church at Faith Mennonite Fellowship had been sup-portive of my ministry from the beginning. They gave generously, both in congregational offerings and in personal gifts, and frequently asked for reports of my work. Pastor Isaac Gehman and Deacon Levi Brubaker each visited the prison with me several times, and we talked of the advantages of credentialing.

Discussion began about licensing me for prison ministry, with the pos-sibility of ordination at a later date. Although it was clear the credentials would apply only to prison ministry, and that I would not be a part of the church ministry team, Esther and I were expected to dress in accordance with their requirements for ministers and their wives. That meant Esther would be required to wear cape dresses and I would have to wear a "plain suit," an altered suit jacket fashioned into a clerical-type collar and worn without a necktie. I had one in the back of my closet that I had worn to a service at the Alabama Work Release Center.

"What do you call that?" an inmate had asked in puzzled derision.

I replied with the typical conservative Mennonite response, that my plain coat symbolized our separation from the world.

"I don't get it," he said, shaking his head.

Other conversations in the same vein left me with the stunning real-ization that a cultural symbol I had grown up with made no sense to men outside my community. My insistence on wearing it would only muddle and distract from the message of the Gospel.

My pastors, however, didn't see it that way. Eventually, Esther and I decided it best to leave our church family at Faith. Ministerial credentials would have to wait.

What paralyzing fears are keeping you from fulfilling God's purposes? Can you trust Him with those fears for the sake of the Gospel's advance?

CHAPTER TEN

The Call Expands

In the summer of 1987, Chaplain McMillian, a friendly pastor in the African Methodist Episcopalian (AME) church, began as a contract chaplain at Camp Hill. He verbalized how impressed he was that Jubilee would pay someone to work in prison at no cost to the state. A few months later he applied for the position as Facility Chaplaincy Program Director (FCPD) at SCI Retreat and was offered the job. "If I accept it, I want you to come with me, Nelson," he said.

Given the two-hour drive, I knew that was not practical, nor was I interested in leaving the work at Camp Hill to go to Retreat. However, I was excited about the potential for Jubilee's expansion into another facility. Would the board be interested? I talked over the possibilities with Director Donald Martin and volunteered to make the two-hour drive once a week to keep the door open until they found someone to fill the spot. Don shared the vision with the board and soon acquired their approval.

I had other irons in the fire at that time, however, so I would not go to Retreat on a regular schedule until the spring of 1988. Chaplain Widmann, a former Clinical Pastoral Education (CPE) instructor, had been urging me to enroll in the fifteen-week CPE classes offered at Philhaven Hospital, a mental health facility near Lebanon. I took his advice and enrolled.

Halfway through the classes, on March 21, 1988, Esther gave birth to our third child, Renee Joy Zeiset, another precious little red-haired daughter. I was humbled at God's blessings poured out on me.

Those years in the late 1980s were busy ones. In 1986 we sold our house at Schoeneck and rented a house while having a new home built on a one-acre lot in the southeastern corner of Lebanon County, in the "suburbs" of Kleinfeltersville. The town claimed to be the smallest town with the longest name in the United States, and I accepted that assertion. Now, after thirty-some years of residing here, I find that Wikipedia ties Kleinfeltersville with Mooselookmeguntic, Maine, for the longest one-word name given to a U.S. Post Office.

The building contractor of our new house allowed us to help where we could to cut costs. Nelson lent a hand with hanging drywall, and we both painted trim work and walls, simplifying the process by painting all the rooms with the same white paint.

Just after we moved in, I dragged through nine months of pregnancy fatigue beyond anything I'd ever experienced. Joel was not yet five years old, and Emily was twenty-six months when Renee was born. Now we had three preschoolers and a twenty-year house mortgage. I began babysitting to supplement Nelson's income, and cared for more than twenty different children in our home over the next seventeen years.

Nelson had taken a pay cut when he reduced his hours at the hardware store to work at Jubilee, but we both felt God directing us to take the step. You could call it faith. Or naivete. One of Nelson's coworkers at the store called it stupid and risky. "What if things don't work out?" he asked. "You're crazy to let this job fizzle to chase after something unproven."

Nelson and I didn't think about it too hard. We'd been praying for the opportunity, and when God provided in a manner beyond our wildest imaginations, I don't think it crossed our minds to not proceed.

At a time when we most needed help, Lester Miller, a pastor and counselor, presented a series of financial seminars at our church. He provided us with invaluable information for navigating our financial path on a shoestring. Pastor Miller emphasized that it's not a matter of how much you earn as it is how you manage it. "Tell your money where to go rather than wonder where it went," he said. At his advice, we created a budget, a practice we still use today.

Maybe that seminar was also the force behind generous giving on the part of our church family at Faith, which backed us with monthly support during the time we worshiped with the congregation. Individuals also slipped us money—a twenty-dollar bill in a Christmas card, or an anonymous gift left in our church mailbox. The auto parts store owned by a member of our congregation and the mechanic who worked on site gave huge cost breaks on chronic repair problems with our vehicles.

One Sunday morning I found a pack of six full-sized Snickers bars on my car seat. Someone had heard me say how much I liked them, and accurately guessed our grocery budget didn't allow for such extravagance. Those six candy bars nearly brought me to tears. That small gift felt huge!

People not affiliated with our church—Nelson's coworkers at the hardware store, relatives, and mere acquaintances—gave generously too. One day a visitor at church interrupted Nelson's conversation with friends by leaning in to shake his hand, and with little more than a quick hello, she pressed a hundred-dollar bill into his palm. One hundred dollars! It was more than a day's wage!

Even our family doctor said that we need not hurry to pay the bill for his services at our daughter's birth. We paid as we could, and after a few months, I dropped by the office to pay off the balance of several hundred dollars. The receptionist smiled broadly. "You don't owe a red cent. Someone paid your bill in full just last week."

In spite of the generosity, I caved to discontentment far too often. When we belatedly turned in our dented and rusting Toyota Corolla for a used Chevy Cavalier station wagon, I savored the glamour of our upgrade—until I compared it with the shiny new minivans on the church parking lot. And every time someone handed me yet another Home Interior catalog and an invitation to the home parties so popular in the '80s and '90s, I cringed with embarrassment. How in the world could my peers afford those crazy-priced accessories or the patterned wallpapers that covered their living rooms? What of the name-brand sweaters, regular lunches at McDonald's, and their children's Christian school education? It hardly seemed fair.

Thankfully, I adopted a better mindset over time. Not that discontentment didn't gnaw at me at times; sometimes it bit hard. But I remembered an incident while in Alabama when a woman mentioned having had bacon for breakfast. In that unguarded moment, the wife of a We Care staff person gasped. "Bacon?! There hasn't been one strip of bacon in my house for years!" Her voice had a bitter edge. I didn't want to be like that.

Nelson worked for Jubilee Ministries for nine years until he was hired as a state chaplain in 1994, and from that time, it was as though a financial faucet turned off. As it should have. God had prompted His people to give generously while we had needs, but as soon as Nelson's new job paid a competitive wage and adequate benefits, our benefactors moved on to help someone else.

But I'm getting ahead of the story.

Winter gave way to spring, 1988, and I told the chaplains at Camp Hill of my plans to go to SCI Retreat one day a week.

Chaplain Widmann sat up stiffly. "To Retreat? With McMillian? Why?"

I assured him the arrangement was temporary and that I would be back on my regular four-days-a-week schedule at Camp Hill as soon as Jubilee hired someone for Retreat. He was not impressed.

Chaplain Bryant strode into my office a short time later. "What's this I hear about you going to Retreat?"

I was unsure of the reason for the chaplains' displeasure. Rivalry between them and Chaplain McMillian? Annoyance that I was cutting my time at Camp Hill by twenty-five percent? Whatever. Apparently, they valued my ministry at their institution more than I knew. I chose to take their disapproval as a compliment.

Every Thursday, for three months in the summer of 1988, I made the two-hour trek to Retreat Prison, a facility converted from the former Retreat State Hospital and opened in 1986. It was situated about ten miles southwest of Wilkes-Barre, in the shadow of Shickshinny Mountain, and accessed from a single narrow road crossing a steel grated bridge over the Susquehanna River. From a security perspective, it seemed odd that a prison would have only one possible exit.

The chapel at SCI Retreat could hold about a hundred men and was housed in a third-floor classroom in an old building at the far end of the prison compound. All the staff chaplains shared a single office. My assigned spot by a long row of windows at the front of the chapel lacked in space and privacy, but afforded a scenic view of the area. My Bible class and counseling sessions with inmates competed for space with choir practices, Bible studies, and a host of other activities.

"Can you round up some of your Mennonite pastor friends to preach here one Sunday every month?" asked Chaplain McMillian.

Among the pastors willing to make the long drive with me from the Lancaster and Lebanon areas were Jim Hess, Fred Heller, Marvin Reed, and Isaac Gehman. When Jubilee hired Glen Souder, pastor at East District Mennonite Church, near Watsontown, I was happy to leave Retreat's work in his capable hands so I could return to Camp Hill four days a week.

In 1989 the inmate population at Pennsylvania's fifteen state prisons rose to an all-time high of more than 20,000, thanks to get-tough-on-crime policies. Overcrowding posed a serious problem throughout the state. At Camp Hill alone 2,600 men were crowded into a space designed to hold 1,826.[15]

The fields were white with harvest and there was much work to be done.

---

[15] Deb Kiner, *Penn Live Patriot News*, "Camp Hill Prison Riots in 1989: 'It Looked Like Vietnam'" https://www.pennlive.com/life-and-culture/erry-2018/10/11a5f30a832610/camp-hill-prison-riots-in-1989.html

How can you show care and support to someone who is fulfilling God's purposes? Something as simple as a favorite candy bar? A cash gift? A service such as mechanical work?

A coworker thought Nelson acted irresponsibly in taking a pay cut to fulfill God's call. What risks and sacrifices do you need to take to step out in faith?

CHAPTER ELEVEN

Before the Chaos

Warm sunshine streamed on me as I walked toward Camp Hill's chapel on the morning of October 25, 1989. Weather forecasters predicted the afternoon would see unseasonably warm temperatures into the seventies, and that was fine with me. The longer winter could be delayed, the happier I was.

The day began ordinarily enough, without a hint of the chaos and terror to strike later in the day. I started the morning in a meeting with Chaplain Favers, who had been hired as a contract chaplain a year earlier. The two of us collaborated on "C Ward Project," which was to provide structured chaplaincy programs for inmates on the unit.

At the time, SCI Camp Hill was one of three classification prisons in Pennsylvania. New inmates coming from county jails in the state's central region were placed in C Ward, a unit segregated from the rest of Camp Hill's prisoners. For three to six months they underwent extensive psychological evaluations, medical assessments, educational testing, and the like. The results determined each new inmate's correctional plan and prison placement.

Chaplain Favers and I ended our meeting that morning feeling satisfied that we would soon be ready to launch "C Ward Project." I went back to my office and prepared for the day's first inmate appointment by reviewing my notes on previous sessions with Robert.

My file was thick with notes on inmates whom I had counseled during the past four years. I'd met all sorts of criminals—drug dealers, rapists, child molesters, kidnappers, burglars, and murderers. Every day I heard dark stories of unimaginable violence.

Robert's story was typical. For nearly four years, we had engaged in conversations about cults, Satan's tactics, and end times. He asked for Bible study courses, and kept me abreast of his persistent and mostly unwelcomed efforts to witness to guards and to pray with them. His mutilated self-esteem evidenced itself often, in spite of the spiritual façade he adopted.

Over time, he gave voice to a deep anger toward his parents, and admitted to what I had suspected—that he had been sexually abused repeatedly while still in elementary school. He alternately raged at his molester and defended him, and at times Robert assigned blame to himself, citing a degree of personal pleasure. I spent hours with him, trying to help him sort through a tangle of lies and vacillating emotions that bound him.

Several weeks earlier, my appointment with Robert had ended badly, and I felt like we had to tie up a lot of loose ends that had come unraveled. That day I had walked Robert to the door after an hour in my office. Greg, my next appointment, had already arrived and stood in the hallway awaiting his turn. He raised a hand in greeting and suddenly dropped it to his side. His face turned ashen, and he shrank in the shadow of Robert's retreating form.

I swept my arm toward my open door. "C'mon in, Greg. Have a seat."

But Greg pivoted away, staring after Robert until he vanished from view. When Greg slowly turned back to me his eyes blazed with anger and his chin quivered. "That guy . . . he . . . he molested me when I was a kid!"

I steered Greg into my office, and his story of violent abuse tumbled out.

I contemplated my response to this new information. As much as I wanted to help Greg to wholeness and healing, I also had an obligation to report the incident to prison security. I called Mr. Jamison, the therapist who ran Robert's sex offenders' group.

He let out a sigh. "I'll have to look into this. One thing for sure, the DOC can never allow the victim and his offender to have contact with each other here."

Later that same day, Mr. Jamison called me back and said he had acted on a hunch and ordered a search of Robert's cell. Officers discovered a ton of alarming information. The therapist called an emergency meeting with

Robert's sex offender group, and he insisted that Greg and I also attend the meeting.

About twenty men in brown prison-issued uniforms sat in a circle in the therapy room where Mr. Jamison confronted Robert with Greg's allegation of molestation. Robert folded his arms across his chest, his face void of all emotion. Mr. Jamison pressed the issue, but Robert remained stoic. Greg's head, however, hung low in an attempt to hide raw emotion. A few men in the circle, moved by the drama, began crying. "C'mon, man, 'fess up!" they pleaded.

Robert remained unmoved, offering only vague excuses and dismissals.

Mr. Jamison strode into the center of the circle, two grocery bags in hand. Angrily, he turned them upside down and flung the contents into the circle. A blizzard of magazine and newspaper insert clippings—images of children clad only in underwear—fluttered to the floor.

"Look at this! Just look at this junk confiscated from Robert's cell!" Mr. Jamison screamed.

Momentary astonishment gave way to collective disgust and indignation. Some inmates turned away from the silent, vulnerable images lying on the floor. Others raised angry voices and flung hot accusations at Robert.

He didn't break.

And now, a few weeks after that dramatic confrontation, Robert sat in my office again. He was still defensive and angry at Mr. Jamison, at the men in his therapy group, and at me. He insisted he didn't remember the sexual encounters with Greg. "If I did it—*if I did it,*" he raised his voice and deliberately drew out each word, "it's in the past and it should be left there! I don't know what the big deal is anyway."

"You've got to come clean," I urged. "You're in denial, and you will never better yourself from that place."

He worked his jaw and glared at me. A cocky grin spread across his face. "I'm gonna deny that I'm in denial."

I raised my hands in surrender. "Have it your way, Robert." I glanced at my watch. "It's time for you to get back to your block. Just do me and yourself a favor, and give serious thought to two things. One, you seem to be out of touch with your feelings about the pain in your life. Maybe I can help you work through that. And two, I want you to consider the pain you've caused your victims."

Robert swallowed and gave an almost imperceptible nod. He agreed to see me again in November. I had no reason to believe that we would not meet again.

Clair came into my office next, offering a lame excuse for having skipped our last appointment. "It wasn't really my fault," he said.

"It's never your fault," I returned with a smile. Clair was a master at shifting blame.

Before I took my next breath, he launched into his favorite topics: that the charges against him were false, that his arrest was a sham, and that his ex-wife had it in for him. He still loved her, he claimed, but desperately wanted to marry his girlfriend of seven years.

Of course. I'd heard his spiel so often I could almost recite it for him. We spent the rest of our time talking about his sexual addiction.

Over lunchtime, I cleared my head and then met with Tim, who was twenty-one years old and serving a six-to-twelve-year sentence. At the earliest, he would be twenty-seven before his release, but depending on his behavior and compliance with programs, he could be into his late thirties before he got back on the streets again. He struck me as sincere and committed to Christ, but ongoing struggles regarding sex and authority made it difficult for him to keep his head above water. Tim left my office assuring me he'd put extra effort into reading his Bible until our next appointment.

It had been a full day of interacting with inmates, and they had all shown up as scheduled. Until now. John was the last appointment of the day and he was late. I looked at my watch impatiently. It was almost three o'clock.

And that's when I heard the gunshot.

Robert denied the effect of sins done against himself, as well as the sins he had done to others. His refusal to acknowledge and deal with it immobilized him. Are there things in your life that need to be faced head-on? What will it take for you to find freedom?

CHAPTER TWELVE

Riot!

*C**rack!*
            I shoved away from my desk and turned to the window behind me, trying to determine the source of the gunshot. It had to have come from a guard tower, the only place on prison grounds where guns were carried. From my window I could see only one of Camp Hill Prison's ten towers, about two hundred feet away. There the guard stood on the catwalk, cradling his gun, and looking intently into the courtyard between inmate housing units.

The unit buildings blocked my view of the area that held the guard's attention, but I could imagine how crowded it was now. "Yard" had just ended, and nearly a thousand men were beginning to stream back to their cells. The movement of so many men at one time always heightened the chance of trouble. Added to that, the gorgeous weather would undoubtedly factor into inmates' reluctance to leave the recreation yard.

Except for that unmistakable gunshot, nothing seemed amiss. I turned back to my desk and checked my schedule again. John still had not shown up for his appointment. I picked up my desk phone and called B Block to check on his whereabouts.

"He's not coming. We're having an emergency," the guard responded tersely and hung up.

Emergencies happen in prison. A fistfight here. Contraband discovered there. But that gunshot bothered me. Something didn't seem right.

Voices drifted from the chaplains' offices. Maybe they knew what was going on. I walked past the rows of pews and the conference room where Mr. Binkley, a Jehovah's Witness volunteer, was leading a Bible study for his denomination's inmate devotees. Beyond the conference room, Chaplains Bryant and Widmann stood outside their offices, silhouetted in afternoon light at the chapel's glass-fronted door. Chaplain Beeman emerged from his office as I drew near. "What's happening out there?" he asked in a slow drawl.

Chaplain Widmann drew on his pipe and exhaled blue curls of smoke. "I guess there's a fight going on somewhere."

"Did anyone else hear a gunshot?" I asked.

"Sure did. It was probably a warning shot, but that's troubling," said Chaplain Widmann. He strode to the door and pressed against the glass. "I'm not seeing anything out of the ordinary from here."

Chaplain Bryant paced the hallway, his finger raised to his lips in thought. "Seems odd," he said, and pointed toward the conference room. "We have, what, eight inmates in there with Mr. Binkley?"

Chaplain Widmann cradled his pipe. Smoke encircled his head, clouding his drawn face. "Yup. Three inmate clerks, too."

Chaplain Beeman moved to my side and gestured toward the sanctuary. I matched his slow amble between the pews where colorful patches of sunshine streamed through the stained-glass windows and danced on the tiled floor. He pointed toward a set of north-facing doors. "Maybe we can see something from there."

Outside the chapel an expanse of lawn stretched to a wide pavement, a main thoroughfare for inmates walking to and from appointments with various departments—medical, educational, and religious—and for vehicles coming onto the prison compound. Now the walkway was deserted.

A quick movement at the corner of the Education Building caught my attention. A knot of inmates ran helter-skelter like kids at a playground. A few broke off the group and bounded up the steps of the building, cupping their hands around their eyes to peer through the glass door. Others ran from one window to another and pulled themselves up to look inside.

"What do you think they're up to?" I asked.

"It's hard to tell." Chaplain Beeman fumbled in his shirt pocket to retrieve a fat cigar. Anticipating a smelly light-up, I stepped aside without taking an eye from the activity across the walkway.

"Looks like they're trying to break in!"

"O Lord!" His voice trembled. "They've lost control of the prison!"

A month earlier he had complained to me of an administrative memo that denied inmate families from bringing in their favorite foods on "family days." I had seldom seen Chaplain Beeman so agitated.

"Look at this!" He had pushed the memo across the desk to me. "Security says there's too much contraband hidden in the food. Maybe so. But they can't just yank this from deserving inmates. We've got to find another way to deal with contraband! If this doesn't cause a riot, nothing will!"

Now his words sounded prophetic. A chill ran up my back. Looking across the lawn to the activity at the Education Building, there was no denying that serious trouble had come to Camp Hill. I only hoped it would soon be contained.

Chaplain Beeman gasped and pointed to my left. "Look at that!"

Two guards raced down the walkway. Behind them came another dozen or so uniformed officers, dashing en masse, their legs and arms pumping furiously. A guard at the rear of the group frequently looked over his shoulder without losing stride. The officers tore past the Education Building, obviously intent on reaching safety in the Control Center.

I needed no interpretation to understand the unfolding situation. In a split-second decision, I turned and sprinted to my office, snatching my briefcase from my desk. Back into the chapel I ran, around the altar and between long rows of pews, and set my sights on the exit beyond the chaplains' offices. It was already clogged with chapel staff, and Chaplain Bryant stood in the center of the maze, waving his long arms and yelling, "Move it! Now!" He herded the three inmate chapel clerks into the conference room with the Bible study group. Mr. Binkley stood outside the door, looking befuddled.

The chaplain locked the door behind the last inmate, and in one fluid movement, stepped into my path to block my escape route. "Zeiset, you can't leave now! It's not safe out there! We'll get you out when we can, but not now!" he barked, and simultaneously motioned to Mr. Binkley. "For your safety," he said, waving us both into his office. "I'll get you an escort as soon as it's safe. Hurry!"

He slammed the door behind us. His keys jangled in the lock. *Click.* I stared at the door, a symbol of the distinction between me, a volunteer, and the chaplains on the other side of it.

Across the room, an east-facing window had been opened to let in the unseasonably warm October air. From this vantage point, I had a view of a short walkway that led from the chapel steps to the main thoroughfare. Beyond it was a grassy area and the infirmary and visiting room. On the left, the driveway stretched out of my view to extend the full length of the prison compound. Not far to my right, it ran to the front gate, flanked by towers and a connecting catwalk where a guard stood holding a rifle.

The air was still, eerily quiet here near the front gate, and in stark contrast to the violent chaos that had broken out somewhere in the back of the prison compound, out of sight and out of earshot.

Sirens wailed in the distance. Time seemed to stand still. Suddenly a tangle of police cars gathered by the front gate. State police, local police, and sheriffs hurried from their cars to form a human perimeter around the outside fence.

I turned to tell Mr. Binkley of the activity outside our window. He sat stiffly on an office chair, his legs crossed at the ankles, and a book opened on his lap. "Hmmm," he said without looking up. "I guess we're in a riot." He pressed his dark tie against his chest and continued reading.

I went back to the window, wondering how he could possibly concentrate on reading in this situation. Didn't he care what was going on around him? Could he truly be unaffected by the madness unleashed beyond the confines of the chapel walls?

Fire trucks rolled in, followed by more police cars. In gaps between buildings, I saw them racing to the back of the prison grounds, lights flashing, sirens wailing. More policemen with shotguns and rifles in hand rushed to tighten the line around the fenced perimeter.

A fresh commotion stirred at the guard tower. Up on the catwalk the guard raised his gun and bellowed, "Stop right there!"

I pressed my face against the window to see a prison maintenance truck roll slowly toward the front gate. The tower guard screamed a second warning. The truck crept closer still, and now I saw its shattered windshield. The two occupants commandeering it both wore brown uniforms and with a shock, I realized they were inmates. Would they try to ram the fence?

"No closer!" The guard's shouts split the air. He steadied his gun at them. "I'm gonna shoot! I will! Stop now!"

The inmates tumbled from the battered truck and raised their hands in surrender. "No! Please! Don't shoot!" the driver called back in a shaky voice. "We got a maintenance dude on the truck. He's hurt bad and needs help!"

The tower guard fell silent, as though weighing truth, and kept his gun leveled at them. Seconds ticked by. "Get moving!" he barked. "Out of here!"

The men sprang to the back of the truck, lifted a khaki-uniformed man off, and laid him on the grass. Then they sprinted back in the direction from where they had come and disappeared from view. The man on the grass lay motionless.

My mind raced to process the unfolding chaos. Without doubt, the injured man wore the uniform of a maintenance worker. Did that mean that two courageous inmates had rescued him from further violence and risked their own lives to do so?

Nurses emerged from the infirmary with a stretcher and sprinted across the grass, hastily lifted the man on, and hurried back to safety. The infirmary door had barely closed behind them when the guard at the front gate bellowed more warning shouts.

Again, I strained to see action on my left. A man ran across the grass, zigzagging his way toward the front gate, and screaming incoherently.

"Stop! I'll shoot!" the guard yelled.

The man kept coming, close enough now that I saw he wore only a ragged undershirt and blue shorts. Shorts? I couldn't make sense of it. With a jolt I realized they were but tatters of a guard's uniform pants. One pant leg was gone, the other shortened to mid-thigh. Had they been torn off? Cut off?

"Stop now! Stop!" the tower guard bellowed again.

The man wasn't far from the chapel now, close enough that I could see his face was contorted with panicked terror. A thousand thoughts assailed me at once, but predominantly, I realized that the tower guard didn't recognize the terrorized man as a fellow guard. Or maybe this was only a ruse! Could it be an inmate posing as a guard? Obviously, the tower guard was uncertain and kept up his threats to shoot.

Suddenly the running man changed course, but not momentum. He ran in a tight circle now, shrieking, "No! Don't shoot! No-o-o!" Around and around and around he spun, his frantic cries escalating into a piercing primal scream.

My head pounded with the horror of the moment. What terrors drove him to the teetering brink of insanity, I wondered. And now, this unspeakable horror—that he could be mistaken for an inmate and shot by a fellow guard with whom he sought refuge!

Suddenly the guard at the front tower stopped shouting.

Eerie silence returned. My heart throbbed.

And mercy came.

Finally.

Two officers dashed across the grass and took their panic-stricken fellow guard by the arms. His wails faded as they hurriedly escorted him to the front gate.

I drew a long breath and turned from the window.

Mr. Binkley turned a page in his book.

The sun sank low in the western sky, casting autumn's long golden shadows across the lawn. Such beauty seemed incongruent amidst the violence around me.

I glanced at my watch and realized almost two hours had passed since we'd been locked in the office. It was nearly time for me to be at home eating dinner with my family. It would be very late before I got home tonight.

If I got home.

Esther would be worried. I hoped she wasn't listening to the news.

A wave of helplessness hit me. I knew there was no way I could reach my wife. The cold fact that prison phone lines were off limits during emergencies had been made clear in periodic training. I could not call out, and Esther couldn't call in. Had I ever thought to tell her that? And if I did, would she remember?

I ached to let her know I was all right, at least for the moment.

What happens when circumstances suddenly turn crazy, and life as you knew it is upended beyond recognition? When events shake loose all the controls you ever held and you are completely helpless to right the wrongs surrounding you?

Jesus' followers can find comfort and peace in knowing that He has no *oops* moments. Nothing catches Him off guard. He sees all, He knows all, and He is a good God. Thank God for His gracious oversight of every moment of every day!

CHAPTER THIRTEEN
The Aftermath

*N*elson was late. I'd expected him more than half an hour ago. This was so unlike him; I could nearly set my clock by his schedule. The last time he'd been this late was while we were dating. He'd had a car accident on his way to my house and was hospitalized for a week.

I cast a nervous glance at the kitchen clock again and turned off the oven to hold dinner. Renee impatiently banged her spoon on the high chair tray, and her red curls bobbed in time. I handed her a cracker. The wall phone rang, and I sprang for it, my heart in my throat.

"I'll be home late tonight," Nelson said above the noise of traffic in the background. "Sorry I couldn't call earlier. I'm at the turnpike now, calling from the first phone booth I could find."

"What happened?" I asked.

"Um . . . a problem at the prison. I'll tell you about it later. I'm okay, and I'm on my way home now, but it will be nearly an hour till I get there."

He sounded upbeat, and he was on his way home. It was all that mattered. That, and getting dinner for my hungry children. No sooner had I spooned chicken and rice onto their plates before the phone rang again.

"Is dinner over?" my father asked in an obviously forced attempt at small talk.

I tensed. Something was up. Dad never called just to chat. "The kids are eating, but Nelson isn't here yet," I said.

"Oh." It was just one little word, but heavy with emotion.

I filled in the awkward silence. "But Nelson just called, and he's on his way home."

Dad sighed heavily. "Oh, that's good to hear. I just heard there's a problem at the prison. But Nelson's okay?"

"Yes. He should be home in an hour."

"That's good," he paused and then quickly said, "I'll let you get back to the kids now."

Almost before the phone was back in its cradle, it jangled again. I recognized the voice of Donald Martin, Director of Jubilee Ministries. "Is Nelson at home?"

"Not yet, but he's on his way home."

"I see . . . well . . . have you talked to him this afternoon?"

I tucked the phone into the crook of my neck and sat down by Renee. She reached eager hands to the dish I held, and nearly knocked it to the floor.

"Um, yes, just a few minutes ago." I spooned another helping into Renee's open mouth, thinking this stilted call was as odd as my dad's.

"Well, I'm glad to hear that," he said, adding that he didn't have many details about a disturbance at Camp Hill, but he would talk with Nelson later.

A chill swept over me as I hung up the phone and turned my attention back to feeding our three young children.

Joel studied the clock with a first grader's concentration. "Daddy's late."

I swallowed. "Yes. But he's coming." He's coming. He's coming. The words spoke assurance to my pounding heart.

"Can we still go to Leesport tonight?" Joel asked.

"We won't have time anymore," I replied reluctantly.

Joel's face fell. He and Emily had anticipated getting ice cream cones at Leesport Farmers Market, the place of my own childhood memories. My dad would go upstairs to the auction barn to pick up a check for the calves he had sold that day, while we six kids browsed among the familiar market stands and deliberated about how to spend the quarter Dad doled out to each of us. Sometimes I chose pink cotton candy, savoring its sweet, sticky nothingness. More often, I bought a popsicle smothered in a chocolate shell and studded with crunchy peanuts. And always, we ended the evening at the candy stand where we kids gathered around our parents, giggling and grinning as they chose spearmint leaves, broken Fifth Avenues, and anise bears.

Joel broke in on my memories. "Well, then can we go fishing tonight?" It had become his favorite activity with his daddy since he caught a six-inch sunny and proudly held it aloft so I could snap the picture that now hung on his bedroom wall.

"No, play Candyland!" three-year-old Emily shouted in gleeful anticipation of her favorite game.

The phone rang a third time. "Esther!" My neighbor's shrill voice blasted through the line, and I jerked the receiver away from my ear. "I sure hope Nelson's not at the prison!"

I didn't have a chance to tell her that he was fine and on his way home.

"You should see the pictures on TV!" she crowed. "They're burning the prison down! There's cops all over the place!" She described in horrifying detail what she was seeing on her living room screen.

She's being overly dramatic, I told myself. Still, I didn't turn on the news when I hung up the phone. It hardly sounded like something I wanted the children to hear. I only wanted to hear Nelson's truck pulling into our garage.

After two and a half hours in Chaplain Bryant's locked office, Mr. Binkley and I suddenly received notice to leave the prison under escort. We hurried through the front gate, beyond the double fence, past a line of police in riot gear, and into the parking lot jammed with police cars.

Black smoke billowed from the back of the prison complex. A police helicopter circled overhead, pulsating with a *whop, whop, whop* that made my ears ache. There was so much to see, even more to imagine, and so little comprehension. The chaos was unbelievable.

I climbed into my Datsun pickup truck, pulled the door shut on the mayhem around me, and drove out of the parking lot. Near the turnpike I stopped at a phone booth to call Esther and then headed homeward. Deep numbness settled in. Images of the terrors I'd seen spun in a mind-boggling mass, and every few minutes another state police car screamed past in the oncoming lane, interrupting my jumbled thoughts.

I wondered what this meant for my future at Camp Hill. I'd been so certain that God wanted me to minister there. He'd flung doors wide open to make it possible, hadn't He? Now the future seemed uncertain.

Cheers of "Daddy's home!" greeted me as I stepped through the door of my home. My family's welcome never felt so good.

Esther set a plate of warmed-up chicken and rice in front of me and shooed the kids into the living room. Then she pulled up her chair at the table and placed her warm hand on my arm. "So tell me . . . what happened?"

I shrugged. Words couldn't describe what I had witnessed. "They rioted. Burned some buildings."

Esther waited for me to go on.

"Some guards got hurt. I don't know how many or how bad." I knew my answers were insufficient to satisfy Esther's questions or to recount the scene at Camp Hill.

"Are you all right?"

"I'm fine." Suddenly I felt drained of every ounce of strength.

When Esther got the kids ready for bed, I scanned the radio dial until I found a Harrisburg news station. This was one of those times I wished we had a TV. Neither Esther nor I grew up with it, and were very happy to keep it that way until something newsworthy happened. Camp Hill's riot certainly qualified.

The radio wasn't reporting much that I didn't already know. I flipped it off and dragged upstairs for our bedtime routine. Scenes of the day's happenings crowded in as I absently read a Bible story, prayed with the kids, and tucked them into bed. Then Esther and I sat on the living room couch together, listening to live coverage of the breaking news story.

Reporters said the incident had started at E Gate when an inmate assaulted a guard. Within minutes the fracas veered out of control. Inmates took eight prison guards hostage and set four major fires. Four hundred state police converged on the scene, and dozens of injuries occurred.

By eleven o'clock, I'd heard enough of the endless loops of the same stories, and I felt a weariness beyond anything I'd ever experienced. But merciful sleep was a long time in coming.

Thursday morning's news was more encouraging. Officials had regained control of the prison where 1,200 inmates had run wild throughout the facility, burning the commissary, furniture factory, and a cafeteria. Forty-five staff and inmates had been injured, two of them critically. But, thank God, the long night of terror was over.

After breakfast I called my friend, Chaplain Beeman. He answered sleepily, but silenced my apologies. "It was only fitful sleep, at best," he said. "Given all I saw, I can't imagine that I'll sleep well for a long time to come." He told me how inmates had overpowered maintenance workers and stolen their equipment. "They ran a circular saw at full tilt at the necks of guards and flung sawblades like frisbees at firemen. They doused mattresses with gasoline and lit them. I never would have guessed steel and concrete could burn like it did." He said that staff chaplains had remained at the prison until five o'clock that morning. "The prison is a mess. Don't even try to get in today," he said.

I'd figured as much. I spent the day at Lebanon Prison instead, where I went through the motions of teaching a Bible class. Uppermost in my mind was Camp Hill, and wondering what changes the riot might mean both for the men who lived there and for me. Donald Martin and I discussed it at length, and then I went home early to take Joel fishing. Even there, along the quiet pond's edge, my mind revisited Camp Hill's devastation. Later that evening, a stream of friends called to offer their support and prayers.

We went to bed at nine-thirty. I tossed and turned for an hour, but sleep was still far from me when the phone rang. It was my friend and Jubilee coworker, Leon Zimmerman. "Nelson, I thought you'd want to know that they're rioting at Camp Hill again!"

Stunned, Esther and I went downstairs, and sat in the dark living room listening to unthinkable news. At seven o'clock that evening, inmates had escaped by tripping locks on their damaged cell doors, and within hours they gained access to nearly every section of the prison, taking five new hostages and setting more fires. This time more than eight hundred state police responded to the crisis. It would be another long night of terror at the prison.

Esther and I both tossed throughout the dark night's few remaining hours, and Friday morning came too soon. My thirteen-hour workday at the hardware store looked impossible. We listened to the radio as we picked at our breakfast. Every spoonful seemed to catch in my throat as reports of Camp Hill's destruction came in. There were conflicting reports of injuries. "It looks like a war zone," reporters said over and over.

Zimmerman's hardware store was abuzz that morning with news coming from the Harrisburg area. Many of the store's regular customers knew of my prison work, and that morning it seemed they all wanted to talk about it. Around noon, a customer told me the sixteen-hour riot was finally quelled, but that most of the prison was destroyed, and more than sixty people were injured. Miraculously, there were no fatalities.

I called Chaplain Beeman after I got off work that night. He described how he'd gone into the prison during the riot and milled with inmates who had surrendered and lay in long rows on the cold ground, their hands cuffed behind their backs. Their cells, their clothing, and their blankets had all been destroyed. On that chilly October night, they lay outside shivering and crying, many of them wearing only underwear. Chaplain Beeman's voice broke as he told me of the need for chaplaincy to both inmates and staff. "Try to get in on Monday," he said. "We sure could use your help."

Chaplain Beeman's description of the situation at the prison gripped me. It was heartrending for Nelson. He personally knew some of the injured staff. He had counseled some of the inmates who, for two chilly days and nights now, lay outside on the grass with little to eat and wearing little clothing. Nelson had visited them on their blocks, encouraging and mentoring them through the dark places in their lives. And now this. How many of them had participated in the rampage? Who among them stood against the violence, pleading for calm and surrender?

The Camp Hill riots made headlines in the national news and became fodder for local talk shows. One caller said that the prison had been free of disturbances in the days when it was surrounded by peaceful farmland.

"So, bring back the cows!" the host whooped and broke into laughter.

Disgusted with the circus of sensationalism, I snapped off the radio.

Nelson and I had talked of little but the Camp Hill riots in the past few days, and my heart stopped when he talked of going back on Monday. It sounded terrifyingly dangerous. Yet I had no doubt of God's calling on Nelson. God had made it possible for him to minister at Camp Hill, and I would need to trust him into God's care.

On Monday morning, October 30, I encountered a police blockade a mile from the prison entrance and talked my way through it. Officers at a second blockade were more wary. They radioed to the main gate, and resolutely shook their heads at me.

Discouraged, I drove to Jubilee and phoned Chaplain Bryant.

"They're not allowing any volunteers into the prison yet," he explained. "We're under a state of emergency. Try again next Monday."

A whole week loomed ahead of me, without a schedule. How would I fill my time? Donald assured me Jubilee would find work for me until I could get back to Camp Hill.

I went back the next Monday, on November 6 (thirteen days after the first riot broke out), parked my truck among a mass of police cars, and strode to the front gate where I opened the drawer and pulled out my identification tag. Act as though you belong, I told myself. The guard at the desk nodded a greeting. Emboldened, I weaved my way among prison officials and state police clustered on the walkway, right up the steps to the chapel, and swung open the door. Chaplain Widmann looked up in surprise.

He allowed me to stay only an hour, and I felt both unnerved and comforted by the armed police presence, some patrolling on horseback. Inside the chapel, a trooper roamed about with a shotgun at his side. The purpose for his being there was unclear. Was he protecting? Surveilling? Controlling? Rumors had it that Muslim inmates had incited the riot and that their chaplain was sympathetic to the cause. The ensuing investigation brought the chapel under scrutiny, and more than three months later, the Muslim chaplain was fired.

The chapel had suffered minimal damage on the second night of the riot when inmates broke into it. The rest of the prison, however, lay in shambles. Almost half of the thirty-one buildings had been destroyed, including 1,200 cells. Damage estimates from the three-day riot stood at fifteen million dollars, with an additional fifty million payout for state police and correctional personnel wages.[16] About a thousand inmates were shipped to federal prisons throughout the country. SCI Waymart, a newly-renovated state facility in Wayne County, Pennsylvania, opened ahead of schedule to accommodate more than two hundred men. The remaining inmates were crammed with three or four men in Camp Hill's most usable cells.

The next week, I went back to Camp Hill again. Nearly three weeks had passed since the riot, and the place was still a mess. Inmates were scheduled to begin getting showers and clean clothes that day. Rifle-toting state police still followed staff chaplains around the prison. I wasn't allowed outside of the chapel, and after a few hours, I got word that I needed to leave the institution. "It's nothing personal," said Chaplain Bryant. "All contract chaplains have been terminated for the time being. I'll call when we can use you again."

---

[16] Bert Useem, 1993, *Resolution of Prison Riots,* https://www.ncjrs.gov/pdffiles1/
       Digitization/147708NCJRS.pdf

That next call was an invitation to help pack and distribute Christmas bags to inmates on December 23. Cell blocks were once again controlled by guards, but a large presence of state police still hung out in the dayrooms and in the basement of the Administration Building. Distribution of the Christmas bags was hurried and allowed no time to talk with inmates.

I left Camp Hill Prison that day, not knowing when I would be allowed back in. Nor did I have a clue of the detour on which God was about to take me.

V. Raymond Edman, a former president at Wheaton College, said, "Never doubt in the dark what God told you in the light." Clearly, God had opened doors for Nelson to minister at Camp Hill, but now they suddenly slammed shut. It was time to reevaluate and to trust that God had all under His control.

Has your call been upended? The disruption could well be God's way of moving you on to discover another aspect of His purpose for your life.

CHAPTER FOURTEEN

Detoured to
Lebanon County Prison

I spent the rest of 1989 and most of 1990 at Lebanon County Prison, all
the while keeping my ears to the ground and seeking God for direction
until I could get back to Camp Hill. It didn't seem likely that the day was
coming anytime soon.

When I joined Jubilee in 1985, the ministry had operated for almost a
decade and had gathered an unlikely conglomerate of personnel.

Donald Martin had been a part-time pastor and full-time landscaper
when he was asked to be a chaplain at the Lebanon County Prison in July
1980. "No way!" he said. A few months later he relented and agreed to fill in
temporarily—just until spring—when he planned to resume landscaping.
After that reluctant start, however, Donald found that he enjoyed teaching
and mentoring, and by spring he admitted to his wife, Mary Ann, that he
would be disappointed if someone else were hired for the position. He became Jubilee's second Director of Prison Ministry.

Around that same time, a board member asked Mimi Keller to lead a
weekly Bible study for female inmates. She was deep into graduate courses
at Lebanon Valley College to further her nursing career, and protested that
she'd never even seen the inside of a prison before. Nonetheless, Mimi consented, and prayed for the ability to see inmates through God's eyes.

Only three women attended her first Bible study in July of 1981, and
in the following weeks, prison staff often refused to allow Mimi onto the
cell blocks. But she didn't quit. She went back again and again, and slowly

won the staff over with her persistent grace. A year later, more than twenty women regularly attended her Bible study, and eventually Mimi's volunteer one-night-a-week Bible study grew into a full-time job.

In 1984, Jubilee asked Helen Hess to consider a part-time chaplaincy role to women. Helen and her husband, James Hess, bishop of the Lebanon District of Mennonite churches, had just entered the empty-nest phase of life. Helen had lots of plans, and none of them included prison chaplaincy. Excuses aside, she agreed to give it a try, and ended up staying for nine years.

Leon Zimmerman's involvement with Jubilee followed more of a natural path, in which one step led to another. After he became a Christian at nineteen years old in 1974, Leon was hungry to grow in his knowledge of God and zealous to share it with others. He connected with Lebanon District youth who had recently begun ministering in the prison and in street evangelism.

In 1981, Leon was licensed as the assistant pastor at Lebanon Christian Fellowship, a Mennonite church at 14th and Willow Streets. Some of the attendees had served time at Lebanon County Prison (LCP) or had incarcerated family members. Those associations led Leon to part-time chaplaincy at the prison.

Neal Eckert joined the Jubilee team in 1990 as counselor and case worker. His dry humor and infectious laughter were magnets for clients who sought hope and change in their lives.

Jubilee personnel also included John Landis, who played a primary role in the ministry's beginnings, and Jan Savercool, a former inmate who was later employed in Jubilee's Material Assistance Program. Others joined in various facets of ministry as Jubilee expanded.

Weekly staff meetings became vital times of praying together and of challenging and daring each other to dream about the ministry's future. We had a common love for people and a desire to help them discover the freedom in Christ that could loosen them from life-controlling issues. Too often, however, new converts got off to a running start, only to abandon their new-found faith in rough times.

At some point, either Leon or I came across Stanton Samenow's book,

Inside the Criminal Mind. Each of us credits the other for finding it. It doesn't matter. To both of us, Samenow's insights made sense and brought together the pieces we were looking for. Although a secular book, it is based on scriptural principles. It helped solidify what we'd held to be true: that many criminals hold a fundamentally different view of the world from that of responsible, law-abiding citizens. They are masterminds at minimizing, rationalizing, and denying responsibility for their crimes.

Since the Camp Hill riots, I had extra time on my hands to help develop the program at Lebanon Prison. Leon suggested that we try out some of Samenow's philosophy on a group of inmates. I began by interviewing men who professed a desire for change, and asked them to list all of their arrests.

"All of 'em, or just the ones I was convicted of?" Claude asked.

I knew where he was going with that question, for I had often heard the assertion that an unconvicted crime is as good as an uncommitted crime.

My purpose in ministry to inmates was not to make judgments on either guilt or innocence but to deal with the inner person and the thought processes that lent to criminal thinking and behavior.

So, if Claude hoped to ignore arrests for crimes that stopped short of charges, or of charges that were dismissed, I saw value in exploring the possible reasons behind him attracting police attention in the first place. What was it about his associations or his behavior that drew suspicion?

Another set of questions explored their job histories. Barry, age twenty-five, recalled fourteen jobs. His longest stretch of employment was eight months; another job lasted a mere two days. Typically, interviewees had a string of short work stints interspersed with multiple lapses in employment. Explanations included, "The boss didn't show me respect," or "I'm made for something more than flipping burgers!"

I also asked inmates to describe themselves. Adjectives like kind, compassionate, cheerful, hard-working, honest, and selfless peppered the interview forms of men whose lives were characterized by violence, uncontrolled anger, and general lawlessness. Ken's arrests included several assaults, but he argued that he truly was kind. "I only hit my girlfriend twice. *Twice!* That's all!"

During the weeks-long interview process, while preaching at LCP one Sunday evening, I read the compilation of positive traits. "Who do you think this group of people is?" I asked.

Immediately several inmates called out, "People at your church."

I shook my head.

"Your grandma," someone else guessed.

The men reacted in surprise when I told them I had gathered the list of complimentary traits from their fellow inmates. They were quick to think of other prisoners as "losers" and "scuzzballs," but reserved positive descriptions for themselves alone.

The inmate interviews continued among twenty-six men and included the question, "Are you a criminal?" John was among the twenty-one who answered, "No." His record, however, told a different story. Forgery, theft by unlawful taking, indecent assault, and three counts of delivery of cocaine were among his charges. "But I didn't *push* drugs. I only sold," he protested.

Cliff admitted that he might be a criminal—but only when he drank. "Society thinks I'm a criminal and maybe I've acted like one," he said, "but in my heart of hearts, I really am not a criminal."

Ken's record included twenty-eight simple assaults, fourteen aggravated assaults, and one burglary. "Yeah, ok, maybe I am a criminal," he said. "But I'm not a *hardened* criminal."

And Ed, a twenty year old with drug charges said, "But I never forced drugs on anyone, and I never sold to anyone younger than myself."

"How do you think your victims feel about your crimes?" I asked. Many of the men looked at me in utter befuddlement. They spoke of "victimless" crimes. "I didn't point a gun at nobody," one man protested, and another said, "I broke into the garage after hours when no one was there."

Brian, charged with two robberies, arson, and forgery, said, "I never hurt anybody." He paused and clarified, "Well, I never set out to give anyone permanent damage."

And Corey grew indignant. "Victims? I'm the victim in this story!"

I asked my interviewees how they felt about their crimes.

"I wouldn't have done them if I hadn't been drunk," said one.

Another blamed his crime on drugs.

Bill, whose record included a string of assaults and gun charges, a kidnapping, and third-degree murder, shrugged off all personal responsibility. "You see, I got mental problems that I have no control over."

Carson said, "I try not to dwell on the past. I don't feel good about my crimes. I'm not really ashamed, but neither am I proud of them. I guess it's something to grow from."

Jeff grew more defensive. "I did it to survive," he said, "and I don't feel sorry for it because my punishment don't fit the crime."

"Yeah, it was stupid, but at the time I thought it was fun," Mark admitted.

Ashton agreed. "Yeah, it was fun to do, all except the manslaughter."

Some said they wished they hadn't done their crime, that they were stupid and not using their head, but only a few said they felt terrible, it was wrong, or acknowledged the degree to which they hurt other people.

The interviews often revealed inmates' disdain for authority in statements like, "No one's gonna tell me what to do! I'm my own man."

When I asked them what they wanted to do with their lives post-jail, they typically vowed to "settle down, get a job, marry a woman, and have some kids." Some dared to dream bigger—to become a company CEO or a veterinarian. Never mind that they'd dropped out of school and couldn't read beyond a fourth-grade level. Their only plan was, "I'll figure something out." Clearly, they wanted the benefits of a responsible life, but without assuming responsibility. They scorned the hard work necessary to attain their dreams, and remained convinced of shortcuts to success. Somewhere out there at the end of a rainbow was their pot of gold. Their ship was coming to port. Success was just around the corner and they could smell it already. And most of all, they were entitled to it.

When the interviews were complete, Leon and I selected four men for the group. We alternately called it a "confrontation group," or the Life-Controlling Problem Group (LCP), which borrowed from Lebanon County Prison's acronym. Our purpose was to confront the issues in men's lives that kept them bound by changing the way they thought of themselves, their behavior, and the world around them.

The meetings were lively exchanges where we chipped away at faulty thinking patterns. John came to the group full of himself, and related the story of his most recent arrest, that of stealing a taxi. "The cab driver left it running on the street," he explained, "so I took it for a drive around the block. That's all. Just to teach him a lesson!"

"How noble of you!" I responded. "I'll bet that taxi cab driver fell at your feet, thanking you for saving him from future stupidity!"

Leon backed me up in mock breathless wonder. "John, the whole world of taxi cab drivers will fall at your feet when they learn of this!"

We kept up the sham a few minutes longer, agreeing that never again would a cab driver leave his cab unattended, all because John had jumped in to save them from themselves. And at such a great cost to himself, we exclaimed. John was willing to expand his rap sheet and to go to jail on principle! How selfless! How honorable! The other three inmates in the group saw through the ridiculous scenario, but John couldn't.

Group meetings often got heated in our single-minded attempt to bring the men to a point of accepting responsibility. If humor and rhetorical questions got us nowhere, Leon and I employed tough talk to cut away the rationalizations and excuses. But before dismissal we took time to check in with the participants. "How are you?" we asked. "It's okay if your toes hurt, but do you feel loved and cared for?" Tough love, not shame, was our goal, and it was gratifying to see the light bulb of truth come on for those men who had the courage to shine it on themselves.

Later, when Leon left Jubilee to become a full-time pastor, Neal Eckert took his place. He also had read Samenow's book and was convinced that inmates needed bold but loving confrontation to expose deeply woven paths of deceitfulness and excuse-ridden mindsets.

Those groups provided a necessary component in the rehabilitation of men. Allen wrote me a letter after he left LCP. "I can hear you now sticking to your guns [in the confrontation group], when I tried to use all kinds of worldly rationalizations as the basis for excuse of why I won't serve our Lord wholeheartedly . . . Well, Nelson, right now I feel love in my heart for you because you gave me the bare uncompromising truth . . ."

Another inmate wrote, "I felt loved in your presents [sic]. You treated me like a human being instead of a criminal."

Jerry was another product of the group. I first met him while making my rounds on the blocks at Lebanon Prison. He leaned against a wall with his muscled arm draped possessively over the dayroom TV. I walked around him and rested my arm, thin and pale in comparison, on the other side of the TV. A man his size could rip me apart in no time. He didn't acknowledge me, intent as he was on watching the show. I waited for a commercial and asked, "So, tell me, what's the soap about?"

I didn't care one iota about the show. It was only an attempt to connect with Jerry. He gave me a quick rundown of "The Young and the Restless" and then asked, "So what do you think about masturbation?"

There it was, without lead-in. It wasn't the first time I'd gotten the question. I just never had it hurled at me so suddenly from out of the blue. But that was Jerry. He asked direct questions and expected direct answers.

Jerry soon began attending Bible studies, accepted Christ, and joined the confrontation group, where he took his turn in the hot seat as we whittled away at his thinking patterns. Some had to do with his drug use.

"Yeah, I use drugs," he said with crusty smugness, "but I'm not like those dumb junkies who show track marks all up and down their arms." Jerry described how he injected into his legs, making his habit less noticeable, and in his mind, more principled.

"So, you're sort of an elitist drug user?" I asked.

"Yeah. I'm elitist." He pushed his sleeve up and examined his arm with satisfaction. "See, my arms are clean. I can go shirtless in the summer, and you know, the girls just drool when they see a well-built man." His thinking still subscribed to worldly sensuality, especially regarding the girl of his dreams.

"She's poison, and she's going to take you down, right back to drugs and your crazy lifestyle," we warned.

Jerry eventually accepted our challenges and determined to truly make Jesus the Lord of his life. His transformation and bold witness were astonishing. He had a way of engaging people and working his testimony of

Christ's power into conversations. After his release from prison, Jerry sometimes came to our house carrying a large casserole of his delicious stuffed peppers. And when he met a lovely Christian girl, I was privileged to participate in their wedding, which was a joyous celebration of God's redemptive work. Nearly two decades later, Jerry is an example of a life changed by the power of Jesus.

Had I not been displaced at Camp Hill, I would not have met Jerry. I have every confidence that he would have come to Christ through someone else's influence, yet I'm humbled that God chose to use me. And it's a reminder that life's detours sometimes offer memorable sights we may otherwise have missed.

The Camp Hill riots marked a watershed, not only in the history of corrections, but also in our lives. Nelson was unsettled. Working at Lebanon County Prison was only a temporary fix until God directed elsewhere. In the meantime, Nelson took additional CPE classes and long-distance college courses, attended Mennonite Chaplain's Association meetings, and spoke about Jubilee's prison work in various churches. The children and I tagged along whenever we could.

As we had opportunity, Nelson and I mentored released inmates and their families. Pete and Sheila were one such couple. We made several trips to their home, more than an hour's drive away, or invited them to ours. Sheila had, of necessity, become independent during Pete's prison term, and they both had been changed by the experience of his incarceration. Like so many others, they struggled to get their footing after Pete's release from prison.

Quite a few of the men being released from Lebanon County Prison lived closer to our house. I think it was for Nelson's thirtieth birthday that I invited a group to celebrate with us. Two carloads of men arrived, some of them beyond giddy with the invitation to a surprise party. The bigger surprise may have come to our neighbors, had they known most of our noisy guests were ex-cons and parolees.

In the late 1980s, we began attending New Covenant Mennonite Fellowship where Pastor Dave Myer, a chaplain at Lancaster County Prison, understood the need for ministerial credentialing. On May 20, 1990, Nelson was licensed for prison ministry. From the church's perspective, a license was viewed as a temporary commission and a testing of the ministerial waters, and it satisfied the state's requirements for chaplains.

That July, We Care (formerly New Life in Atmore, Alabama) asked Nelson to consider chaplaincy in Blountstown, Florida, so we flew there to size it up. Soon thereafter, Gospel Express, another prison ministry, also approached Nelson about the opportunity. Other invitations had come to us in the past decade: teaching at a Christian school, chaplaincy at the Bowery Mission in New York City, VS in Kentucky.

Exciting possibilities for ministry were everywhere, and we could be pulled in any direction. What was the best fit? Where did God want us to serve to the maximum? As much as we might have been drawn to the sunny south, we lacked a clear sense of God's leading, so we hunkered down for the time being, praying and waiting for a revelation of His purposes.

Late in 1990, Bishop James Hess asked Nelson to assist Richard Newswanger in pastoring at Roedersville Mennonite Church, near Pine Grove. From our house, we had a forty-five-minute drive over the Blue Mountains on Route 501 and into Schuylkill County. The fifty or so congregants welcomed us, graciously allowed Nelson to cut his preaching teeth there, and kept us posted of houses for sale in the area. But we were quite happy, thank you, to remain in Kleinfeltersville, close to our families and to Lancaster County. It was akin to the Promised Land for Mennonites and offered more options for our children's future Christian schooling.

The original plan was that we would split Sundays between Roedersville and New Covenant churches, but by early 1992, we attended Roedersville every Sunday.

We could not have known then how familiar Schuylkill County would become during the next twenty-five years.

Self-perception and reality are sometimes at odds with each other. That's why we need to invite God's perspective as the psalmist did when he cried, "Search me, O God, and know my heart! Try me and know my thoughts! And see if there be any grievous way in me, and lead me in the way everlasting!" (Psalm 139:23, 24; ESV)

A detour is seldom fun. It is an inconvenient time-waster; an out-of-the-way route to the destination. We're usually too peeved and hurried to enjoy the scenery along the way. Are you on a detour, not of your own choosing, of your life purpose? Can you trust that God will refresh and renew you along the way?

CHAPTER FIFTEEN

At Frackville Prison and Beyond

Time spent in the county jail is short term, often for just a few weeks or months. Inmates are caught up in the crisis and the questions: *Will my girlfriend stick with me, or will she clean out my apartment and run? Will my employer send me my paycheck? Will he hold my job until I get out? Who is looking after my apartment? What will happen to my car that's parked along the street? Will it be towed away? Will the bank repossess it? How do I claim it when I get out?* County jail ministry involves "putting out fires" and helping inmates to deal with all the loose ends of life on the streets. It's also a jarring wake-up call for some, and an opportune time for chaplains to share the hope of the Gospel of Jesus Christ with them.

By the time men get to the state prison they have moved beyond the crisis of the moment. The reality of long and lonely years behind bars is setting in, and the focus shifts from life on the outside to surviving and re-building life in "The Big House." One man who had a long-term sentence told me, "My parole papers will come from a tree that is just a small sapling now." State prison chaplains have time to mentor and disciple men over a number of years.

In the late 1980s, I began attending the annual meeting of the Pennsylvania Prison Chaplain Association (PPCA) and gained some understanding of the vast harvest field behind state bars. In 1985, the year I began working with Jubilee, the state housed 14,260 inmates.[17] Five years later the popula-

---

[17] 1985, *1980-85 Annual Report, Commonwealth of Pennsylvania Department of Corrections Statistical Report,* p. 4, https://www.cor.pa.gov/About%20Us/Statistics/Documents/Old%20Statistical%20Reports/1980-85AnnualReport.pdf

tion ballooned to 22,325.[18] Between 1980 and 1989, Pennsylvania built six
state prisons: Cresson, Frackville, Retreat, Smithfield, Waymart, and Waynes-
burg.[19] The building boom alleviated overcrowding, but could not keep up
with the numbers of incoming inmates, and made prison officials jumpy.

The Department of Corrections recommended a ratio of one chaplain
to every five hundred inmates,[20] but the numbers fell woefully short of that
ideal and left even the most enthusiastic chaplains overwhelmed. It troubled
me that the potential for a great spiritual harvest among state inmates was
not being realized, and I left each chaplains' meeting with an increasing
desire to see godly chaplains flood the state system.

Late in 1990, Clair Weaver assumed the role of Executive Director
with Jubilee Ministries, and he shared my vision with enthusiasm. Much
of Jubilee's efforts were funded by its thrift store sales, which had increased
from $20,000 in 1980 to $94,000 in 1989.[21] The increase made it possible
for Jubilee to explore various opportunities at both state and county prisons. Already, the ministry operated at Lebanon County, SCI Retreat, and
SCI Camp Hill, and its reputation was growing among officials within the
Department of Corrections. Chaplain Menei, head of all state chaplains,
worked from the Department of Correction's Central Office next door to
Camp Hill Prison. He had occasionally dropped by the prison chapel where
he saw firsthand the work I did with Jubilee, and he lent an ear to my desire
for further ministry.

At PPCA's meeting in the fall of 1990, I spoke with Chaplain Ennis from SCI Frackville, a maximum-security prison in the coal regions of
northern Schuylkill County that housed just over a thousand inmates. He
asked a lot of questions about the work I'd done at Camp Hill. That night
he called to invite me to help him at Frackville.

---

[18] John C. McWilliams, *Two Centuries of Corrections in Pennsylvania: A Commemorative History,* Commonwealth of Pennsylvania, 2002, p. 84.

[19] Ibid., p. 83.

[20] Jubilee Ministries Board of Directors, *A Mustard Seed: The History of Jubilee Ministries,*
2008, p. 25.

[21] Ibid, p. 18.

On October 25, 1990—exactly one year after the Camp Hill riot—I drove to Frackville to further discuss Chaplain Ennis' invitation. In a windowless office that reeked of cigarette smoke, the white-haired chaplain and I worked out the details for my ministry at Frackville through Jubilee. I would work there every Tuesday and Wednesday and remain at LCP on Mondays and Thursdays. I would also pursue a return to Camp Hill.

At the chaplain's suggestion, I submitted a proposal to Frackville's Deputy Superintendent that requested privileges for ministry at the institution. I had not yet received a response when Chaplain Ennis invited me to attend a Sunday afternoon service on December 2. He introduced me to the prison congregation and told them that I was to join the chapel staff.

I surveyed the eighty or so men sitting shoulder to shoulder in the small chapel. "I'd love to meet you, and we can talk about whatever's on your heart," I offered. "If you're interested, see me after the service."

Two days later, when I began working at SCI Frackville, I already had a list of men to put on my call line. I was disappointed, although hardly surprised, that the Deputy Superintendent shot down two main points of my proposal. I would not be permitted to do block visitation, nor to have access to chapel keys.

I had never officially been issued keys at Camp Hill, but after chapel staff came to know and trust me, they handed the keys to me. Otherwise they were inconvenienced numerous times a day to unlock doors within the chapel at my every move. I hoped and prayed for similar autonomy at Frackville.

Chaplain Ennis showed me to an office tucked at the far end of a hall in the education department. Isolated as it was, no inmates had business to walk into the area except those who were scheduled to see me. I felt like I was in jail! At those times when contract chaplains were in the office, I got bumped to the chapel, which was in a short hall between the education building and the gym. There was a bit more foot traffic in that location but men were not permitted to stop to talk for long.

In time, Chaplain Ennis would arrange for a supply closet to be turned into an office, which I shared with a Catholic contract chaplain.

But that was short-lived. I was only a volunteer, so he got priority. Back to the chapel I went, this time with room dividers to form an L-shaped office behind the last row of chairs. But, more often than not, other activities took place in the chapel and created distractions that hampered meaningful conversation.

It was like starting all over again. The less-than-satisfactory office arrangements—being pushed from one area to another and the inability to leave the chapel—were reminders of my volunteer status and stoked my desire to become a "real" chaplain. I longed to move freely about the prison, to be able to interact with the men on their turf, and to invite them into mine where they might open up and share without distraction.

The present reality was that many times men didn't show up for their appointments and I was left with nothing to do but to develop more call lines, to talk with Chaplain Ennis or the Catholic chaplain, to journal, or to read. Often, I had to wait for someone to unlock my office. One day I wrote in my journal, "Nobody showed this morning. Did some reading and odds and ends. Bum morning. Wish I could change this."

The first change caught me off guard. At lunch with Chaplain Ennis in January, 1991, he said in his customary brusque manner, "I need to visit someone in the infirmary. Come along. It will go faster if you visit some and I visit some."

And it did go fast. It was basically a nod here and a hurried how-do-you-do there, and in no time at all, we left the infirmary and rushed through the Mental Health Unit in the same manner. Throughout the next year, he occasionally invited me to join him on those obligatory rounds.

In an apparent vote of his confidence, the chaplain asked me to conduct and preach at Sunday services in April and in October, 1991. Chaplain Ennis served two small Lutheran congregations in the area and arrived at the afternoon prison services just in time to escort guest pastors to the pulpit. He seldom preached there himself. His apparent lack of enthusiasm for the men and the ministry at Frackville fueled my desire to be cut loose to minister to inmates.

But even after a year of working at the prison, my request to do block

visitation was shot down again. It would be an additional year—in the fall
of 1992—before I was granted permission to visit in the new modular units
that housed about 150 minimum-security inmates. To my surprise, I was
also allowed access to the RHU. It didn't make sense that I could go there
but not to the general population. However, I wasn't going to make a fuss
about it for fear that all privileges would be retracted.

Although changes in rules governing my involvement at Frackville did
not come as I had hoped and prayed for, I was grateful for the change I saw
in some of the inmates with whom I met regularly.

Mike accepted Christ and grew by leaps and bounds, and eagerly applied godly principles to his life. His transformation was a joy to behold. So
was Jerry's, the inmate I had gotten to know over a soap opera at Lebanon.
His sentence at Frackville gave opportunity for continued discussions and
growth in his faith.

Phil also came by my "office" on occasion and the seed of the Gospel was planted, but I was unaware of the extent until his release several
years later. Wanting to honor a now-deceased Mennonite woman who had
showered him with kindness as a child, Phil chose to attend a church of
her denomination. By that time, I was assistant pastor at Green Terrace
Mennonite Church, and Phil recognized me as soon as he stepped into the
foyer. His toothless mouth dropped open and he pointed at me excitedly.
"Chap . . . Chap . . . Chaplain Z!" he stuttered and engulfed me in a bear
hug. Phil became a member at the church and attended faithfully.

In April 1991, one and a half years after the riot, and after many phone
calls to Chaplain Bryant, I finally gained approval to go back to Camp Hill
Prison—but for only one day a week, and with very tight controls. "I'm not
too confident this will work," I wrote in my journal. It felt like I was back to
square one. I was restricted to the chapel where I taught two Bible studies,
and filled the rest of my day talking with inmates on my call list.

Camp Hill Prison was still recovering from the damage incurred during the riot. Sometimes on lunch breaks, the staff chaplains invited me to
walk outside with them to view progress on new buildings. With the inmate
population climbing again, Chaplain Bryant suggested I submit a non-

monetary contract to the administration, requesting privileges for ministry on the cell blocks. I waited and prayed for a response for several months.

In the meantime, I explored other possibilities that seemed to be popping up all over. Pennsylvania's burgeoning prison population had lawmakers scrambling for solutions to overcrowding. At the end of 1990, housing capacity was at an alarming 155.7%.[22] By 1993, eight years after I began at Camp Hill, the number of inmates across the state had nearly doubled. The six new prisons opened in the 1980s were bursting at the seams. Six more were to open by 1993, and plans were in place for two additional institutions in 1995 and 1996.[23]

Cambridge Springs was among the new locations, and it would become the second institution in Pennsylvania to house women inmates, who account for less than five percent of the state prison population. Female prisons hire men to be chaplains, just as male prisons hire women, but I didn't give it a moment's consideration. It just didn't seem like a good idea to me.

Of the other prisons slated for opening in 1993, all but SCI Mahanoy would require moving our family, and neither Esther nor I wanted to do that. Mahanoy was being built just three miles north of Frackville, but it would still be two years before construction was complete. The wait seemed interminable.

Although I preferred state chaplaincy, I chased after openings at both Dauphin County and Monroe County Prisons. When the job at Monroe County came through in October 1991, I turned it down. I still hoped for the contract at Camp Hill, and while it was under consideration, Chaplain Widmann retired. I interviewed for the vacant position but came up short on the educational qualifications. In a double whammy, the contract was also denied—on the very night that I was honored as Frackville's Volunteer of the Year. It was all a mixed bag of emotions.

---

[22] Commonwealth of Pennsylvania Department of Corrections, *1993 Annual Statistical Report*, p. 18, https://www.cor.pa.gov/About%20Us/Statistics/Documents/Old%20Statistical%20Reports/1993%20Annual%20Statistical%20Report.pdf

[23] McWilliams, *Two Centuries of Corrections in Pennsylvania*. Commonwealth of Pennsylvania, p. 59.

Chaplain Smith, a contract chaplain from SCI Greensburg, got the Camp Hill job. I was glad for the energy and fresh evangelical flavor he brought to invigorate the chaplaincy program. At his invitation, I preached on several occasions where three Sunday services (two in the morning and one in the afternoon) drew about six hundred men.

It seemed as though I had little to show for the nearly three years I spent at Camp Hill in the 1990s. However, in later years, I would reconnect with men in whom God had begun a good work.

Faithfulness is all that God asks of us—persistent faithfulness in the face of obstacles, and even in the absence of success stories. He simply asks us to plant and to water faithfully and to pray that He will bring the increase.

Are you discouraged about your call? Do you feel like restraints beyond your control are hindering you from reaching your potential? Pray for wisdom to discern what your next steps should be through the wasteland. And trust that, even now, God is working out His best plans for you.

CHAPTER SIXTEEN
Beginning at SCI Mahanoy

Starting in 1991, there was much talk at Frackville of the nearby prison under construction. SCI Mahanoy would be Schuylkill County's second state prison, and some of Frackville's staff eyed better positions there. I made a few quick lunchtime trips to the construction site myself. From Frackville, the new location was just a short jog away: under the Interstate 81 bridge and onto Morea Road, past the state police station, through a wooded area, and there—tucked behind a knoll and hidden from view, the prison complex slowly took shape. The facility was built atop a scrubby-brushed mountain on more than two hundred acres, sixty-seven of which are inside a fourteen-foot-high double fence.

I prayed and dreamed during Mahanoy's construction, wondering whether God would open the doors of ministry to me there. The past years had seemed a bumpy ride of bouncing from one institution to another and never really feeling settled nor granted freedom to be a "real chaplain."

SCI Mahanoy opened in July 1993, at a cost exceeding eighty-three million dollars. It was to eventually house one thousand medium-security inmates. Two months after the prison opened, a twenty-hour contract position was posted, and I wasted no time applying for it. While awaiting the outcome, I was ordained as assistant pastor at Roedersville Mennonite Church on September 12, 1993.

Late in September, while working at Frackville one morning, I heard that Mahanoy's Chaplain Whalen was in the prison for a meeting. He caught up with me, flashing a wide smile and extending a firm handshake.

"Mr. Zeiset, I want to be the first to tell you that you got the contract at Mahanoy. I look forward to working with you!"

I had a hard time concentrating on my work that afternoon. Was my dream actually taking shape after all this time?

A week or so later, I learned that the contract had been split between myself and a chaplain from Philadelphia. Oh, well, I was grateful for even ten hours on a contract.

On the morning of October 26, 1993, Chaplain Whalen met me at the front gate, gave me a tour of the prison, and introduced me to other staff. I was impressed with the good rapport he had with them, and it was easy to see why. This tall, jovial Irish Catholic was friendly to all.

We stopped at an office for my identification badge, made our way through a few gates, and out onto a long walkway. "There it is," he said, pointing to the chapel. We passed through another gate, exchanged greetings with the guard stationed there, and on to the building's entrance.

Chaplain Whalen swung the door open and ushered me into a wide lobby, pointing out the Education wing on the left and a classroom on the right. "Straight ahead is the chapel clerks' work area, and the chaplains' offices are to the right side," he said, offering a peek through the door's window. "But first I want to show you the chapel."

Double doors opened into the large sanctuary. Light filtered through patterned glass brick windows that flanked the pulpit and from windows around the perimeter of the recessed ceiling. The wooden pews, I estimated quickly, would seat about 150 men.

Near the front of the chapel, Chaplain Whalen unlocked a second entrance that circled into the clerks' area and waved me through it. "Right now we employ only one inmate clerk, but in time, as the population grows, we'll have several working out here." He swept his hand toward four doors lining the exterior wall. "My office is the second one on the right. You get to pick yours."

My office!

My very own space that still smelled of new carpet! Remembering the converted cramped broom closet and the shared offices I had occupied over the years, I felt abundantly blessed.

The advantage to working at a new institution was that I had a blank slate. There were no previous programs or expectations to fill, and Chaplain Whalen encouraged my innovations in developing the Protestant chaplaincy program. I set up a directory of volunteers by drawing on those I had met at other prisons and invited them to teach regular Bible studies at Mahanoy. The owner of the Christian bookstore in nearby Pottsville provided names of local pastors who might serve as additional guest speakers and volunteers. I drew up a list of traveling prison ministries to call on for weekend seminars. My inmate clerk wrote letters to organizations willing to stock the prison library with Christian literature.

From the time I got the contract, I stopped going to Lebanon County Prison but continued at Frackville and Camp Hill. I was at Camp Hill, in the middle of teaching a Bible study, when Chaplain Bryant stuck his head in the door to tell me I had a phone call.

"For me?" I asked.

He nodded. "It's the deputy from Mahanoy."

Oh. That didn't sound good.

It wasn't.

The deputy explained that the Central Office in Harrisburg had just caught up on the particulars of the contract that Mahanoy's business office had split between the Philadelphia chaplain and myself. It was to have been awarded to only one person, the deputy said, and consequently it was being yanked from both of us. "I'm so sorry," he said. "We really like the work you're doing here. Is there any way we can keep you?"

I thought fast. "I think it could be worked out." Confident of Jubilee Ministries' vision to expand into state prisons, I was certain that they would just as soon pay me to work at Mahanoy as at any other prison.

The deputy seemed glad for a solution to the sticky situation. Jubilee agreed, and I continued at Mahanoy. The Philadelphia chaplain remained, too, hoping against hope that the contract would be reinstated. We never met because our hours did not coincide, but I wondered why he would drive more than two hours to a job. But then, hadn't I done the same during the summer that I drove all the way to Retreat Prison?

Christmas approached, and Chaplain Whalen said that the Philadelphia chaplain wanted off two Sundays. Would I conduct the services in his
stead, he asked. So, on the day after Christmas, I drove to the prison for an
evening service. A week later, with permission to hold Mahanoy's service at
noon, I preached to about fifty men, and wrapped the service up in time
to fulfill a promise to Chaplain Ennis at Frackville, where a hundred men
showed up for the two o'clock service.

For the third week in a row, the Philadelphia chaplain asked whether I
would fill in for him. The following week he was nowhere to be seen. Nor
the next week. And then he officially called it quits.

I'd seen it coming, and started thinking about what time of day would
be best to hold prison church services. Some prison chaplains choose the
traditional Sunday morning slot, while others claim the afternoon. A few
opt for Sunday nights. I weighed the pros and cons of my choices. Our
children were young—nine, seven, and five years old—and I thought it
important that they see their Daddy worship at church, and that I stay
connected to a local church body for support and accountability. It seemed
Sunday afternoon at one o'clock would work best for both the prison congregation and for my family.

*We had a problem. I agreed with Nelson that afternoon ser-
vices at the prison would be the best option for our family, but
how would we work out the logistics of time and distance? Roedersville Church was a forty-five-minute drive north from our
house, and Mahanoy Prison was an additional thirty-five minutes
farther. How could Nelson drive us home and still clock in at
work on time?*

He couldn't.

That meant we needed to drive to church in separate vehicles.

*"That seems silly," I said. "We'll burn a lot of extra gas and cut
out an hour and a half of family time on the road."*

"What choice do we have?" asked Nelson.

I hatched a brainy solution. "The kids and I can camp out at

*church until you're finished at the prison, and then you can swing by
to pick us up and we can all come home together!"*

*Nelson raised his eyebrows. "You know you'd be there almost
four hours?"*

*"We'll eat lunch. We'll nap and read. And then we'll play games
till you get back."*

He shrugged in quiet surrender.

*I packed lunches. "I'll have to eat as I drive, so mine needs to be
easy to handle on those hills and curves," Nelson said.*

*Thus began his standard Sunday lunch of Diet Coke, carrot
sticks, and pretzels—a menu that lasted for twenty-three years, with
little variation. The lunch I packed for the kids and myself was a
bit more conventional, featuring sweets and snacks to give it a party
flair.*

*But the party fizzled in a short time. The church grew cold. The
wooden pews were too hard. We couldn't get comfortable to nap or to
read. By the time Nelson picked us up, we were out of sorts.*

*We tried my plan a few more weeks until my friend, Jean Hurst,
learned of our being marooned at the church. "That's nonsense!" she
said. "You're coming to my house so our girls can play together and
you and I can gab the afternoon away!"*

*That was that. After church, three adults and seven children
crammed into Jay and Jean's van for the ride to their house for good
food and gracious hospitality. By late afternoon Nelson came by to
pick us up.*

*As the reality of Nelson's schedule sank in, he and I began driv-
ing both the car and truck to church so the children and I could spend
time at home, and Jean could do likewise with her family.*

*For six years, Nelson worked every Sunday afternoon. I felt
badly for him. He preached twice a month at Roedersville, and had
time for only a few hurried handshakes before rushing off to work. He
no longer enjoyed either church fellowship meals nor Sunday dinners
with family and friends. No longer did he have the glorious luxury of*

crashing on the couch for a Sunday afternoon nap. I went to family
reunions without him.

    Easter Sunday was the only exception; every year he held early
morning services at the prison so he could join me at my family's
dinner.

When I arrived at Mahanoy in the fall of 1993, only two of the seven
units housed inmates. At year's end the prison population stood at 382
men. Legislators had approved costs for building the prison, but not for
staffing it. Additional blocks opened as funds became available, and men
came from prisons throughout the state, an average of ten per week. By the
end of 1994, Mahanoy housed 886 men.[24]

In the spring of 1994, the prison posted a full-time Protestant chaplaincy position. I'd been praying about this for years and thought I had a
pretty good chance at it. If there were any obstacle, it would likely be my
lack of a college degree. For nearly a decade, I had been patchworking my
education and had acquired about seventy credits, but that was barely half
of what I needed to earn a bachelor's degree. To my knowledge, no one had
ever been hired for chaplaincy without it.

The interview took place in the superintendent's conference room
where four of the prison's top officials, including Chaplain Whalen, were
seated around a massive table. Chaplain Menei, the head state chaplain
from the Central Office in Harrisburg, wasn't far into the interview when
he asked, "Mr. Zeiset, if you are granted this position, will you pursue your
education?"

I felt all eyes turn on me. "Yes," I answered evenly. "I have been pursuing my education and I will continue to do so."

I wasn't sure how I would fulfill that promise to ramp up my educational progress.

---

[24] Commonwealth of Pennsylvania Department of Corrections, *1994 Annual Statistical Report,* p. 21, https://www.cor.pa.gov/About%20Us/Statistics/Documents/Old%20Statis-
tical%20Reports/1994%20Annual%20Statistical%20Report.pdf

"Where there's a will, there's a way," Esther said.

We'd figure it out somehow. Otherwise I probably didn't stand a chance of ever getting a chaplaincy position.

Opportunities seldom avail themselves without our preparation. How are you preparing to fulfill God's purposes? Paramount, of course, is the development of godly character. What steps will you take—today—to pursue it?

What other training will you need? How can you adjust your schedule to prepare yourself to carry out God's plans to the fullest?

CHAPTER SEVENTEEN

"Real Chaplain" Challenges

I got the job!

For years I sensed God's leading in that direction but never guessed it would take so long. As impatient as I'd been, I was grateful now for the ten years of experience I gained in prison chaplaincy—one year in Alabama and nine years with Jubilee Ministries.

I was thirty-two years old, and possibly the youngest chaplain in the state when I began as an employee on June 20, 1994. From that day, I ended my employment at the hardware store and at Jubilee. All my involvements at Frackville and Camp Hill came to a close. Now my full-time job would be at Mahanoy alone.

My family was with me on the evening when I went by the hardware store to pick up my last paycheck. We had just come from my uncle Reuben's car lot where we bought a 1993 Plymouth Acclaim, the previous year's stripped-down model. Our children were disappointed that it had crankdown windows, but Esther and I agreed we didn't need bells and whistles. It was simply a car with low mileage and within our budget.

My friends at the hardware store saw us pulling into the parking lot, and a group gathered around to banter in the customary manner of the employees.

"What in the world?" one said loudly. "You land a new job and right away you run out to buy a fancy new car!"

Oh, boy. Just what I had feared—that people might think we upgraded our car to celebrate Nelson's new job. Our purchase had nothing to do with that. We run our vehicles till the wheels fall off, and our truck was shot. It had nickel and dimed us far too long. The station wagon was also gasping its last breaths.

And fancy? Hardly. One of the first things I said when we took the Acclaim for a test drive was, "It looks like a state car. Boxy and plain white."

My friends thought the same. "Looks like just the thing for a state worker!"

Laughter erupted at the reference to PennDOT workers who had recently worked on a road project near the store and who became the brunt of jokes for their lack of a git 'er done work ethic.

One of my coworkers suddenly turned and jogged away. Seconds later, he returned holding a shovel aloft. "Here you go, Nelson!" he said with a wide grin. "Every state worker needs a shovel to lean on."

Merriment broke out again around the circle.

"Jokes aside," the shovel bearer said, "I'm happy for you. I know you're following God's leading, and we all wish you the very best."

The send-off felt good, a fitting end to my years of part-time employment at Zimmerman's.

My memories of Nelson's time at Frackville and his beginnings at Mahanoy seem a bit hazy, maybe in part because of distracting events that transpired in May of 1993. Nelson's father attempted to remove overgrown shrubbery from their landscape with a tractor and chain when the chain snapped and hit him with blunt force on the back of his head. A shaken family gathered in the trauma unit at Lancaster General Hospital and took turns standing by his bedside throughout the afternoon and evening.

Back home late that night, we comforted our children and dragged to bed. Before we fell asleep, the phone rang with more bad news. My mother, who had endured weeks of lethargy and other baffling symptoms, had just been admitted to Reading Hospital. Blood-

work was thus far inconclusive, but she would undergo a battery of tests in the morning.

My stomach was in knots when I left home the next morning to make good on my promise to drive Nelson's mother to the hospital in Lancaster and to stay with her until other family came by. Throughout the day, Dad Zeiset showed signs, however small and tenuous, of improvement. When I left that afternoon, I had no doubts that the road ahead would be long and difficult.

And what of my mother? Cell phones had not yet gone mainstream so I hadn't heard anything of her condition all day, and I was eager to get home for news. On the flat stretch of road approaching our house, I caught my breath at the sight of Nelson's truck on the driveway. He had five hours left on his work shift. Instinctively, I knew his early arrival had something to do with bad news about my mother.

He met me on the driveway, his teary eyes filled with pain, and he wrapped his arms around me. "Is she—is she gone?" I whimpered. He shook his head, led me inside, and gently broke the news. My mother had leukemia.

Numbly, we drove forty minutes to Reading Hospital, trying to comprehend the gravity of my mother's condition. At worst, the grim-faced doctor said, she had only a few days to live. Possibly, given a miracle, she might linger a few weeks.

A grueling marathon of visits between two hospitals ensued. Every phone call held the threat of dreaded news.

After six long days, the doctor discharged Nelson's father, and except for lingering headaches, he recovered fully.

My mother spent nearly a month in the hospital and cycled through remissions, relapses, and lengthy hospital stays for the next seventeen months.

In May 1993, when it looked as though Nelson and I could both lose a parent in the same weekend, Renee was wrapping up kindergarten, Emily was in second grade, and Joel was nearly through fifth *grade at Schaefferstown Elementary. The next year he transferred to Ephrata Mennonite School, and his sisters followed him there a few years later.*

Life had gotten busy. Far too busy. The demands of babysitting for several families while raising our own young family, the responsibility of pastoring at Roedersville, the weight of a twenty-year mortgage hanging over us, the concern for my mother's diminishing health, and the added work of Nelson's college classes all piled up. Yet I didn't realize that joy had slinked away and left drudgery in its place until one hot summer Saturday afternoon.

The day and my energy were both nearly spent, and I still had a to-do list longer than my arm. I trudged upstairs to clean our bathroom and was quietly going about the task when a blast of cold water hit me square on my back. Puzzled, I whirled around to the window. Nelson was on the driveway below, garden hose in hand, feigning attention to washing the car.

So he wanted a water battle, did he? I wasn't in the mood, nor did I have the time!

But memories of long-forgotten water battles overtook me. Oh, the fun we had in those carefree days of another lifetime! Before I thought better of it, I quietly removed the screen from the front window, filled a cup of water, and flung it at him. I missed him by a mile, but he jumped up, pretending surprise, and aimed the hose upward in retaliation. I slammed the window shut. The water's blast splashed against the pane and dribbled onto the porch roof.

Thus began an epic water battle in which we ran up and down the stairs dripping wet, and shushed each other so as to not awaken the children from their naps. After we spent ourselves with laughter, Nelson went back to washing the car, and I changed out of my drenched clothes. And then, completely bereft of all sense, I threw them out the front window at my unsuspecting husband.

They were still parachuting downward, one piece after another, when a long-nosed brown Buick rolled by our house. The elderly cou-

ple in the front seat sat stiff as corpses. He gripped the wheel as though he were riding a bucking bronco, and she sat primly at his side, boring her gaze through the windshield—until she caught sight of the spectacle in our front yard. Her head whipped around, her mouth flew open, and her eyes grew as large as Buick hubcaps.

The driver never flinched. He held tight to the steering wheel and silently glided by. I bowled over the open window, laughing till my sides ached, while Nelson nonchalantly continued washing the car.

I didn't get much else done that afternoon. What did it matter if my living room wasn't dusted? Who cared about the cobwebs on the front porch? So what if I didn't prepare a salad for dinner? I savored the unfamiliar cleansing effect of laughter, and contemplated the dissipation of my joy. It had always been my belief that God meant for family and ministry responsibilities to be a joyous calling. But for me, they had become an obligatory cross to bear.

I mulled this over for some weeks and months. I knew, of course, that joy cannot be manufactured and that it springs from a living relationship with Christ, but I hadn't noticed how the cares of life had crowded Him out. That became crystal clear to me in a week that I'd packed to the gills. I didn't plan it that way; it just happened.

On Monday, I had taken a meal to my parents after another of my mother's lengthy hospital stays, and remained a few hours to weed their garden. On Tuesday, I babysat for a neighbor, fulfilled my volunteer obligations at the school library, and rushed home to prepare for out-of-state guests who were staying with us for two nights.

By Friday morning, after the whirlwind died down, I sat down to have my devotions and realized I hadn't opened my Bible all week. And then I remembered that I was to teach the ladies' Sunday School class, only two days out, and I hadn't a clue what the lesson was about!

I opened my study book and stared at it in disbelief.

Flabbergasted *might be a word to describe my feelings.* Convicted *is another.*

The lesson passage in Luke 10 described Martha's frenzy upon welcoming Jesus into her home. I pictured her—like myself—mixing, sautéing, baking, smoothing the wrinkles from the tablecloth, fussing with the flowers, lighting the candles, and growing increasingly anxious. Where was her sister, Mary, anyway? Didn't she know there was work to be done? Martha peeked into the next room and there sat Mary, at Jesus' feet, captivated by His every word, and oblivious to all else but basking in the Lord's presence and learning from Him.

Martha exploded with indignation. "Lord, don't you care that my sister has left me to serve alone? Tell her to help me!"

Jesus turned compassionate eyes on her and said, "Martha, Martha."

Suddenly it was as though He turned His eyes on me. His gentle rebuke addressed my misplaced priorities and my neglect of Him.

I saw it clearly now. Little wonder that my frantic pace left me depleted and stripped of joy.

I could have learned this lesson from Nelson. From the day we got married, he set a good example of spending consistent and regular time with God every day. He didn't approach it legalistically, as though God were poised to bonk him on the head if he skipped a day or two of Bible reading and prayer. Nelson viewed daily time with God as being absolutely essential, that without it he would shrivel and die as surely as if he refused physical food.

I was also glad for Nelson's common sense in setting parameters for himself. In a prison that eventually housed up to 2,500 men, the needs were endless. Only in cases of extreme emergency did Nelson stay after hours. At times I thought him a bit heartless to not attend to those needs on the spot, but came to understand that otherwise he would not have lasted through more than three decades of prison ministry.

Early in Nelson's ministry, a pastor advised us to get away for at least one night every year. "Just the two of you," he said. "I know you think you can't afford it but the truth is, you can't afford not to. Ministry is demanding and it takes a toll on a marriage." It was good advice.

And then there was Nelson's sense of humor and fun. To this day, he still struggles to restrain himself when he has a garden hose in hand.

A week into my new role at the prison I wrote in my journal, "Now the buck stops at my desk."

I was tested from the start. That Sunday an inmate jumped to his feet midway through my sermon. He waved his arms, and shouted, "Jesus, Jesus, thank you, Jesus!"

Sensing that his outburst had more to do with his habit to showboat than with a moving of the Spirit, I asked the inmate to sit down. He ignored me.

I repeated my request.

Men in the congregation began nudging each other and whispering.

For the third time, I asked the inmate to be seated. He finally complied, and I breathed a sigh of relief. I was shaken by the public showdown and so were the inmates.

I called the offender to my office the next day.

He was defiant. "I'll stand when the Spirit tells me to stand."

I ignored his sham of spirituality and told him I expect cooperation and order during services.

"I won't make any promises about anything," he answered and stalked from my office.

Inmates arrived at Mahanoy with expectations and ideas about how church services should operate. "That's not how we did things at Graterford Prison," one complained, and another countered with a completely different concept from Greensburg.

"My word, if I followed all their ideas it would be a zoo!" I wrote in my journal.

Mitch said I ran my Sunday services too much like the Catholics. "They're boring and put me to sleep. All you do is read the Bible and I can do that just as well in my cell. You really need to work at becoming a man of God."

Maybe Mitch was in cahoots with Jack, who sent the prison super-

intendent a complaint against me to say I didn't meet his "Baptist needs."
The next week Jack told me that a large group of disgruntled inmates had
planned to stage a protest against me in a service. "But I talked them out of
it," he said with an air of heroism. "They agreed to put up with you until a
more charismatic chaplain comes."

I had no idea whether there was any truth to his story, but the possibility unnerved me. I sure didn't want to garner the prison administration's
attention over such a disturbance.

My biggest headache came from the choir, a mishmash of men from
varying musical backgrounds and religious traditions. They each had their
ideas about what to sing, how to sing, and mostly, *who* should sing. Each
wanted the lead solo, and collectively, they wanted more and more "show
time."

Randy sent me a two-page request slip describing a particularly tumultuous choir practice. He'd been under the impression that he was to open
with a song. It didn't happen, he wrote in his complaint, and the director couldn't control the group. Songs were eliminated on someone's whim,
words were changed, and there was too much emphasis on blending the
guitars. He blamed the chaos for both his and a friend's headache. "Guys
were in and out of the room," he reported, "and a certain individual made
fun of you in prayer." But Randy's sensibilities reached a breaking point
when "someone kept passing gas and leaving a foul odor in the room . . . I
will not be [at church] on Sunday and I'm not going to sing with the choir
anymore."

One day I had an issue of a different sort with an inmate who regularly
attended church services. I happened to look up as Troy walked by my office
door. He had no reason to be in the area.

I opened my door just as he scooped a handful of sugar packets from
the coffee-making supplies. "Whoa, what are you doing?" I asked.

He looked at me as if I were a complete idiot. "I'm getting some sugar
for my coffee."

"Where's your coffee?"

"Back in my cell."

"Let me get this straight—you're taking my sugar back to your cell to put in your coffee?"

"Yeah."

I pointed to the sugar dish. "Put it back."

"Aw, Chaplain—"

"I said, put it back."

I'm not that stingy that I wouldn't gladly give sugar to someone, but the coffee supplies Troy dipped into were strictly for staff use. If he were caught with those contraband packets of sugar, the officers could trace it back to me and I'd have some explaining to do.

Troy turned slowly, stuffed the sugar packets back into the container, and stalked off, muttering under his breath.

About a week later, he came by my office and said, "Chaplain, I gotta talk to you."

"Sure," I replied and invited him to take a seat, expecting to hear an apology.

"Chaplain, I gotta tell you, I was really disappointed in you last week."

I leaned back in surprise. "Oh? How so?"

"You disrespected me."

A chuckle escaped before I could squelch it. "Really? I disrespected you? Wasn't that *you* stealing *my* sugar?"

"Well, no, I was just helping myself, and you disrespected me."

Obviously, this discussion wasn't going anywhere. "I'm sorry you felt disrespected," I said, "but I don't even feel guilty about not feeling guilty." I showed Troy to the door, steered him past the sugar pot, and sent him on his way.

The inmate population doubled in 1995, and the facility's census topped at 1,735 men by the end of the year.[25] New staff also arrived steadily. Some subscribed to get-tough ideology. Others viewed inmates as hapless

---

[25] Commonwealth of Pennsylvania Department of Corrections, *1995 Annual Statistical Report*, p. 26, https://www.cor.pa.gov/About%20Us/Statistics/Documents/Old%20Statistical%20Reports/1995%20Annual%20Statistical%20Report.pdf

victims of societal failings and took a softer approach. Inmates sized up staff and pounced on new employees perceived as malleable.

Within one week in late 1994, I learned of three people (some of them in other institutions) who got tripped up by inmates. One was caught smuggling drugs into prison and another was discovered having a sexual relationship with a prisoner. They both lost their jobs. A volunteer minister got kicked out of the prison when he unwittingly (I hope) handled money for a drug deal. He'd fallen for the inmate's Christian talk, unwisely trusted him, and became putty in the inmate's hands.

Another time, a sharp-eyed officer noticed a toothbrush sticking from an inmate's shirt pocket. "What's with the toothbrush?" the officer asked. "You know you're not allowed to bring personal items to chapel."

The inmate reluctantly confessed that he had sweet-talked a young volunteer into bringing her used toothbrush to a Catholic Bible study group. I guess the handoff was the ultimate romantic gesture in their covert relationship. The offense earned him time in The Hole, and the volunteer was banned from returning to the prison.

The manipulation and games were relentless. "It's pretty scary," I wrote in my journal. "Working in prison can make one cynical. Lord, I need wisdom!"

Late in 1994, two sergeants intervened in a fight between inmates over the choice of television channels. One officer suffered a broken nose and got fifteen stitches, and the other was hospitalized with head injuries.

The next day an inmate confided to me that he knew where the blades were hidden that had been used in the scuffle. "But man, I don't want to get in trouble," he said. "You know how it goes for prison snitches."

I assured him I would do my best and thanked him for his courage in reporting the matter. Shortly after I reported it, the Security Lieutenant and two plainclothes state police came to my office for more information. I assumed that they would protect the snitch, but I was wrong. They left my office, promptly went to his classroom, and pulled him into the hallway where they questioned him in view of fellow inmates.

Understandably, the snitch was upset with me. And I was just as per-
turbed that Security handled the matter so flippantly and without regard
for his safety.

Those kinds of situations did little to ease the insecurities I fought. In
many of my journal entries I cried out to God for wisdom to present the
Gospel message in an effective way, guidance in treating men with compassion, and the spine to deal with ecumenical issues that confronted me. Muslim, Protestant, Catholic, Jewish, Wiccan, Rastafarian, Jehovah Witness,
Seventh Day Adventist, Satanists—each group and their multiple variants
demanded representation. Chaplains and volunteers of all religious stripes
vied for office and chapel space.

For the stretch of my employment at Mahanoy, I struggled with the
tension of interacting with other faith groups. "Some of it makes me sick," I
wrote in a journal entry. "I must always respect other faiths, but that doesn't
make us brothers! I never want to compromise Jesus and the truth of the
Gospel message. No job is worth that."

Perhaps a dormant fear of reliving the Camp Hill riot lurked within
me. During my first emergency drill at Mahanoy, all the staff from the edu-
cation/chaplaincy departments were escorted to the administration building. We each were briefed on our responsibilities in the event of a real emergency, and I waited out the rest of the afternoon contemplating my primary
duty: notifying families whose loved ones were taken hostage.

I could only pray that I would never see the day.

**What joy-stealers have sneaked into your life? Take steps to recapture the joy of
basking in the presence of Jesus, beginning with regular time in His word.**

**Some inmates tried to dictate the direction of Nelson's call to ministry at the
prison. In the same way, others may try to steer you off the course to which God
has called you. Stand firm and never compromise on the truth of the Gospel.**

Nelson Zeiset, at 12 years old, in 1973.   *Esther Allgyer, age 15, in 1974.*

Ellis and Lois Zeiset family in November 1973 – (back): Nelson, Nevin, Arlene; (front): Joanne, Lois, Marlin, Ellis, Elaine.

Melvin and Nancy Allgyer and children (from left): Michael, Melvin Jr., James, Esther, Nancy, Anna; October 1971.

Nelson and Esther's wedding day on February 14, 1981.

The house trailer near Atmore, Alabama, where Nelson and Esther lived while serving at New Life/We Care from January 1983 – February 1984.

Chapel at G. K. Fountain Prison, Atmore, Alabama.

New Life's Chaplain's Assistants share the Gospel with inmates in a dormitory at G. K. Fountain. Circa 1980.

Martin Weber, founder of We Care Foundation/New Life Program.

New Life's Chaplain's Assistants in 1983 – (back): Nelson Zeiset, Tommy Rudolph, Aaron Martin, Darwin Hochstetler, John Hurst; (front): Anthony Swartzentruber, Mark Miller, Marvin Reed, Ken Wanner.

Homemade "shanks," like these confiscated from Alabama inmates, were possibly fashioned from a bed rail, a kitchen utensil, and a pitchfork tine.

Chaplain Widmann, Nelson (seated), Esther (with back toward camera), and other guests at a picnic outside the Camp Hill prison chapel in May, 1985.

A storage closet at SCI Frackville was converted into an office that Nelson shared with another chaplain. Circa 1991.

Leon Zimmerman, Nelson, and Donald Martin confer in the chapel at Lebanon County Prison. Circa 1990.

Nelson at Jubilee's office. Circa 1993.

Staff at Jubilee Ministries included Nelson, Mimi Keller, Clair Weaver, Marilyn Nolte, Neal Eckert, and Art Bomberger. Circa 1993.

Nelson and Esther, Joel, Emily, and Renee at Nelson's ordination in September 1993, at Roedersville Mennonite Church, near Pine Grove, PA.

Nelson and Esther with their children: Emily (9 years old), Joel (11), and Renee (6) in February 1995. Four months later Nelson was hired as chaplain at SCI Mahanoy.

Nelson and Esther at his graduation from Lancaster Bible College in January 1999.

Joy marked Michael Clancy's baptism in 2002, performed by Chaplain Guy Giordano (right) and Nelson. Michael is now a pastor and an EMM field worker in Lebanon, PA.

Chaplain Giordano (right) and Nelson celebrated Chaplain Whalen's retirement from SCI Mahanoy in 2008.

Chaplain Kevin Dobbs assists Nelson in an inmate baptism at SCI Mahanoy. Circa 2015.

Nelson, behind the pulpit in SCI Mahanoy's chapel. Circa 2015.

The Zeiset family in October 2020. Left to right: Andrew and Renee Stauffer and two sons; Kenton and Emily Bucher and four children; Nelson and Esther; Joel and Anita Zeiset and five children.

CHAPTER EIGHTEEN
Obstacles and Growth in Mahanoy's Prison Church

*O*n Nelson's first day as a state employee in June 1994, I was occupied with mowing the lawn and pulling weeds at my parents' house. Mom and Dad were 4,000-some miles from home, belatedly fulfilling their dream of touring Alaska. They had purchased a motorhome thirteen months earlier, in the same week that Mom fell desperately sick and learned she had leukemia.

In the summer of 1994 she felt reasonably well, and they left for six weeks to explore the Last Frontier. I think my parents knew it was now or never. By the time they arrived back home Mom's rapidly declining health was evident. Doctors confirmed her leukemia was back with a vengeance and on November 8, 1994, my parents' thirty-ninth anniversary, Mom lost her courageous battle against her illness.

Around that same time Nelson resigned from the ministry at Roedersville Mennonite Church, but he promised to remain until other leadership was in place. Freed of pastoral responsibilities, Nelson could finally step up his educational goals. Within a year, he completed four distance-learning courses from Southeastern College.

Our children got their first look at Daddy's workplace in May of 1995, when Mahanoy prison held a Family Visit Day to coincide with Corrections Employee Week. Joel was almost twelve years old, Emily nine, and Renee seven. The following fall, Renee described *her momentous visit in a second-grade writing assignment. The title, "The Day I Went to Prison," drew horrified gasps from her classmates.*

Several years later, when the girls were in junior high, I took them snow tubing at Blue Marsh Ski Area. Nelson worked at the prison that night, and was perfectly happy to avoid the snow and cold weather. The resort was packed with families who, like us, had earned free Monday night tickets by submitting UPC symbols from store-brand groceries.

We stood in a long line awaiting the ski lift when a voice called out above the crowd, "Hey, Mrs. Zeiset!" Nearer to the front of the line, the father of Renee's school friend waved his arms above his head. Satisfied that he had my attention, he hollered, "Is that husband of yours in jail tonight, Mrs. Zeiset?"

A sea of faces pivoted toward us. I could only imagine what they might be thinking of me and my felonious husband. My mortification should have silenced me, but before thinking better of it, I yelled back, "Yes, but he'll soon be home!" And then I realized I'd only worsened a bad situation, and wished for an avalanche to swallow me up.

I couldn't be upset with our friend. I had heard that kind of question before, asked in jest. "Your hubby isn't here tonight? Don't tell me he's in jail again!"

On occasion, I instigated the jokes and whispered with feigned embarrassment, "Nelson couldn't come because he's, ahem, locked up again."

But this is no joke for inmates' families. They bear a heavy burden of pain and humiliation.

After that first Family Visit Day, the age requirements for children changed, and Renee, who hung just below the minimum age, was not permitted to visit Mahanoy again for more than a decade. While Nelson worked at the hardware store, the children and I could stop by to see him. We knew his coworkers, and we understood the nature of his work. But it was different now. The children and I felt detached from Nelson's ministry.

He had some tough going in those first years at Mahanoy. Tougher than I knew. He sailed uncharted waters, his small boat bobbing on a vast sea.

In March of 1995, Gospel Echoes Prison Ministry Team, led by Todd Neuschwander, presented a weekend seminar at the prison. Gospel Echoes had been to Camp Hill and Retreat Prisons on several previous occasions, but this was their first visit to Mahanoy. The inmates connected well with Todd's teaching on godly manhood, and between sessions, Nelson bounced ideas and vented his frustrations to this man familiar with prison chaplaincy. Todd lent a listening ear and advised Nelson to move forward in confidence as he waited on God to establish the prison church. Todd's caring friendship proved refreshing and encouraging in subsequent visits to the prison and to our home.

A variety of prison ministries regularly provided encouragement, teaching, and fellowship for Mahanoy's Protestant inmates. Streams of Life, founded by Del Burkholder and aided by Delmar Weaver and other volunteers, taught Monday night Bible studies. A Yokefellow group taught another class every week; a Baptist Laymen group conducted classes once a month. Other ministries including Second Chance, Outward Focused, and Rock of Ages also provided biblical resources to the chaplaincy program, often in the form of weekend seminars once or twice a year. The support and friendship of each group proved valuable to Nelson.

In the early 1990s he learned of Aurora Ministries, whose focus centered, not on prisoners, but on the chaplains who served them. The organization believed that the success of a chaplain's ministry was related, at least to some degree, to the spouse's support. Their Chaplain Enrichment Seminars qualified for part of the mandatory training that Nelson was to acquire each year, and he excitedly showed me their brochure. "You can go to the conference with me," he said. "The ministry will cover my costs, and they ask only a nominal fee for your lodging and meals."

> *So off we went to picturesque Schroon Lake in New York's Ad-*
> *irondack Mountains for three days of solid Bible teaching and fellow-*
> *ship with other evangelical chaplains and their spouses. Mealtimes*
> *were lively exchanges where I gained perspective on the nuts and bolts*
> *of Nelson's ministry that I otherwise would not have experienced.*
>
> *In the next few years, we would take in additional Aurora con-*
> *ferences—at Sandy Cove in Maryland, on a cruise to the Bahamas,*
> *and lastly, in North Carolina. Around 2011, Aurora fell victim to*
> *the economic downturn and folded. Yet for a season God used them to*
> *encourage many godly chaplains with respite and valuable resources.*
> *We felt so blessed to be among them.*

Chaplain Whalen, the Facility Chaplaincy Program Director (FCPD), was a great sounding board and advisor as I tried to gain my footing at Mahanoy prison. He gave me free rein in developing programs and services for the Protestant community. I was saddened when his bishop reassigned him to another location in September 1995, and it fell to me to assume the role of Acting FCPD. The position involved the supervision of all chaplains at the institution, too many meetings for my liking, and administrative responsibilities that robbed me of time to do the ministry work to which I felt called.

A portion of the role involved dealing with grievances filed against the religious department. One involved an inmate who demanded vegetarian meals in keeping with his religious beliefs. Administration advised him that at last record he had identified as Protestant and would need to verify acceptance into the Krishna faith before accommodations could be made. His last name was—no kidding—*Crook*!

Native American inmates also came out of the woodwork to claim mental anguish and stress when some of their sacred religious items, those that prison policy deemed "excessive," were confiscated from their cells. The prisoners also lodged complaints and boycotted the spiritual advisor who was not to their liking.

Muslim men filed grievances to avoid trimming their beards.

And then there were the haircut exemption grievances. A large percentage of those filing for exemptions claimed religious belief but seldom attended the services connected to those religions. I had to carefully pick my way through the game to sort out the players who only wished to grow their hair longer than the general prison population.

In June 1996, Akra, a Cambodian inmate who practiced the Buddhist faith, requested the "religious materials" his family had sent to him. They were Buddhist chants, he said. Because of their purported religious nature, it was my responsibility as acting head chaplain to review them.

Akra's home-recorded cassette tapes did not sound like anything Buddhist to me. I asked the Catholic chaplain for his opinion. He was also skeptical so I pulled the music director in on it. "I don't think so," he said. Just to be certain that all my bases were covered, I asked a Buddhist unit manager to lend his ear. He rolled his eyes and said, "That only sounds like Cambodia's top ten."

I denied the cassettes on the premise that they were not religious and notified Akra of my decision. In accordance with policy, he had a choice— he could either pay to have them shipped out of the institution or sign off to have them destroyed. He had thirty days to decide; I gave him an additional month. In the meantime, Akra appealed to my supervisor, who also denied his request.

Akra came by my office to plead his case and I repeated my position. His dark eyes narrowed. "I'm going to sue you for them."

I had heard such threats before. Maybe he would sue, and maybe not. I couldn't let it worry me.

During the next eleven months, Akra pursued a string of actions, beginning with a grievance against me. It was denied. He appealed to both the prison superintendent and the office of the Commissioner of Corrections. When they both upheld my decision, he wrote to Father Menei, the head state chaplain at Central Office, to request reimbursement for the tapes that by this time had already been destroyed. Finally, when all administrative remedies were exhausted, he filed a lawsuit in which he named Superintendent Dragovich and myself as defendants. He and his co-plaintiffs—all "currently incarcerated Asian prisoners held at SCI Mahanoy"—sued for denial of the right to practice their traditional religious beliefs. They sought $15,000.00 in compensatory and punitive relief, a jury trial, and reasonable attorney's fees.

I filled out a ton of paperwork from the state attorney general's office and opted for the attorney assigned to me by the Commonwealth. After reviewing my trail of documentation, the judge ruled that Akra's lawsuit was frivolous. The case had dragged on for nearly eighteen months.

My role as Acting FCPD stretched into fourteen long months. Administration offered me the position, but I turned it down flat. They couldn't have paid me enough for the headaches, and I was relieved when the prison hired a replacement near Thanksgiving in 1996. Finally, I could get back to my previous role as Protestant Chaplain.

My relief was short-lived. My new supervisor, whom I will call Chaplain B, was an eccentric man who spoke in low tones and drew out every syllable in maddening form. I soon learned his favorite topic concerned the Catholic church's authority. "You protestors—" he spat out the word and narrowed his eyes. "You know, don't you, that the term Protestant arose from the fact that you protested against the one true church?"

I didn't answer, nor did he give me a chance. He was into a full rant mode. Even so, he didn't hurry but deliberately enunciated each word of his long diatribe. He claimed the Catholic Church endowed him with responsibility to censor all religious materials and the right to hold suspect Protestant literature hostage in the corner of his cluttered office.

He held all faiths in disdain and demeaned each at every opportunity. When a Catholic inmate converted to Islam, Chaplain B unnecessarily picked a fight with the Muslim chaplain, asserting that the inmate belonged to "The Church" and always would.

Chaplain B nearly came undone when I began planning for Mahanoy's first baptismal service and mentioned my intent to publicly invite men to join the instructional class. He shook a wagging finger at me and warned, "That is tantamount to casting pearls before swine, and you know our Lord warned against that."

He stonewalled every aspect of the process, including arguing against the soundness of the baptistry. He entertained notions of it breaking and flooding the chapel. Never mind that it had been purchased only a year earlier. When all of his excuses were finally exhausted, he fairly shouted in four syllables, "No-o-o-o! I will *not* allow baptism into the protesting church!"

Chaplain B would not budge. No amount of coaxing or reasoning changed his stubborn mind. I appealed to the deputy superintendent, but he was unwilling to side against a priest, so I took my case to Chaplain Menei at Central Office in Harrisburg, and at long last, the baptism took place.

I paid a price, however, for going over the deputy superintendent's head. Chaplain Menei called him about the matter and the superintendent gave me a tongue-lashing. Sometime later, I submitted a request to attend a pastors' conference at Rosedale Bible College (formerly Rosedale Bible Institute). The conference would have fulfilled part of my yearly mandatory training, but the deputy superintendent denied permission.

"It's been approved before," I reminded him. "Is there a reason for it being turned down this year?"

He stepped close and drew himself to full stature. "Yes, there's a reason." He pinned me with a steely glare. "Just because I can."

Throughout the wearisome three years of his employment, Chaplain B nursed a paranoia against both inmates and staff. He called me into his office one day to divulge the extent of it in conspiratorial whispers. "You know how I keep the lights off in here?" he asked.

Of course I knew. His office was always darkened, his door half closed. For the life of me, I had no idea how he filled his hours. He seldom had inmates in his office and rarely visited the RHU or other blocks.

"I keep the door at that precise angle," he said, demonstrating the distance with outstretched arms. "It reflects in the window like a mirror. I can see movement out there in the clerks' area. Not a person goes in and out that I don't monitor."

Oh. So *that* was what Chaplain B did with his time! That, and inventing obstacles for the Protestant community, including pushing through a new policy that dictated the chapel be used only for weekly worship services. Suddenly, Bible studies had to be rescheduled to coordinate with available classrooms in the education department. Some studies got canceled altogether for lack of space, while the chapel remained vacant.

In spite of Chaplain B's efforts against the Christian church at SCI Mahanoy, the fellowship began to experience significant growth. Early in 1998, I started two prayer groups of four inmates in each one. We met once a week and devoted the entire thirty minutes to earnest prayer for the church at Mahanoy. From that, a closeness grew among the men and they began speaking freely of their struggles and the ways in which God was teaching them godly living.

Drew shared how he had waited to get called to the visiting room on a Saturday afternoon. He expected his wife and daughters, but minutes dragged by without a call. *Did they have an accident? A flat tire? Were they sick? Did they not love him anymore? Was his wife about to draft a Dear John letter and move on to someone else?* A thousand negative thoughts flooded his troubled mind. When he finally got called for the visit, Drew couldn't get there fast enough. But visiting hours were nearly over. He had only fifteen minutes with his family—hardly time for a greeting, let alone an explanation about their tardiness. He went back to his cell and sulked.

That evening, when chapel services were announced over the loudspeaker, Drew decided to kick aside his pity party, but his face still bore his dejection as plain as a billboard. Shane, a Christian brother, read it a mile away. He fell into step with Drew on the walkway and asked, "Hey, man, why so glum?"

Drew spilled his frustration, and Shane listened without comment. They walked in silence for a while and then Shane said in a husky voice, "I'm not sure I understand. I've been locked up for fourteen years and haven't had a single visit." His voice held no bitterness. He only spoke the bare fact.

"The Spirit convicted me for pouting," Drew told me. "At least I had fifteen minutes with my family. God has blessed me abundantly!"

Time and again, I marveled at how the Holy Spirit worked in the lives of men who came to Jesus in confession and repentance. Each time I led someone to Christ, I said, "Brother, there are two things I want you to do as you begin your walk with Christ. One, tell someone else of your decision to follow Jesus, and two, read your Bible every single day." I might have pointed out a truckload of issues that needed to be addressed but left that to the convicting work of the Spirit, confident that He would lead them into all truth as they sought Him for it.

Sure enough, the men came back to tell me about it.

"You know how my cellie runs a store?" Max asked.

Yeah, I knew. Every block had its men who "ran a store" by stockpiling items from the commissary and exchanging at exorbitant prices to someone who, for instance, was three days from going to the commissary but dying for a bag of chips. The practice was illegal, and if caught, could land a man in the RHU.

"I used to help my cellie out," Max said, "but now that I'm a Christian, I don't want to do it anymore. It's just not right. He's putting a lot of pressure on me though. What do I do?"

Other men shared how God worked in their lives.

Chip said, "I never knew I had such a foul mouth! It's disgusting, the things that come out. How come I see it now, but never did before I accepted Jesus?"

Brian told me he got rid of the smut in his cell. "All those girlie pictures on my wall—they went out with the trash yesterday. I couldn't stand to look at them anymore."

And Jeff grew bothered by his smoking habit. "Every time I light up I get this nagging feeling that it's not right. What's that all about?"

"That's the Holy Spirit in your life!" I told the men. "It's the assurance that you're a man of God, and He's working on you to become more and more like Himself!"

I began holding communion services for the Christian inmates. It was not without its glitches. Policy did not allow me to take anything into the prison, so I ordered the bread and grape juice from the food service department. On one occasion, the juice could not be found anywhere.

The food service manager admitted that it had most likely been stolen.

He apologized, but what could be done? The service was to begin in thirty minutes. "We have some powdered orange drink here," he offered hesitantly.

"I'll take it," I said.

"Really? You want orange drink for communion?"

And that's how it happened that artificially flavored orange drink stood in to represent the Blood of Jesus Christ.

The annual Maundy Thursday service was only a few weeks away when William, a new believer thirsty to learn and eager to live out his new-found faith, came by my office.

"Chaplain, I need to sort something out," he said, and his story of indoctrination into white supremist ideology tumbled out. From as early as William could remember, his father raged against Blacks and shoved Ku Klux Klan literature at him. William joined a militant branch of the KKK and worked his way up in the organization. He gave speeches, wrote articles, and incited others to hatred.

"It seemed normal and right. But now . . ." William paused and rubbed his chin thoughtfully. "I don't get it. Seems like God is telling me that I have it all wrong . . . that He loves Black people and wants me to do the same. But, man. . . ." He broke off again. His struggle was real.

We talked for more than half an hour before I had to draw our conversation to a close. "I have an idea for you, William, something I want you to think about and pray over," I said. "You know that we're having a communion service in two weeks?"

William nodded. "And we're going to wash feet?"

The practice has its roots in the John 13 account that tells of the upper room Passover meal Jesus shared with His disciples mere hours before His arrest and crucifixion. Jesus humbled Himself to do the work of a servant by lovingly washing his friends' feet. The practice of feet-washing is a part of my Mennonite heritage, and I incorporated it into the annual Maundy Thursday prison service to symbolize servanthood among the brotherhood. It had become a highlight with the men.

William knew where this was going. "You want me to wash a Black man's feet?"

I shrugged. "It's your call. Yours and God's."

Sixty-some men showed up for the communion service, and when we commenced with the feet-washing part, William approached a Black man, eager to prove he'd shucked off racism through the act of washing his feet. But the Black inmate insisted on washing William's feet first.

As the man knelt before him, William's mind went down a foreign path, a road on which he had never allowed himself to travel. He thought about how the man's enslaved great-grandfathers had no choice but to serve their White masters. *Perhaps those masters had been his own great-grandfathers,* William thought. He contemplated the prejudice and hatred and brutality heaped upon Black people throughout generations, and suddenly he was overcome by shame at the sins of his forefathers and at his own sin of hatred and superiority.

It was now William's turn to wash the other man's feet. He knelt by the tub of water and grasped the black feet in his white hands. Tears streamed down his face as he tenderly washed and dried them. When he got up from his knees, William threw himself into the embrace of his Black brother in Christ. The two men sobbed together.

The holy moment was not lost on other men who looked on at the emotional symbolism of mutual love and service. A pattern was set for subsequent communion services. Racial walls among the Christian brothers at SCI Mahanoy began crumbling. It was beautiful to watch.

God had work to do in my heart, too. At one communion service a grizzled inmate sought me out. "Chaplain, I'd be so honored if I could wash your feet," he said.

Bad breath wafted from his toothless mouth, and I drew back, noting all at once his stained and misbuttoned shirt, his ragged coat, and a repulsive stench of body odor. I tried to think up a plausible excuse, but in that moment, God broke through my own superiority and I heard myself saying, "Sure, I'd like that."

As I washed the smelliest, dirtiest feet I'd ever seen, I felt humbled by the experience of seeing my own filth for what it is in the sight of a holy God who loves me unconditionally. I can't say it was an easy thing to embrace my brother, but it was the hug my soul needed at that moment.

We chaplains were sometimes called "hug-a-thugs." Skeptics rail against jailhouse religion which, they say, is just a crutch and a coping technique that lasts only as long as the incarceration.

"Once a criminal, always a criminal!" an officer griped to me. "These guys come to church, find religion, and blab all about Jesus, but they lie and steal and give me lip like anyone else. And when those 'Christians' leave the prison, they dump their Bibles in the trashcan at the front door. Then they go live like the devil until they get thrown back into prison."

Sadly, his charges were true all too often. I understood the cynicism because I also wrestled with it. Many prisoners, overwhelmed with despair and regret, have made quick commitments to Jesus without understanding or thinking through the implications of discipleship. When their fervor dies out and they fall away, a watching world sneers at the idea of redemption and lasting change.

Although my confidence in man is shaky, my faith in the transformation that Jesus Christ can bring to a yielded heart is solid. Teachability is the most essential factor in producing life-altering change. Responsibility is a close second. Most criminals have shut both characteristics out of their lives.

A man once told me that by the time he reached first grade, he didn't know a single person he could trust. My experience was worlds apart—at that age I didn't know anyone that I *couldn't* trust. A lifetime of betrayal and abandonment resulted in him closing off his heart to others. They had nothing to offer him. He became his own master.

Such a person typically throws off personal responsibility and blames his environment for his criminal behavior. I generally offered two responses to that assertion. "Really?" I asked. "Does everyone who grew up as you did turn to crime?"

Invariably, they admitted to knowing guys from the hood who turned out to be productive citizens.

Alternately, I might ask, "At the time that you committed your crime, did you know it was wrong?"

"Well, yeah, but . . ." Too often they were quick to justify, rationalize, and minimize their actions.

However, I held out great hope for those who were both willing to learn and to assume responsibility. They were on track to lasting rehabilitation through the power of transformation in Christ.

Sometimes we try to play the role of the Holy Spirit for a new convert. We expect immediate and dramatic change. Our task is to faithfully teach, rebuke, and encourage. To pray and to trust that the Spirit will bring conviction in His time.

And what of ourselves? Are we teachable? How readily do we accept godly counsel from others? Do we assume responsibility for our unwise choices, our failures, our sins?

CHAPTER NINETEEN

Co-laborers for the Ministry at Mahanoy

Early in 1998, Chaplain Menei called from Central Office. "A pastor contacted me asking where he can volunteer as a prison chaplain," he said. "You came to mind right away. I think you and John Ritchey would work together well."

John pastored an Assemblies of God church, and he had a big heart for people and a passion to lead them to Jesus. I was thrilled at the prospect of working with him! John went through a lot of rigmarole to gain approval and began volunteering at Mahanoy in May of 1998. He was restricted to the chapel, however, and denied clearance to visit on the blocks or to conduct Sunday services. It brought back memories of when I was stuck with similar frustrating limits.

By then, the inmate population at Mahanoy edged toward 2,000 and I was the only Protestant chaplain. I sure could have used his help in a larger capacity, but John made the most of his time in the chapel and connected well with both inmates and staff. Almost a year later, he got a contract chaplaincy position at the prison through Jubilee Ministries, and his restrictions were lifted. He operated in his element when making rounds on the blocks and in the RHU. John was the first in a succession of Jubilee chaplains to work with me at Mahanoy.

Around Thanksgiving in 1998, attendance at Protestant services hit an all-time high of 168. In December it spiked at 182. Increased numbers were nothing new during the holidays. Every December we distributed a small handful of Christmas cards to attendees. Many men could not afford to buy cards for their loved ones, and they appreciated the giveaway, but there were always some who tried to sneak through the line a second time or otherwise attempted to con a few extra cards from us. The giveaway became a hassle, and I complained in my journal that too many men came to church services only for the freebies.

And then I remembered. John and I and a few of the inmates in the congregation had been praying that more men would come to church. In spite of my limited expectations, God was obviously answering our prayers, and I felt convicted for my lack of faith. Near Christmas, I wrote in my journal, "Even if they come for the wrong reasons, I pray that the men will allow the seed of the Gospel to grow in their hearts."

· · · · ·

George had the marks of a man who had borne too much in his lifetime. Downcast eyes. Slow shuffle. Flat, garbled speech. He had been locked up for thirty-nine years, he said.

"Since 1960?" I asked.

He nodded. "You probably weren't even born yet."

"Not till a year later," I said. *1960!* That was the year my oldest brother was born! 1960 was before President Kennedy's assassination. Before men landed on the moon. Way back in the day when the phone system had party lines, and Russia had Nikita Khrushchev.

George broke in on my thoughts. "I was sixteen when they locked me up the first time."

Sixteen? Only sixteen? My son, Joel, was counting down the months until his sixteenth birthday!

I could not wrap my head around it. George had thrown away a life of promise and potential for choices that landed him in the wasteland of human warehousing, without a chance of ever seeing the streets again.

My encounter with George was a reminder of the passage of time. At the beginning of my prison ministry, many inmates were my age. Now, more and more, I met those who were young enough to be my sons.

Early in 1997, Nelson had begun a degree completion program at Lancaster Bible College (LBC), and for two years, he juggled classes even while working full time at the prison. His graduation in January 1999 was cause for great celebration. Nelson's parents, my father and his new wife, Dorothy Groff, and our three children cheered Nelson's accomplishment of graduating with high honors. His mother, unfamiliar with graduation traditions, eyed the gold honor cord that the college president draped around Nelson's neck.

"It looks like a curtain tie-back, don't you think?" Nelson teased.

She fingered the shiny tassel. "Well, yes, sort of, I guess."

"It would look good on your living room drapes, huh, Mom?"

"Indeed not!" she sputtered. "You worked hard for it. You can hang it on your own drapes!"

He had worked hard and we both were glad that he had finally fulfilled the educational requirements that he promised four years earlier when hired at Mahanoy. Soon after graduation, he took a few master's level courses, but eventually gave it up. He had only so much time and energy.

Since the fall of 1997, we had begun attending Green Terrace Mennonite Church, a small church tucked into the hills near Wernersville. The move shortened our drive to church considerably. When Joel got his driver's license a few years later, I was relieved that he would not be making the forty-five-minute trek across the mountains to Roedersville's youth group activities.

I had long ago gotten used to driving two vehicles to church so that Nelson could leave directly after dismissal to go to the prison. He and I both still felt strongly that he should attend morning services with our family. Over the years I'd met many chaplains' wives who attended church services alone because their husbands were occupied with their prison congregations. I couldn't imagine their loneliness, nor their husbands' feeling of disconnect and lack of accountability from a local church.

In 1999, plans were made to transition leadership at Green Terrace church. Leon Stauffer served as lead pastor, and Harold Martin, the assistant, wished to retire. In seeking to find a replacement for Harold, discussion turned toward Nelson, already an ordained minister. On May 21, 2000, he was installed as assistant pastor at Green Terrace Mennonite Church.

The potential for trouble in prison was always present, even at church services. Usually one or two officers remained in the building during services, but one Sunday about eight officers scattered throughout the chapel and lobby.

"There's a rumor afloat that a fight is coming down in your service, Reverend," the lieutenant said. "We're going to do random pat searches as the men arrive, and throughout the service we'll have a strong presence and sharp eyes on the chapel."

Was it a baseless rumor, or did the increased officer presence squelch a dangerous plot? All I know is that the service went off without a hitch, and I was more than grateful.

Security presence was strongest at Muslim Jumah services. On one occasion, count time was called before the service had ended. Nothing stops count times in prison; all activity ceases when the call is made for the regular accounting of prisoners.

The Muslim contract chaplain was on a tight schedule and needed to leave the institution to hold the Friday service at the Pottsville mosque. "I can't hang around until count clears," he said. "We didn't have time for elective prayers but the obligatory prayers are finished, so it's okay to conclude the service with that."

In retrospect, I should have insisted that he explain it to his congregation of 150 men. They were already disgruntled at the hurried conclusion to their service and didn't want to take it from me. And then a muscular officer stormed into the chapel, stepped onto their prayer rugs, and ordered them to sit down for count.

I don't know whether he didn't think about the disrespect he showed by stepping onto their rugs or if he didn't care, but the inmates were offended and slow to comply with his order.

He repeated it. "I said to sit down so we can take count! Y'all just a bunch of convicts!"

His use of a derogatory term added fuel to the fire, but he didn't hang around for the explosion. He stalked out and left me to supervise while two guards prepared to take count.

The agitated inmates crowded around me. "How dare he step on our holy rugs?" complained one man.

"He can't get away with that!" another growled.

My heart pounded. I motioned for quiet. "You're right. I apologize for his disrespect, and I assure you that this will be addressed." Somehow, I calmed the men down and they dispersed without incident. I shuddered to think how close we'd come to disaster. And for no reason.

This situation was only a practice run for a later near-catastrophe.

On a hot July afternoon in 1999, nearly two hundred Muslim inmates streamed into the chapel for Jumah. A female officer called out a prisoner for not having his shirt tail tucked in.

He ignored her.

She persisted.

He gave her lip.

A male sergeant fell into step beside him and said, "Hey, she gave you a direct order!"

The inmate swung around and shoved him. Immediately, tension electrified the place.

I didn't know anything was amiss until an inmate clerk stepped to my office door. "Chaplain, there's a big problem out here!"

I sprang from my desk and into the clerks' area. At the far end of the room was a single door with a large window, and it alone stood between me and the milling crowd that moved in waves around an inmate and a sergeant. The two gripped each other in a struggle for dominance—twisting, turning, and banging against the door. I quickly locked it and ran back to my phone to notify the control center.

"Help is on the way, Chaplain," the officer said.

It couldn't come quickly enough. Even before I hung up my phone, I heard someone say, "Let's get 'em!" and the refrain passed among the crowd. "Yeah, let's get 'em!" In an instant, a tangle of men pounded and yanked on a second door that accessed the clerks' area and chaplains' offices. Their efforts were fruitless. It was already locked, but clearly, the group was bent on violence.

My heart pounded in my head. Memories of the Camp Hill riot flooded me.

The seconds dragged interminably until the major arrived, backed up with a small army of officers. He engaged a few of the more vocal inmates in conversation, and after some tense minutes, he managed to restore a tenuous calm. Negotiations were made to allow the Muslim service to proceed.

And then the major motioned to me. "Reverend, I want you to go into the chapel to supervise."

I swallowed the bile rising in my throat. He couldn't be serious!

But he was.

"Yes, sir," I mumbled and followed the crowd of inmates into the chapel as if on legs of lead. The door closed after us. I stood beside it, determined not to allow a prisoner to get between me and my escape route.

Wilson, the Muslim inmate leader, gruffly directed the men to the prayer rugs and raked the inmates over with dark, flashing eyes. Murmurings died down. "That was not acceptable behavior and it was most un-Muslim!" Wilson growled. "A situation unfolded between *one* prisoner and *one* staff person. It did not concern you, yet you used it for violence. That's no way to act! You should be ashamed of yourselves!"

I could scarcely believe my ears! Wilson continued to berate his fellow inmates at length, and they took it from him without a word. Finally satisfied with their cooperation, Wilson commenced with the Jumah service and it went on for forty-five minutes.

Even while I kept a sharp eye on the group for the slightest hint of a disturbance, I was aware of movement out in the lobby, and learned later that all available officers were called to the chapel. Thankfully, the fracas happened at shift change, so additional officers were available. They gathered in the building, and not knowing what to expect from the inmates at

Jumah's dismissal, hastily took precautions. Anything that could potentially be used as a weapon—trash cans and chairs—were stashed into a locked classroom. Officers cleared the education wing. They sent inmates back to their cells and locked teachers and non-uniformed staff into a room farther back in the wing.

By the time the Muslim service ended, tempers had cooled, but the officers took no chances. They spread apart, two or three at intervals along the routes to the cell blocks. When the last inmate left the chapel, I took a deep breath and thanked God that it was over.

Three officers had suffered minor injuries. While the female officer's order may have been justified, she was reprimanded for unwisely pressing the issue in the presence of a large group of inmates.

An officer groused to me later, "All she had to do was write the inmate up! She could have even done that in the comfort of an air-conditioned office, and just like that, he would've been hauled off to the RHU. But no, she went on a power trip that could have gotten us killed!"

I resented being thrown into the chapel with two hundred angry men, like fresh meat to ravenous lions. In hindsight, I understood the major's reasoning—a chaplain did not present the threat that a uniformed officer might have. It was little comfort, though, and another reminder of the volatile nature of working in a prison.

• • • • •

The summer of 1999 morphed into fall and with it came the welcome news that Chaplain Whalen would return to Mahanoy. The Catholic bishop had decided to move Chaplain B to a parish. I was elated with the decision.

Three months later, I heard that Chaplain B was removed from the parish and transferred again, this time to a program for troubled priests. I shook my head at the news. "Are you serious? We had to put up with him for three long years, but the parish tolerated him for only four months!"

Chaplain Whalen chuckled. "Yeah, from what I hear, he gave a lot of people fits around here."

For sure.

• • • • •

Joel wrapped up his senior year of high school in 2001. Since tenth grade he had used Abeka homeschool video courses produced by Pensacola Christian College in Florida. The college planned a two-day celebration for graduates, and we made a family trip to participate. It was almost like going home again.

During our time in VS in 1983, we had made multiple trips to Pensacola's white sandy beaches only an hour south of Atmore, Alabama. Now, three days before Joel's graduation, we drove by the prisons where I got my start in ministry, stopped in at We Care Prison Ministry offices, and visited with Martin and Anna Weber. The two-week trip was the beginning of a tradition that we would continue for our daughters' graduations.

About that time, John Ritchey left Mahanoy and took a chaplaincy position at SCI Retreat. I was happy for him. Retreat Prison was much closer to his home and he was excited to be cut loose for ministry in another institution.

But I would miss him, and I feared that his replacement might not be a godly man. "I'm reminded repeatedly how I need to trust God," I wrote in my journal.

In my wildest imagination, I never would have guessed the method God would use to bring John's successor to Mahanoy. John Ritchey drove truck as a side job, and while traveling on Interstate 81, he struck up a conversation with a fellow trucker on his CB radio. When John mentioned that he worked in part-time prison chaplaincy, the other trucker was all ears. He had been pondering a call to prison ministry but had no idea where to get started.

"Oh, listen, man!" John said. "You gotta call Jubilee Ministries. They'd love to talk with you!"

By June, Guy Giordano had been hired by Jubilee to serve as a contract chaplain at Mahanoy. He was almost like John's clone. He, too, was a member of the Assemblies of God church, had an easy way of relating spiritual truth to inmates, and possessed a great sense of humor. And like John, Guy would also eventually move to Retreat. But first he would work with me at Mahanoy for ten years.

I was blessed beyond measure to work with both John and Guy.

Who would have thought that God could orchestrate a conversation between two truckers to bring a new godly chaplain to Mahanoy? His ways are beyond astounding!

CHAPTER TWENTY

Life in The Hole

I n Alabama they called it Segregation or Lock-Up. At Camp Hill it was referred to as Mohawk. Journalists might call it Solitary Confinement. At Mahanoy we knew it as The Hole or Restricted Housing Unit (RHU). Call it what you want, but it's all the same—a prison within a prison.

Almost five percent of the prison population is housed in the RHU. Policy mandated that a chaplain make daily visits to the unit. An entry from my journal on January 12, 1994, described the chaos that often erupted when I entered the unit. "That Christian's here again!" someone shouted and others echoed it.

"He's a blue-eyed devil!" another yelled, and the refrain passed among the cells. But they all fell silent as I approached.

"They're like puppies who strut around thinking they own the place," I wrote, "but as soon as you stamp your feet at them, they go running."

Guy Giordano, Jubilee's contract chaplain, had his own unique welcome on the block. Inmates thought he looked like Jerry Springer, and often met Guy's arrival on the RHU with raucous chants of "Jer-ry! Jer-ry!" and a wild banging against the cell doors.

If Guy and I didn't already know it, being likened to Jerry Springer and a blue-eyed devil reminded us of how much work we had to do in the RHU.

• • • • •

Men are locked into their RHU cells around the clock, except for one-hour exercise sessions in a caged "dog run" five days a week, and to get a shower twice a week. In either case, men need to strip down and hand their clothing through the wicket for the officers' inspection. That done, officers visually scan the nude inmate, hand his clothes back to him, watch him dress, and handcuff him behind his back before letting him out of his cell. Two officers, one on either side of the inmate, escort him to his destination. For some inmates, it's too much hassle, and they snub the opportunity to leave their cells.

Hands down, Kevin was one of the prison's nastiest RHU inmates and seemed proud to hold the title. Staff called him an animal. His time on the unit probably began with the typical sentence of thirty to ninety days, but because of ongoing misbehavior, his time on the unit stretched into nine long years.

At some point, Kevin stopped talking except to scream dark curses, vulgarities, and death threats at no one in particular. He refused to leave his cell for exercise, seldom showered, flung unwanted food against his walls, and took pleasure in throwing feces and urine at unsuspecting guards when they opened the wicket on his door.

Often, he refused to flush his toilet for long days at a time, apparently playing some twisted game to lure staff into his cell even while screaming that he would kill them if they did. After one particularly long non-flushing stint, I walked onto the block, and the nauseating stench nearly turned my stomach inside out. Inmates covered their faces with blankets, coming up for air occasionally to yell obscenities at Kevin. He didn't care. What harm could they do to him? The maintenance department eventually devised a way to flush his toilet remotely.

Months in the RHU dragged into years, and Kevin decided to quit walking. Most likely, it was for the same reason that other inmates cited: "They aren't gonna tell me what to do!"

That declaration never failed to both rankle and amuse me. "What do you mean, *they* aren't going to tell you what to do?" I'd ask. "Look at you! You're in the cell that *they* put you in! *They* gave you the clothes you're wearing! *They* tell you what to eat and when to eat it! *They* tell you when you can shower and *they* tell you when to exercise! Whatever do you mean about them not telling you what to do?"

Few inmates got that. They lifted their heads higher and responded with something like, "Yeah, well, they can make me do it on the outside but they aren't gonna get me here!" And thumping on their puffed-out chests, they declared, "Deep down, they're not gonna break me!"

I grieved for men like that. Unteachable and unbroken hearts cement the path to chronic incorrigibility.

That was Kevin.

Whatever his reasons, he quit walking. For six years, he spent his days sitting on the floor with his back to the cell door, scuttling on his buttocks only as far as the toilet in his cell and back again to his post. In time, Kevin's leg muscles atrophied to the point that he no longer had the ability to walk, even if he had wanted to. On the day that he maxed out on his sentence straight from The Hole, guards lifted him into a wheelchair and pushed him from his cell door to the front gate where he boarded the prison bus that drove him out into the free world.

I could only pray he didn't move into my neighborhood. Nor into yours.

• • • • •

Paul's original crime in 1993 involved a convenience store robbery. A parole violation resulted in him coming to Mahanoy in early 1998. A year later, he earned time in The Hole for molesting a nine-year-old girl in the prison visiting room. His crime was made more despicable by the fact that the assault happened multiple times, with his wife's full knowledge.

The story made it into the news, and inside the prison, everyone talked about Paul. I was as repulsed by his actions as anyone. When I entered the RHU the first time after he was sent there, I prayed for wisdom and for compassion. I reminded myself of Paul's value in the sight of God, no matter the depth of his depravity.

I was not prepared for the electric charge of hatred on the unit. All along the tier, on both sides of the corridor, men stood at their doors, screaming threats and insults at Paul. And as I approached his cell, they banged on their doors and screamed at me, "Chaplain, don't you go near that *blankety, blankety, blank-blank's* cell!"

I did go by Paul's cell, but it was impossible to talk with him above the din on the block, and I soon left. Remaining there would have only incited the men further.

Paul was in the RHU only a few months before his transfer to another institution. He'd fallen to the bottom of the brutal prison pecking order. Life would have gotten really nasty for him at Mahanoy.

• • • • •

An inmate in The Hole asked me to bring him a pack of cigarettes.

I shook my head.

"What? You won't bring me a pack? Just one measly little pack?"

I'd had encounters with this man before and knew it was a waste of my breath to argue against the hazards of smoking or to remind him that his request violated policy. I simply said, "Nope."

"Why not? Don't you care about people?"

"I'm here, aren't I?" I asked. "Do you think I'd come onto this block if I didn't care about you?"

"Nah, you come to this hellhole only because the big guns say you have to. You're just here for the money. If you really cared about me and my needs, you'd get me some smokes."

I knew he was just messing with me and returned with a stab at humor. "Man, why don't I feel guilty for not feeling guilty?"

He chuckled and walked away from his door. He'd had fun while it lasted.

"You have a good day!" I called after him.

He grinned and gave a thumbs up.

• • • • •

In August 1999, a four-time killer fashioned a life-size dummy in his bed at SCI Huntingdon, cut through his cell bars, and made his way to freedom by way of a rope. Two weeks later, two inmates escaped from SCI Dallas.

Three prison escapees, and all of them on the lam, reflected poorly on the Pennsylvania Department of Corrections. Governor Ridge ordered a complete lockdown and security audit of all Pennsylvania prisons. Inmates were confined to their cells twenty-four hours a day while security personnel scrambled to check and double-check against potential security lapses. At Mahanoy, maintenance workers checked every bolt on the fence surrounding the 67-acre prison compound. Staff were assigned to perform all the jobs done by inmates—janitorial tasks, delivering mail, washing dishes, and preparing more than 6,000 meals every day. I was off work for my Grandpa Beyer's funeral when lockdown began, but for two days afterward, I was tasked with packing food and distributing it on the blocks.

Mike, one of the Dallas escapees, was captured and brought to Mahanoy's RHU. Seven years later, he still had no indication of when he would get back into the general population. Mike took it with uncommon composure. "So my timing was off," he said with a shrug. "I shouldn't have run when another guy was already out."

"Yeah, you put me on kitchen duty for two days," I returned good-naturedly. "I came here to be a chaplain, not to scoop out applesauce for two thousand inmates!"

Mike told me that the prison deputy periodically came by his cell. "Before my escape, I shed some pounds so I could wiggle through my window and scale the fence. Now the deputy often says I look a little thin and asks if I'm gaining weight. I think I make him nervous."

"Can't fault him for doing his job," I said.

"Nah, I don't blame him none. But you know what I tell him? I say, 'Deputy, the way your staff is feeding me, it's really hard to gain a pound of weight. Tell your kitchen staff to add a little to my tray.' That always makes him chuckle a bit."

Mike joked that his escape charge tacked an additional three-and-a-half to seven years on top of his life sentence. "What are they gonna do?" he snickered. "Stand me up in the corner when I die so they can get another seven years out of me?"

Mike's laid-back nature, however, had its limits. Near the end of his time in RHU, a newly-enacted law required certain inmates to provide a DNA sample. Mike refused. After exercise one day, his escorting officers bypassed his cell and headed to the infirmary. Realizing their intent, Mike dropped to the floor. A scuffle ensued and more officers piled in to subdue him.

"You know," he told me later, "that touch felt sort of good. Sounds weird though, doesn't it?"

No, I assured him, that didn't sound weird at all. Human touch is essential to our well-being, and deprived of it for so long, even the rough handling felt good to Mike.

· · · · ·

Travis flagged me down from his cell. "Hey, Chaplain, I requested some religious books from the library but they didn't come yet. Any chance you'd check on them for me?"

Sure, I told him, I would look into it.

The prison librarian nodded and raised an eyebrow. "I remember that request slip and kept it because I thought I might hear from him again. Here it is, Chaplain, at the front of my file. Take a look."

She pushed Travis' request slip across the counter to me and I read, "Greetings to you in the lovely name of Jesus . . . Please send me any books about terroristic threats . . . May God richly bless you."

"Any incongruencies there?" she asked. "Jekyll and Hyde, maybe?"

Yeah, maybe just a little.

· · · · ·

Ingenuity reigns in the RHU. Prisoners passed long hours playing chess from their single-man cells without being able to see their opponents. They had a system of drawing a chess board on a piece of cardboard, often from the back of a tablet, and numbering each square. Shouts of "fourteen to nine" and "twelve to sixteen" volleyed between cells as the game progressed. Most often, playing pieces were simply labeled scraps of paper, but some men carved intricate pieces from soap or rolled thin paper strips into unique masterpieces held together with toothpaste.

Although hampered by limited resources, men in RHU nevertheless turned out lovely artistry with nothing more than a scrap of paper, a No. 2 pencil, and perhaps markers or crayons.

The most intriguing innovation on the locked unit involved the operation of "Cadillacs" that were used to exchange items between cells. Base-line models were typically constructed from cardboard while flattened toothpaste tubes fashioned top-of-the-line vehicles. A long rope of bedsheets, torn into thin strips and fastened securely onto the Cadillac, provided the "gas."

In amazing shows of skill, inmates flung their cars from their cells so that they skated through the narrow gap beneath the door and whizzed into the hallway toward their destination at another cell. If a first attempt was unsuccessful, the driver pulled it back and "gave it more gas." Skilled drivers were able to send their Cadillacs down the hallway, over the catwalk lip, and onto lower tiers. When it reached the intended cell, the recipient snagged the incoming Cadillac with his own car. In this way magazines and notes were exchanged between cells. I even saw inmates trade a hamburger for a piece of cake.

When the transaction was complete the owner pulled his Cadillac back to his cell and parked it in a "garage," a hiding place to avoid confiscation by guards, until the next opportunity to drive it on the "streets."

When I first began making rounds on the RHU, men were hesitant to show off their Cadillacs because they knew I had the authority to confiscate them. I saw no reason to do so, and actually, few guards nabbed them unless inmates blatantly drove them beneath their noses or when they suspected that something more than harmless pastime occurred.

• • • • •

Census in the RHU changed almost daily, and I never knew who I would meet there. After a few months out on the streets, Ralph had only recently come back to prison on a parole violation, and already he'd found his way to the RHU. "Ralph! What are you doing here in The Hole?" I asked. "Don't tell me you already got tired of B Block?"

He chuckled and planted his palm between the two narrow windows in the steel door that separated us. "Nah, I just needed a change of scenery. But it wasn't really my fault."

Yeah, yeah. Yada, yada. I cut him off. "It was your pride that got you here, wasn't it? Actually, pride brought you to prison in the first place, right?"

A grin toyed at the corner of his mouth. "You know me pretty well, don't you?"

"Not really. I just know pride."

He stared at me evenly, eyes unblinking.

"Ralph, take a good look at that light above your bed."

He looked up at the ceiling fixture and turned back to me with a puzzled look.

"Unless you change something about yourself, you'll still be looking at that light when you're seventy years old," I said.

Ralph's shoulders slumped in feigned offense. "You think I'm gonna do life on the installment plan?"

I turned my palms up. "It's all up to you, Ralph. It's your call and no one else's."

Like Ralph, all too many men waste their entire lives cycling in and out of prison. National statistics show that within the first year of an inmate's release, 56.7% are rearrested. About two-thirds (67.8%) reoffend within three years, and 76.6% fail within five years.[26] It's a pitiful hamster wheel.

$$\bullet \quad \bullet \quad \bullet \quad \bullet \quad \bullet$$

---

[26] National Institute for Justice, *National Statistics on Recidivism,* https://www.nij.gov/topics/corrections/recidivism/Pages/welcome.aspx

I approached the cell of a man I had never met before. "Hey, how's your day going?" I asked.

"I'm in The Hole, right?" he fired back. "What do you mean, how's my day going? That's the wrong question to ask!"

It wasn't hard to detect anger and bitterness. I ventured to talk with him about it, and he engaged me for a while. But then he veered onto another path. "You know I'm a god, right? I control my destiny."

"Really?" I asked. "But look where you are."

He didn't want to talk about that and preferred to discuss violence instead. "It's one way to get what you want," he said. "You might even need to kill. And if you do, you might as well take as many other people out as possible. Especially if you're gonna die anyway."

Now I wanted to change the subject and talk with him about love. Especially about God's love for him.

"Tell you what," he returned. "You Christians are really violent, too. You tell people that if they don't believe like you do they're gonna go to hell. What's that if it's not violent?"

I wondered where he'd gotten such a distorted view of Christianity, but he steered around that too. "You like violence," he said.

"How so?"

"Everyone likes violence. Books, movies, TV shows—they thrive on violence! Blood and gore sells. You look to bad guys like me to entertain you!"

I couldn't argue with his tragic analysis of our culture, but prayed that someday he would encounter the love of Jesus.

• • • • •

Some people just don't learn.

Bob went to the RHU in 1998. Two years later, with one infraction stacked on top of another, he was looking at June 2013 before his release back into the general prison population. Fifteen long years in The Hole!

But he had a defense. "I wouldn't act out if I was treated right! I ain't the problem. It's the guards. They're the oppressors. I'm the oppressed."

That's not quite the way I saw it. A year earlier, Bob had told me he wanted to kill me. "When I get the chance, I'm gonna cut your flesh up in tiny little squares!"

I could have written him up for threatening me, but saw little point in that. He might have earned an additional ninety days, but what was that when he already had thirteen years to go?

• • • • •

Don also blamed the guards for his own misbehavior. "One day I just had enough of their disrespect. Couldn't stand it anymore, and I sort of lost it," he said.

Sort of? I'd heard about his temper tantrum. He shredded his mattress and flushed it down the toilet, piece by piece. That done, he tore up his legal paperwork, letters, and all his clothing, and flushed it down. His toilet lever worked some serious overtime.

A week later, Don was issued a new set of clothes. He promptly went to the toilet again, and this time he first stopped it up. Then he began flushing, over and over again, until water flooded his cell floor, ran into the hallway, and into his neighbors' cells.

"Something in me just snapped," he said.

I told him he needed Jesus in his life. "He loves you, Don, more than you can imagine. You've trashed your life, but that doesn't make Him love you any less. If you give your life to Jesus, He will help you to deal with things that eat at you."

"Oh, yeah, man, you might be right. I had a Bible, but I lost it in the flooding. Can you get me another one, Chaplain?"

I assured him I would bring it on my next round. He would have a lot of time to read it. He still had to do six months in the RHU, and after that, the rest of his life in prison.

• • • • •

Some men acted out with their food. They smeared it on their walls or threw it at the officer who came by to collect their trays. Perhaps they refused to give up their trays, or worse yet, defecated on the tray before handing it back. Their devious creativity knew no bounds.

Their punishment sometimes came in the form of "food loaf." That hamburger the inmate was to get for lunch? It went into a blender, along with the enriched wheat roll, lettuce, and a spoonful of macaroni salad. Applesauce was thrown in, too, and then a piece of chocolate cake. It was all whipped together with some kind of thickener and shaped into a rectangular loaf for the finest of gourmet dining. The tasty entrees, made of whatever was on the menu, generally continued for three to seven days, in the hope that it would motivate the inmate to start acting like a civilized man.

Maybe.

Maybe not.

It was his choice.

• • • • •

Administrative Custody status was granted to a small percentage of men who needed protection. This was sometimes the situation in a high-profile case, particularly when the crime involved sexual abuse of children. Such offenders find themselves at the bottom of the pile in the prison pecking order and things could get pretty ugly for them.

Some inmates sought Administrative Custody to escape dangerous situations they'd gotten themselves into, most often because they'd run up gambling debts or messed with rival gang members.

Tony was one of the latter. On several occasions, he reported threats on his safety, but for whatever reason the guards didn't take him seriously. One day Tony's antagonist caught up with him on the walkway and drew a shank from his pants. Tony took off running and reached the safety of his cell, where he yanked a razor blade from his shaver and broke it in two. Then he went to a guard on his block and held the razor piece to his wrist. "I'm gonna slice myself. But before I do that, I'm gonna slit you," he said.

"Yeah, Tony," the guard replied. "Quit playing your games. You're not going to do that."

"You're right," said Tony. "I'm not going to get you or me. But I will get that pretty woman deputy. I'll get her good, I will."

Was his threat only a harmless ploy to create distance between himself and a rival gang member? Or might he have been desperate enough to harm staff? The security team couldn't take chances. Tony's threat landed him in the RHU for eleven months.

• • • • •

Rick had already been confined to the RHU for more than a year when he called me to his cell door. I had stopped by on several occasions but he hadn't been very talkative. He was Muslim, he said, and had little use for a Protestant chaplain.

But that day was different. "Chaplain, I want to tell you what happened to me last night. I couldn't sleep. I tossed and turned for most of the night. And then I started to pray. Not like a Muslim, but as a Christian." Rick smiled broadly. "I don't know if this makes sense to you, but I asked Jesus into my heart, and I'm like, floating on the clouds today! I don't remember ever feeling this happy before!"

"Well, this makes my day, man!" I said, wishing I could put my arm around Rick and welcome him in the faith. But the solid steel door stood between us.

"Pray for me, Chaplain. I know I'm gonna get pressure from my friends to go back to Jumah when I get out of here."

I assured Rick of my prayers and promised to see him again soon. As I walked away, I thought of Jesus' words about the fields being white with harvest. "Send laborers here to Mahanoy," I prayed.

• • • • •

Frank was sentenced to thirty-five to seventy years in prison, and it looked like he might become a regular in The Hole. He had just finished a thirty-day stint in the RHU, was released into the general population for four days, and now he was back again to do another ninety days.

He waved me to his cell. "Chaplain, my girlfriend's birthday is coming up. You know how women can get if you miss their birthdays. Can you get me approved for a phone call, Chaplain?"

"What are the rules, Frank? Am I allowed to give you a free phone call to wish your girlfriend a happy birthday?"

"Oh, come on, man. Who's gonna know?"

I shook my head resolutely.

"Well, call her for me from your house. You'd do that for me, wouldn't you, kind Chaplain?"

I shook my head again. "If I'm going to break the rules, I may as well go get a set of browns and find me a cell."

He laughed. "Nah, this brown uniform would look bad on you, Chaplain, and we'd be in bad shape without you. You're the best thing that ever happened to this place. But that buddy of yours, Chaplain Giordano, he never comes by to see me. Does he have something against me?"

"Man, stop trying to butter me up," I said. "And don't trash Chaplain Giordano. You know he's a good man." I was losing patience with Frank and prepared to move on.

"One more thing, Chaplain. Can you bring me some books from your library?"

"Sure, I'll bring you books on one condition. You can't write in them. You understand?"

We had been around on this before, but Frank looked shocked. "Oh, Chap, but that's my ministry, man! I wanna help the brotherhood. So when the Spirit gives me a thought, I want to pass it on to others. It's what I'm on this earth for."

How can so much ego fit into a ten by seven cell, I wondered.

In time, Frank got out of the RHU and came to church services faithfully until some perceived offense soured him. The last I heard, he continued to write in books that didn't belong to him, still trying to pass along his profound thoughts.

· · · · ·

The man in Cell 12 lay on his stomach on the thin mattress, reading a book. "Looks like you got an interesting book there," I called out to him.

His face lit up. He jumped from his bed and came to his door. "Hey, Chap, do you remember me?"

I'm not good in that department, but I tried. I backed up for a better look at him and then checked his name and photo on the door tag. "Sorry, Wayne, it's not registering."

"Yeah, well, a couple of years ago I tried to con a phone call outta you. Told you my grandma was sick or something like that."

"Did I give you the call?"

Wayne grinned. "I couldn't convince you. But I've been doing some thinking and changing. I gave up being Muslim and that was kinda tough because those dudes kept messing with me, threatening me and all. But I don't believe that way anymore."

"Well, praise God!" I said. "Jesus is the only One who makes a difference in our lives!"

"Hey, I need a Bible. Can you get me one? Like today?"

I told him I'd see what I could do for him.

"Hey, Chap, I got a question. Do I have to wait till I get out of The Hole to become a Christian?"

"Absolutely not!" I exclaimed. "You can do it right now. Right here. Do you know what you need to do?"

He shook his head.

I explained that we all are sinners, separated from a holy God, and doomed for hell. "That's the bad news. But let me tell you the good news that comes through Jesus. The Bible says that if we confess our sins, He is faithful and just to forgive our sins and to cleanse us from all unrighteousness!"

Wayne nodded. "I've got a big stack of sins that I need forgiveness for."

In the noisy chaos and irreverence of the RHU and with a steel door between us, Wayne prayed to receive the Lord Jesus into his heart. Tears streamed down his cheeks.

"About that Bible, Wayne. I'm going to check to see if there's one around here," I said, and went in search of my officer friend, Monty.

If there was a Bible in the RHU, Monty would know where to find it. Not that long ago he was hostile toward me and inmates alike, but then he got saved, and what a difference Jesus made in his life! I didn't know anyone who witnessed more often or more effectively than Monty did. He couldn't stop talking about Jesus.

Monty quickly found a Bible and I told him why I wanted it.

"Really? You just led the man in Cell 12 to Jesus? That's great, just great! Let me go with you to meet my new brother!" His excitement knew no bounds. Monty hurried to Wayne's cell, wicket key in hand, and pushed the Bible through the opening. "Man, let me shake your hand! You've made the best decision of your life! Now we're brothers in Christ!"

The two men, officer and inmate, grasped hands through the narrow wicket. Wayne began to cry again.

It was a holy moment in the RHU.

Men in the RHU sometimes felt they'd fallen as far as they could go, and had one of two responses. They either got bitter and blamed the whole world for their problems, or they took an honest look at themselves and accepted responsibility for their choices. If they chose the latter, God could finally get through to them.

It's not only men in prison who have this choice. We all do. What is your response?

CHAPTER TWENTY-ONE

But for the Grace of God

One afternoon in August 2002, a security guard called my office. I stiffened, wondering what trouble he might be sniffing out. Without preamble the guard said, "Chaplain, I need to ask you to confirm your wife's name and your home address."

I gave him the information but couldn't help asking, "What's this all about?"

He was courteous but brief. "At this point I can't tell you that, Chaplain," he said.

A chill swept over me as I hung up the phone. I could deal with work-related questions from the security office, but what did this mean? Had an inmate gotten information about my family?

Some of the prison staff blacked out their listings from phone directories housed in the prison library, but I had never bothered, figuring that an inmate could garner the information from free-world family or friends if he were so inclined. Of course, it's an offense for an inmate to be in possession of a staff person's personal information, but that is hardly a deterrent. Apparently, someone had gotten my wife's name and our address. My stomach tightened.

A short time later, the guard called back. "No worries, Chaplain. We're working on something here, but just so you know, you're in the clear." His message was cryptic and only slightly reassuring. Something was going on, and I didn't like the feel of it one little bit.

Over dinner that evening, I told my family of my concern and reminded them, as I had on occasion, to be guarded about incoming phone calls, of strangers coming by the house, of odd-looking mail, or of any packages that might be left at the door. "It's probably nothing, but keep your radar up," I said.

I don't remember that the conversation went far. The kids had full lives of their own. Joel had just celebrated his nineteenth birthday and was eager to spread his wings for flight. Within days he would leave for a three-week wilderness leadership trip in Ontario and then head to Rosedale Bible College in Ohio.

Emily, sixteen years old and the proud new owner of a driver's license, was primed to make her mark on the world. She planned to jump into her tenth grade homeschool curriculum ahead of schedule so she could juggle youth group, her job, and a public speaking class at Lancaster Bible College. Despite her bravado, I knew she was nervous about making her first-time forty-minute solo commute and finding her way around campus.

Truth be told, maybe I was a bit jittery too about my beautiful red-haired daughter's march into an adult world. "I'd better lock you and Renee into a closet to hide you from the boys!" I sometimes teased.

"Oh, Dad!" fourteen-year-old Renee scoffed, as though boys were the furthest thing from her mind. That summer she had gone to Rosedale's Choral Camp, and was already making plans to return as a counselor next summer. Her energies focused on practicing violin and on a summer job of picking strawberries and vegetables at a nearby farm market. As soon as her job wound down, she would begin her freshman year as a first-year Abeka video homeschool student. Like her older siblings, she had gone to public school for her first years, finished junior high at Ephrata Mennonite School, and now planned to complete high school at home.

I was proud of our three teenagers. Like the apostle John, I found no greater joy than that my children walked in truth. I had always felt that no matter how successful I might be in prison ministry, it would all be for naught if my children didn't honor Jesus in daily life. Now my protective father mode was in high gear. It just stirred my ire to think of anyone messing with my family.

Later that evening Esther asked, "Do you remember that I told you about a weird phone call a week or so ago?"

"Hmmm, yeah, but tell me again. Maybe there's a connection with whatever is happening," I said.

The female caller had said her son was an inmate at Mahanoy and was incredibly blessed by Nelson's ministry. "Your husband is a wonderful chaplain!" she gushed. "I can't begin to tell you of the impact he's made on my son!" She wanted to send a personal note of thanks, she said, and asked me to verify our mailing address.

I hedged, unwilling to dispense personal information to a stranger. "Send the note to him at the prison," I said. "He'll be sure to get it there."

"But that's so cold and impersonal!" she shot back.

I was stunned by her angry injured tone—such a dramatic switch from her former syrupy sweetness. Suddenly she reverted back to her charm. "Really, a card is the least I can do to show my gratitude for the chaplain's kindness. But we wouldn't want my note to get lost in the mail for lack of confirmation of your address, would we?"

I think I rolled my eyes then. We? Since when were she and I in this together? My caution heightened. "Send it to the prison," I said again.

The woman's hard edge returned. "You really could learn a lot about kindness from your husband!" she growled, and suddenly, click, the phone emitted only a dial tone. I stared at the receiver in my hand, wondering what that exchange was all about.

"Do you think there's a connection with Security's concern?" Esther asked me now.

I shrugged. "I'll find out soon, I'm sure."

The following week I got the call that summoned me to the security lieutenant's office. He motioned me to sit down and said, "Chaplain, if my staff hadn't already uncovered some information, you would be in the hot seat right now. For whatever reason, Inmate Hackett has it in for you, and he played a really good game."

Hackett. My mind sped through what I knew of him. He'd been nothing but trouble in his inmate role as the prison choir director. Uncooperative. Back-biting. Critical. Doing his own thing, in his own way, in his own time. When Guy Giordano and I had enough of his manipulation, we relieved him of his position.

Hackett's suspension seemed to be redemptive, and after some time, we reinstated him as choir director. Soon thereafter he sent me a request slip, the official method of written communication with staff, in which he professed a deep respect for me, commended me for an upsurge in church attendance, and expressed his intent to do his best in helping the church at Mahanoy to develop and mature.

I confess—I chuckled when I read it. What is he up to now, I wondered. My most cynical thought would not have imagined his request slip for the Judas kiss that it was.

The lieutenant thumbed through a stack of papers on his desk and said, "We sort of stumbled onto Hackett's scheme." He explained that an officer assigned to monitor approximately fifty phone lines had randomly chosen to listen in on Hackett's line. His conversation with a female friend in Scranton seemed jumbled and curiously interspersed with numerous scripture references. "Our officer was pretty certain they were speaking in code. Here's the transcript of that call." He slid a paper across the desk to me.

I stared at it. How did Hackett and his friend get our personal information and for what purpose? Was it tied to that strange call Esther had taken?

"You can see there that they mentioned both Esther and Newmanstown. It didn't take us long to realize that was your wife's name and your local post office." The lieutenant shook his head. "You're one lucky man, Chaplain. That guard who listened in on that conversation? It was his first day doing phone duty. He's a smart man, and he saved you a lot of trouble."

From that day, the lieutenant told me, the security office began monitoring all of Hackett's calls. They also intercepted his outgoing mail. "We caught a letter sent to his friend in Scranton. He included a really graphic love letter. It was pretty sick, actually. But he didn't write it to her." The lieutenant grimaced apologetically. "Hackett instructed her to type it out to an inmate named Mark, forge your signature, and mail it from the Newmanstown post office."

My head was spinning. "So it was supposed to look like I'd written to a male lover? And mailing it from Newmanstown would have authenticated it?"

The lieutenant nodded. "The letter would have had your town's postmark on it."

"But it's more than a two-hour drive from Scranton to Newmanstown!"

"All the more convincing. But it didn't happen. We confiscated the love letter and the information she needed to mail it. Of course, we knew it was only a matter of time till we got more on Hackett."

I nodded. The trail was getting easier to follow.

When Hackett signed up for his next call to his Scranton friend, the officers were ready and waiting. "That call was something," the lieutenant said. "She insisted she didn't get the love letter or your address, and he blamed her for going soft."

"So he sent the letter a second time?"

"Yup. But that time he put another inmate's return address on the envelope. I guess he hoped to bypass Security, but we caught that one, too, and it was just as lewd. It's here in the file." The lieutenant leaned back and studied me for a moment. "I'm telling you, Chaplain, someone upstairs is looking out for you. Anyway, Hackett changed his tactics then. Instead of risking another letter to Scranton, he sent me this request slip. It was unsigned, but of course, I knew it was from Hackett. It didn't take a handwriting analysis to figure it out."

And the plot thickens, I thought as I took the form the lieutenant held out to me and read of the vulgar accusations against me. Proof could be obtained, Hackett claimed, by searching Mark's cell where Security would find a yellow post-it note containing my address and phone number stuck beneath Mark's desk.

The officer held up a small yellow paper.

I looked it over. There it was—my address and phone number—correct and spelled perfectly. I snorted with disgust. "Why?"

"Give me your ideas."

We compared snippets of information we both had and ran through possible scenarios. I recalled a conversation with an inmate who had come to my office. He had fidgeted with his sleeve as he spoke. "Chaplain, I've heard a rumor, and I can hardly believe it, but I've gotta ask you anyway." His head dropped, and he stammered that he'd heard an inmate and I had something going on.

Prison is a hotbed for rumors, speculations, innuendos, and outright lies. But this was low.

"So that's the scuttlebutt, huh?" I said. "Well, I could defend myself till I'm blue in the face, but that won't do much good. You know me. You know what I stand for and what I teach. And you need to decide what you're going to believe. I can't dictate that."

Now I was certain Hackett was behind the rumor and had been setting the stage to the smallest details. Shuffling through the papers before me, I looked again at the date on the request slip sent to the lieutenant. It was sent within a day of the form he'd submitted to me! A Judas kiss, for sure! He'd buttered me up while simultaneously slaughtering me to Security.

"Why Mark?" the officer asked.

I shrugged. "He's a regular at church and at Bible studies. Probably comes to the chapel as much as anyone."

"Makes sense. We've no reason to believe that Mark is complicit in this scheme."

"So what about the post-it note? How did it get there?"

"Hackett had that covered, too. He slipped into Mark's cell during call-out under the guise of returning a borrowed book. It didn't take but a second to slap it beneath his desk."

The biggest question remained: What did Hackett stand to gain?

"Something surfaced in our investigation," the lieutenant said. "It doesn't make a bit of sense, except maybe to a delusional mind like Hackett's. Obviously, he wanted to get you fired, Chaplain, and it seems he wanted to replace you with a woman friend of his who is a minister."

Oh. I remembered that Hackett had often complained that I wasn't moved and filled with the Holy Spirit which, interpreted, meant that I didn't whoop and holler as he thought I should.

"So Hackett thought his friend would be the savior for my every flaw?" I asked. "But how did he think he could muscle her into the chaplaincy here?"

"Who knows? He's shown himself to be a criminal mastermind. He was the brains behind a string of robberies that got him jail time in the first place, and he got extra time for intimidation of his co-conspirators. Then, at a prison upstate, he finagled the sale of a friend's car to the chaplain. Turns out his friend was an ex-con. The chaplain lost his job over it."

Whew! I was getting a thumping headache.

The lieutenant leaned forward and steepled his fingers beneath his chin. "You were just a pawn in his game, Chaplain."

I left the lieutenant's office with a renewed respect for the security staff and an overwhelming sense of gratitude that the inexperienced officer was so perceptive of the unfolding scheme. It could be nothing less than a monumental prompting of God that made him wise to it, that he spoke up about his suspicions, and that his superiors believed him. Nobody could ever persuade me that the officer had "randomly" picked up Hackett's line. Without God's merciful intervention, I would be on the road right now, heading home to begin administrative leave while an investigation ensued.

How would I have explained to Esther that I was accused of a sexual relationship with an inmate? What would I have told my children? My church? Our families? The implications of Hackett's calculated scheme burned in my frazzled mind as I walked back to my office.

Retreating to its comfort never felt so good. I hurried into the air-conditioned chapel wing, thankful for the welcome reprieve from summer's heat, and hastened through the lobby and past the drinking fountain where an inmate bent over it. He turned as I approached. My heart sank. Mark! Of all people, he was the last person I wanted to see right now! Well, except for Hackett, but the lieutenant had told me that he'd already been sent to the RHU.

Mark looked as rattled as I felt. "Chaplain Z! I was looking for you!" He pulled a confiscation slip from his pocket and held it out to me with trembling hands. "Do you know what this is about? My cell was searched this morning and they found your phone number and address, and I haven't a clue where it came from or anything! Do you know what's up?" His words tumbled over each other, and I thought his distressed look must have mirrored my own.

I wished I could assure Mark that he was clear. But I couldn't talk with him about a case which involved us both. That was the job of the security office.

To this day, I shudder to think about the close call to my career and reputation. I am humbled and amazed at God's mercy and protection. Danger in prison doesn't always wear a violent face. Scheming and manipulation are every bit as malicious.

Mark is a prison ministry success story. I had the privilege of baptizing him and mentoring him in his faith. After his release, he sought out spiritual mentors and continued his walk with Jesus. Today he has a family and serves in full-time ministry.

Hackett, however, forged a different path. His shenanigans against me gained him six months in the RHU. Disciplinary problems tacked on two more months. For my part, I had to decide how to interact with him on mandatory visits to RHU inmates. On my first round, he busied himself in the back of his cell, and I was glad for that. I wasn't yet ready to face him.

On subsequent visits, Hackett complained to the guards that I made faces and laughed at him. His counselor advised me, "I know it's your job to talk with the men, but steer clear of Hackett. Don't engage him in any way."

I was only too happy to comply. But Hackett kept up his game. His continued claims of harassment were disregarded, so he faked a seizure and was taken to the infirmary where he bent the ears of medical staff with nonsense about me making passes at him. Later, he lodged a complaint against me with the Pennsylvania Prison Society, an inmate advocacy group, and I answered some uncomfortable questions. By the time he accused me of sexual relations with a chaplain at another institution, Hackett's claims had lost all credibility. In time he tired of the game, and no one was more relieved than I.

Take the time, right now, to pray for prison chaplains. They are in Satan's dark territory, among men who would stop at nothing to destroy them and the advance of the Gospel. Pray for protection for them and their families, for their spiritual and emotional well-being, and for the courage to continue in their call to prison ministry.

CHAPTER TWENTY-TWO

Never a Dull Moment

*F*or several decades, Nelson drove forty-one miles to work. Round trip, that added up to eighty-two miles, every day, and that translated to over 20,000 miles every year, for work alone. The first twenty minutes of his drive wasn't so bad. Much of Route 419 is flanked by farmland as it threads northward through Newmanstown and Womelsdorf, and brushes by Rehrersburg. It's a picturesque drive through small towns and among rolling hills.

The driving fun begins just outside of Schubert when the road dead ends and Route 183 takes over to cross the Blue Mountains. It alternately widens to two lanes on uphill climbs, narrows to one going downhill, constricts in Cressona, and ends at Route 61. From there the road expands to mostly four lanes, going through the heart of Pottsville and skirting St. Clair before climbing another mountain into Frackville.

The last leg of the trip is a divided highway on eight miles of twisting mountainous road. That is where I lost several years of my life.

I estimate my dear husband drove those wicked turns more than 6,000 times over the course of two and a half decades, and he took them with the confidence of a race car driver. I traveled that stretch of road maybe two or three times a year, and always, on the southbound trip, I tightened my seatbelt, gasping and praying and nearly punching my foot through the floorboard in vain attempts to help Nelson brake.

*I sympathized then, with a terrorized fellow chaplain who hitched
a ride with Nelson down that mountain in a blinding snowstorm.*

I've seen snow at Mahanoy into May and as early as September. It seemed to fall with strange regularity on Monday evenings when I worked late. But often, by the time I drove nine miles south to St. Clair, the snow turned to rain or stopped altogether, and before I reached home an hour later, there wasn't a snowflake to be seen anywhere.

On this particular occasion, snow began early in the afternoon. A Muslim contract chaplain, a native of India, watched it in wide-eyed fascination. At his quitting time at four-thirty, an inch or two had accumulated, and his wonder turned to fear.

He called me shortly after leaving the office. His broken English and obvious distress made for a difficult conversation, but I understood that he had driven only a mile down the road to the state police barracks. He asked whether I would pick him up and take him to his home in Pottsville.

"Sure, I can do that, but I work until eight-thirty."

"Eet ees okay. I wait," he said.

"You'll wait more than three hours?"

"Yes, yes," he insisted. "I not know how to drife in snow. I wait for you at po-leeze station."

I found him there in the lobby, staring into space. He rose slowly as the nor'easter's windy gust pushed me inside and rattled the windows menacingly.

"You think it, how you say . . . safe . . . in snow?" His dark eyes flashed with fear.

"It's okay," I said, one hand on the door. "Ready?"

We ducked into the howling wind and he trailed behind.

He stopped abruptly in front of my car. "Thees ees your car? You no haf beeg truck?"

Irritation rose, and I motioned impatiently for him to get in. The snow was piling up fast, and I had a long drive ahead of me. He was still fumbling with the seat belt when I pulled onto Morea Road. Snow caught on the undercarriage of my car, and it bucked and spun until I maneuvered it into tracks made by previous vehicles.

My passenger gasped. "Thees ees leetle, leetle car for snow."

My Plymouth Acclaim had done just fine in many snows, but I was too preoccupied to answer. Blinding snow pelted my windshield, and I leaned forward to grip the wheel while straining to see the road in front of me.

"You no haf, um, four-wheel drife?"

"No, it's front wheel drive. We'll be okay." The assurance was as much for myself as for him. I picked my way through Industrial Park and under Interstate 81. My shoulders were tight with tension before reaching Route 61, a steep and winding desolate mountain road.

No houses.

No streetlights.

No other cars.

Not one snowplow in sight.

It was impossible to know where I drove on the road—the shoulder, the passing lane, or anywhere in between.

His trembling voice broke my concentration. "We go fast, no?"

"We'll be okay." Oh, I'd said that a minute ago.

"Thees ees leetle car for snow. Very leetle car," he muttered. He'd said that before too.

The defroster hummed on high and the windshield wipers pulsed rapidly. My coworker continued muttering, and I answered in monosyllables, focused on getting down the mountain without loss of life or limb.

Suddenly, a dark object loomed ahead. I swerved around a stranded car abandoned by the roadside, and pity welled within me for anyone caught in this blizzard. Pushing on, my headlights caught the figure of a lone man walking by the side of the road, head hunched down against the driving snow.

Naively assuming he was the driver of the disabled car, I slid to a stop. In an instant the back door opened and a disheveled man jumped in, brushing snow from his bare head onto the seat. "Hey, man, can you take me to Pottsville?"

"We're headed that way." I gingerly accelerated again and snow crunched beneath my tires. "Is that your car back there?"

"Oh, no, no, man. I don't got no car."

That's when the sharp stench of alcohol assailed me, and I wondered what I'd gotten myself into. My front seat passenger sucked in a sharp breath and wrapped his arms around himself.

The man in the back seat said, "I'm just walking. Need to find me some dope in town." He clicked a cigarette lighter, and a flame flickered starkly against the inky darkness surrounding us.

"Hey!" I said, my voice too loud, too harsh. "You can't smoke in my car!"

"Okay, cool. No problem," he said, also too loudly. "You do dope?"

"Nope, never did dope," I answered while inching my way around another slippery curve. "I have Jesus in my life. Don't need dope." I knew it sounded pretty lame, but how was I to converse under these circumstances?

"Cool, cool! Yeah, I'm a Christian too. But, hey man, dope's pretty cool too. You oughta try it sometime."

I think that's when my front seat passenger began pleading with Allah for his life. He and I fell silent for the remainder of the long trek down the mountain, but the backseat drunk kept up a stream of nonsense.

This was like a comedy in which the most unlikely three-some were thrown together—a Christian who was trying desperately to maneuver a desolate mountain road in a raging snowstorm, a Muslim who had by now fallen silent except for heavy breathing and occasional gasps, and a strung-out guy in the back who wouldn't shut up. There had to be a great punch-line to this joke.

Snow was still falling when Pottsville finally came into view, a most welcome sight that night. I pulled into the grocery store's snowy parking lot where my passengers had agreed to be let out.

The back door flung open. "Man, thanks a heap for the ride. Now, I gotta go find me some dope!" the drunk said as he exited my car. He paused to light a cigarette before heading across the street.

The Muslim chaplain sat rigid and still, as though frozen in place.

"This is where you want off too, right?" I asked.

He nodded and stared after the man. "He go that way. Eet ees good." He climbed from my car and hurried in the opposite direction.

My chaplain friend left Mahanoy soon after that memorable drive. Maybe he moved to a snow-free zone. But I'll bet that like me, he has a story to tell of the frightful ride down the mountain in a blizzard.

· · · · ·

By 2002, the inmate population at SCI Mahanoy exceeded 2,000 inmates. Pennsylvania now housed 40,000 prisoners in its twenty-six institutions.[27]

Guy Giordano worked four days a week, and we teamed up to build the kingdom of God behind bars. I was so grateful that he assumed responsibility for two Sunday services every month. The prison church was growing numerically, with the average weekly attendance at 177. Even more thrilling than the climbing church attendance was the obvious spiritual growth among the men. That year we baptized eighteen inmates. Guy and I brainstormed about developing Men of Faith, an inmate church leadership team of six inmates who demonstrated spiritual growth and who were humble and teachable.

We charged them with opening church services, making announcements, reading Scripture, and leading in prayer. Sometimes they involved other inmates, but they understood the need for tight controls and were careful to choose those who would stay on script. Later, we established Men of Faith as overseers of representatives on each of the prison blocks, and tasked them with welcoming newcomers to church, encouraging participation in chaplaincy programming, and holding Bible studies. In this way, we practiced a multiplication of leaders with various levels of responsibility.

At every Sunday service we took time to recognize and pray for those who would be released from prison that week. Happiness aside at the prospect of "going home," most men held fears and doubts about their ability

---

27 Pennsylvania Department of Corrections, *2002 Annual Statistical Report*, p. 30, https://www.cor.pa.gov/About%20Us/Statistics/Documents/Old%20Statistical%20Reports/2002%20Annual%20Statistical%20Report.pdf

to assimilate into life back on the streets. Actually, I had much more confidence in a man's ability to succeed if he was scared about re-entry and lesser hopes for those who arrogantly thought they had it all sewed up.

A common concern was that of employment. "Nobody's going to want to hire an ex-con," they said.

No doubt about it, landing a decent job would be tough. I offered three bits of advice. "First, be humble. Accept any available job, even if it means flipping burgers, or hanging on to the side of a garbage truck at four o'clock in the morning. Secondly, show up for work. Every day. On time. Without exception or excuse. And lastly, have a good attitude, and work as though you're earning twenty-five dollars an hour."

"There's no shortcuts, huh?" one man asked.

"That would be nice, wouldn't it?" I replied. "But if you follow through, I think I can guarantee you this: after three months, one of two things will happen. Either you'll get a raise, or you will have begun a work record that will look good on a resumé for another employer."

· · · · ·

Every week we met with Men of Faith leaders for times of prayer, leadership training, and to talk through issues that arose.

Jim and Tony could not have been more different in personality and background. One was White, the other Black. One was high strung and planned out the minutest of details. The other was laid back and flew by the seat of his pants. It was only a matter of time before conflict erupted between them. With guidance, they talked out their differences, prayed together, and committed to a relationship that would bless the church at Mahanoy.

The Men of Faith team changed as prisoners were released or transferred. When I left the prison in 2017, the team was comprised of five men, four of whom were lifers. Collectively, they had served almost 150 years in prison.

· · · · ·

Outside of prison, it was hard for people to grasp what I did as a chaplain. I once struck up conversation with a graying man whose reputation preceded him. He had long ago abandoned his conservative Mennonite upbringing, and plenty of stories floated about the shadowy world in which he partied. He asked where I worked.

"Pennsylvania Department of Corrections," I replied.

He looked befuddled. "You mean the prison system?"

I nodded. "Yes, I'm a chaplain."

"That's your job? Like, your forty-hour-a-week job?"

I don't know why, but that always seemed to surprise people, especially those in my Mennonite community.

At that time, I had been in full-time prison ministry for about twenty years, counting back to my time with We Care Ministries in Alabama. After that, I had worked for Jubilee for nine years, and now I'd been at Mahanoy for ten or twelve years.

The information seemed to make the man's head spin. His face scrunched in bewilderment. "But I know you're also a Mennonite pastor."

"Assistant pastor," I said.

"Whatever . . . I'm trying to picture it. I mean, there's a huge difference between a quiet little Mennonite church and a state prison. How do you make that jump?"

"Oh, I don't know," I said. "I guess I never thought much of the jump." I looked to Esther for help.

She chuckled. "Well, sure. What was the title of last week's sermon at the prison?"

"Oh . . . yeah . . . it was 'Who's Your Real Road Dog?' "

The man laughed. "Meaning, who's your best friend, right? Yeah, that kind of slang sure wouldn't fly at a Mennonite church."

"And you've never kicked anyone out of a service at our Mennonite church," Esther said. "Nor told them to be quiet."

Indeed. Sometimes I felt more like a policeman than a pastor to my prison congregation. Occasionally, I dismissed men who insisted on talking during the service, or separated lovers who snuggled up to each other. I always had to be on high alert, sniffing out trouble before it found me. The smallest infractions could mushroom into major security issues in no time.

At one service, Cory began laughing and talking to himself during the second hymn. He stepped into the aisle and threw a few punches into the air. His karate-like moves got more exaggerated as he worked his way to the front row of chairs.

I walked toward him. He fastened dead eyes on me, pivoted, and walked back to his chair. The song ended and the congregation sat down. So did Cory—nearly in the lap of another prisoner. The surprised man moved over and Cory followed, smashing tight against him.

I caught the eye of the inmate assigned to read the scripture and motioned for him to proceed. Then I strode back the aisle to Cory. "You can't act like that here. You need to leave."

He jumped up, yelled, and reared back with clenched fists. I braced to feel the force of his blows, but Cory suddenly dropped his arms, and I moved in to escort him out of the sanctuary. He reared back again. I wasn't taking a second chance; I turned and hurried into the lobby to summon help from an officer.

He reached the chapel in an instant.

Cory edged close and whimpered, "Oh, Chaplain, please let me stay. Please, please!"

I left him in the officer's care. On my way back to the pulpit, I tried to clear my head and still my pounding heart. And then I took a deep breath and launched into the sermon.

Another Sunday I observed two inmates, heads hunched together and talking up a storm. I walked over to them, and as I approached, one quickly shoved something into his pocket.

"Okay, what do you have?" I asked, holding out my hand.

He sighed and produced an onion.

Esther screwed her face up in puzzlement when I told her the story. "An onion? Where did he get an onion, and why did he pass it to his buddy in church?"

You may not think of an onion as being a hot commodity either. But in prison, many inmates seem to think that anything that isn't glued down, screwed down, or locked down is fair game. Apparently, a kitchen worker had access to an onion and knew of someone who had a hankering for one. He probably looked to make a trade-off of some kind.

But then I showed up.

The inmate sighed again and plopped the onion into my open palm. I probably should have given him a write-up. I did that only once in the twenty-three years I worked at Mahanoy—and only because I felt pushed into it.

Justin had borrowed two cassette tapes from the chapel library, and when they were long overdue, I asked him about them. He insisted he had returned them and accused my clerk of sloppy bookkeeping.

Another inmate overheard the exchange and came to me later. "Justin has those tapes in his cell. I saw them there yesterday."

I asked the search team to check on it for me, and sure enough, one tape lay in Justin's cassette player, the other on his desk.

An officer brought them to me. "Here you go, Chaplain. I did what you asked me to do. Now, I expect you'll do what you need to do."

I knew what that meant. I had to write Justin up. He got fourteen days of cell restriction because of it. I much preferred pastoring over policing.

One evening I checked in on a Spanish service and saw an inmate trying to stuff something into his pants. At that moment, an officer came up beside me. I told him what I'd just seen.

"You want me to search him?" he asked.

"Better would," I sighed.

He motioned for the inmate to meet us in the hallway. "Okay, what are you hiding?" the guard asked.

"Oh, man, you got me," the inmate said with obvious discomfort.

"Yeah, well, it's pretty hard to conceal a bulge like that. Give it up."

The inmate turned aside and fumbled in his pants. Reluctantly he pulled out a bag of gummy bears, handed it to the officer, and slinked away.

"Can you believe this?" the guard said to me, holding the bag between two fingers at extended arm's length. "Three pounds of gummy bears stuffed in the guy's underwear and warmed to body temperature. Care for some candy, Chaplain?"

"You're generous," I returned with a chuckle, "but I don't have an appetite for them."

My appetite for prison food also diminished after too many unsavory experiences. One day I made my way through the food line in the staff dining room. A kitchen inmate leaned over the counter and spoke in a low voice. "You might want to avoid the salad bar today, Chaplain."

"What's up?" I asked.

He grinned. "A rumor got to the food service manager that someone urinated on the iceberg lettuce."

"You're serious?"

"Well, no one knows for sure if he did or not. But the boss wasn't taking chances, so he ran it through the dishwasher."

"He *what?!*"

The inmate raised an open palm. "Absolute truth. I saw it with my own eyes. And now that lettuce is being served on the salad bar."

That incident coincided with my middle-aged weight gain that I blamed on high-carb fare from the prison cafeteria. More and more, I avoided the dining room except to slip in for packets of peanut butter or a piece of fruit. Maybe that's why I missed out on another gross episode.

"I wish you could've seen it, Chaplain!" a maintenance worker told me. "My boss dug into his stewed tomatoes, brought a spoonful to his mouth, and there, among the tomato chunks, was a dead mouse with its tail hanging off the side of his spoon."

"You actually saw it? This isn't just some rumor floating around?"

"You betcha! I was sitting right there at the table with him!"

Other employees vouched for the story.

The nasty deed was traced to a kitchen worker, an inmate whom I knew pretty well. He wore a chronic chip on his shoulder, but interestingly enough, he admitted to the misdeed and earned ninety days in the RHU for it.

On those occasions when I accompanied Nelson to Sunday services, once or twice a year, he urged me to eat with him in the prison cafeteria.

"It's all part of the prison experience package," he said.

I begrudgingly agreed that it added some value to the visit but adopted a sort of horrored fascination with prison food. Never again did I eat from the salad bar, and I would rather have starved than to eat stewed tomatoes!

Sometimes you just have to laugh about the ridiculous things that come at you. Thank God for humor. It diffuses tension and releases pent up anxieties. Let go and laugh.

CHAPTER TWENTY-THREE

Marriage Interviews

The church at SCI Mahanoy was much like any church on the streets. We held the same services—Easter and Christmas, communion, baptism, and memorial services.

But not weddings—not in the chapel, anyway, and to my knowledge, not by any of Mahanoy's chaplains. However, weddings did take place in the visiting room when officiated by a justice of the peace or a minister of the couple's choice.

The groom would wear his best state-issued browns, and the bride might have a new dress for the occasion and be allowed a small bouquet. If the couple purchased photo tickets in advance, an inmate visiting room worker snapped some Polaroids of the occasion. The couple could exchange rings and vows before a few witnesses, and a kiss was permitted. But that was pretty much it, and then the bride left the institution, and the groom spent his wedding night in the loneliness of his prison cell.

Prior to an in-prison wedding, the inmate had to request permission for the marriage, and staff weighed in on it. This included the inmate's unit manager, counselor, and superintendent. Each person had a specific perspective to consider, such as prison security, the inmate's level of cooperation with programs, and his psychological welfare. As chaplain, I was to ascertain his fiancée's understanding of his crime and length of sentence, and to determine that she entered into marriage on her own free will, without coercion or manipulation.

I believe that marriage is instituted by God and that it is a life-long sacred union. Because the odds are stacked heavily against prison marriages, I could not in good conscience recommend them.

The prison superintendent affirmed my position. "I might do the same, but my role doesn't allow me to turn them down," he said. "The courts uphold an inmate's legal right to marry, and if I vote them down, they'll slap me with lawsuits."

The first request for marriage reached my desk in 1995, and over the next decade, I would conduct about forty interviews.

Bill and his fiancée were both in their early twenties, had lived together for a year prior to his landing in jail, and they had one child together. His minimum sentencing release date was still five years out; his maximum date stretched to eleven years.

"A lot can happen in those years," I reasoned. "Getting married won't change much for you. Use these years to develop your relationship before you commit to a lifetime together."

They didn't want to hear it.

I asked interviewing couples a lot of questions about the reasons for wanting to marry. Most men simply said, "I love her," as though, *duh,* that was reason enough. I talked with couples about their preparedness in making a life-long commitment and about the difficulties of maintaining a long-distance relationship. I told them upfront that I would not recommend their requests.

One inmate was Muslim; his fiancée was Baptist. Neither seemed to think their differing religious preferences would pose a problem in marriage.

Bryce said he was of the Native American faith. When I asked his girlfriend about her religious preference she said, "Whatever he is." She may as well have also said, "Whatever he has," because it became clear that she hoped for access to Bryce's veteran's benefits. He was terminally ill, and they planned to marry within a month.

Gerald also eyed veteran's benefits for his fiancée and admitted as much to his counselor, who uncovered the fact that Gerald's girlfriend had previously been married to his brother. That meant nothing to Gerald. "I love her so much and just want to have God's blessing on our union," he said.

Shane was only two months from his minimum date and two years from his maximum, but he and his girlfriend wanted to marry as soon as possible. "I don't feel like waiting," she said. That was the clearest statement she made during our thirty-minute interview. She seemed unsure of how to answer, maybe because she took cat naps throughout the interview. She sure didn't strike me as an eager bride-to-be.

Mickey met his fiancée while working in the visiting room. His job involved taking pictures for inmates, handing out games, and doing janitorial work. Although he was prohibited from interaction with visitors beyond the confines of his job, he found a way around those inconvenient rules. He had met the woman of his dreams.

She was there to visit an inmate, probably a relative, but for all I know, it may have been her boyfriend or husband. She wouldn't have been the first to jump ship on a prison visiting room romance.

She and Mickey fell in love and now they wished to be married in the prison visiting room where they got acquainted. He was thirty-three years old; she was forty-seven. "My two kids are giving me hassle about a wedding," she said. "They say the same thing you do—to wait until Mickey gets released. But I'm so crazy about him and just want to get married now!"

Bruce met his fiancée a short time before his imprisonment. Turns out she was the ex-wife of his victim. I didn't ask about the twisted circumstances that drew them together.

Delbert filed for marriage a year after arriving at Mahanoy. In that short time, he had already incurred four misconducts. "I think getting married will stabilize some things in my life," he reasoned. I suggested they work at personal growth before jumping into a hasty marriage.

Denny was thirty-nine years old; his fiancée was fifty-three. "I love him and want to spend my life with him," she said.

But Denny had a life sentence, I reminded her, and he would spend the rest of his life in prison.

"Oh, I know *that*," she said, "and it doesn't matter. He's still in my heart."

I talked to couples about the essential ingredient of trust in a healthy marriage. "He let you down and caused you a lot of heartache when he chose to commit his crime," I said to one woman.

She nodded vigorously in agreement. "But you can't trust any man out there on the streets," she said, slipping her arm around her boyfriend and patting his shoulder. "At least I know where my man is!"

It was an *aha* moment for me. The women I interviewed offered glimpses into past relationships. Without fail, they all had suffered some form of abuse by men. Marrying a prisoner would curtail that. Her emotional need for marital status could be met, yet allow her to call the shots in all aspects of their relationship. As long as he was locked up, he could not abuse her physically or sexually. If he bullied her verbally, she could refuse his phone calls and skip visits. She could decide if and when and how much money she would send him. She would never wonder where he was or what he was up to.

The men stood to benefit also, believing that a girlfriend would stand by her man. She would visit him. Write him letters. Send him money. Check in on his family. Follow up on his legal work. Think about him. Believe in him.

But sadly, the fantasies seldom lined up with reality.

Wesley's marriage didn't take long to unravel. I had interviewed him and his fiancée and expressed my objections. They went ahead anyway and found a minister who was willing to officiate. On the day they were to be married, I happened to walk by the visiting room. An officer knocked on the window to get my attention and gestured that I should call him. I did so from the front desk.

"Chaplain, Wesley and his fiancée planned to get married today, but the minister didn't show up. Any chance you would perform the ceremony?"

"Nope. I already told them I couldn't approve it, and I stand by my decision."

"I understand," said the officer. "Just thought I'd ask."

The minister showed up the following day and performed the wedding. Not long after that, the superintendent caught up with me on the sidewalk. "Reverend, remember Wesley and his girlfriend? You're not going to believe it, but we caught him trying to consummate his marriage in the visiting room, *not* with his new wife, but with her best friend!"

That escapade immediately landed Wesley in the RHU. His new bride, suddenly deprived of his phone calls and letters, called the prison. "I'm so worried about my Wesley. Why isn't he calling me anymore?"

"Because he's in RHU," answered the officer.

"What?! My Wesley would never do anything to deserve time in The Hole! He must've been framed! What is his charge?"

"I'll let you talk with the RHU lieutenant," came his simple response.

She assailed the RHU lieutenant with the same questions. But there was no way he was going to get embroiled in the situation. *That*, he told her, was a question she needed to ask her new husband.

I can't imagine what kind of a song and dance she heard from Wesley.

Trenton was also a player. He scheduled visits from his wife and his girlfriend on alternating weekends. All went well until his wife showed up to surprise him on her off weekend. Trenton denied the visit.

His wife was crushed. "Why?" she asked. "Why can't he see me?"

The officer at the desk wasn't about to get caught in the middle. "All I can tell you is that he denied your visit. You'll have to ask him about that."

I never heard the outcome.

Tom's girlfriend was every bit as devious. I plainly told them during their marriage interview that I would not approve their application. Tom got agitated.

"It's gonna be okay, Babe," she said, stroking his arm. "Calm down. We'll figure something out."

Two weeks later Tom flagged me down on the block. "Remember that sweet girl I was gonna marry?" But he used a colorful word instead of *girl*, and his voice was thick with the bitter edge of betrayal. "She stole my mama's credit cards and hiked up a huge bill, and if I got my hands on her now, I'd kill her!"

Listening to Tom tell it, she'd been running up his mother's account for months—long before they filled out the marriage interview forms. "Sweet little lyin' thief, is what she is! I'd kill her, for sure, if I got the chance!"

In time, policy changes relieved the chaplains of doing marriage interviews. It made me a happy man.

Many of the marriages proceeded in spite of Nelson's dissenting recommendation. He could have reasoned that there was little point in obstructing plans that the couple would probably carry out anyway. After all, he would not need to officiate. God's call, however, mandates integrity in all areas, not just in those directly associated with the call.

CHAPTER TWENTY-FOUR
Death Notices

One of my jobs as chaplain was that of notifying inmates of a family member's serious illness or death. In twenty-three years at Mahanoy, I served more than 1,500 notices.

Policy stated that the situation needed to be verified before getting passed on to the inmate. It could not be assumed that the caller was telling the truth, so I needed to verify with the hospital or funeral home that reportedly held their loved one. If that checked out, I called the inmate to my office to offer them one phone call to a relative. An additional layer of security mandated that inmates could not dial out; I had to do so for them. Policy also dictated that I remain with them for the duration of the call and allow them sufficient time to process the tragedy. If the conversation veered from the emergency at hand, I was responsible to end the call. Casual conversation was not to take place on the taxpayers' dime.

There was no lack of manipulative games. If a caller refused to divulge the name of the hospital or funeral home, I could be certain they were up to no good. One man argued that disclosing the information violated his imprisoned relative's privacy. Without the information, I said, I could not grant a phone call. He yelled and swore and threatened to sue me, and I knew it was all a ploy. Legitimate callers provided the necessary information.

• • • • •

214

In my first year at Mahanoy, I bought into someone's game. A man called my office just before a Sunday service, his voice thick with urgency. "My brother, Josh, is locked up in your prison, and his daughter got hit by a car. She's done up real bad."

I didn't have time to verify the information before inmates arrived for church, but because I knew Josh fairly well, I decided to go ahead and give him the phone call. After all, I was a father, too, and I felt for him. I pulled him into my office after church and gave him the few details I had of his daughter's accident.

Color drained from his face. "No! Not my daughter!" Josh slumped in his chair and gave way to heart-wrenching sobs.

I allowed him time to collect himself. "When you're ready, I'll call your wife so you can talk with her."

"Umm, she's not my wife, just my daughter's mother."

"Doesn't matter," I said.

I made the call and heard only his side of the conversation, but it didn't sound good. Josh soon hung up. "It's all a lie! There was no accident. My daughter's fine."

Josh's brother hatched the story in an attempt to get back at him for some ongoing feud between them. I could have saved Josh the emotional distress if I had done my job as policy stated. I was more vigilant after that.

· · · · ·

During the course of verification on another case, I spoke with a funeral director who confirmed the death I inquired about. But something didn't seem right. The funeral director lacked professional demeanor and speech. Still, I had nothing concrete to go on, so I called the inmate to my office and allowed him a phone call. He didn't get far into the conversation before I realized I'd been hoodwinked, and I demanded that he end the call. He sheepishly hung up.

"What are you doing, playing that game on me?" I asked.

He admitted there had been no death. His girlfriend simply wanted to talk with him on a free phone call, so she called in the "death" and enlisted a friend to be the "funeral director."

• • • • •

We staff chaplains (Catholic, Muslim, and Protestant) shared the load of delivering death and serious illness notices. One day I delivered bad news to five different inmates, and got little else done on that eight-hour shift.

Giving the notices to prisoners raised the possibility of a volatile situation. If we knew the inmate to be unstable, or if the caller had indicated that he might take it hard, we usually notified the officer on duty at the chapel entrance so he could back us up, just in case of a problem.

After completing the verification process (a procedure that could take an hour or more), I called the inmate to my office.

"Who died?" some men asked even before taking a seat.

Others, eyes wide with dread, said, "Please don't tell me Mama's gone!"

Some reduced their fears to a single word: "What?"

After delivering the news of a family death to Jack, he became agitated, clenching his fists, and working his jaw. "Noooo!" he wailed. Tears streamed down his cheeks. Suddenly he sprang from his chair. I got up from my desk and stepped back, unsure of his intentions. But Jack's fists were not for me. He slammed them into the wall. *Whump!* The pictures on the wall shifted. *Whump! Whump!*

Within seconds, the Muslim chaplain sprang to my door, ready to tear it open to assist me. It was comforting to know he had my back and would come to my aid at a moment's notice, if necessary.

Thankfully, Jack soon got himself together. When he left my office, I called the officer on the block to ask him to keep an eye on Jack.

Grief is especially acute for inmates, isolated as they are from their families and unable to go home for mutual comfort and support of one another. In the solitude of a prison cell, feelings of helplessness mount. Guilt and anger escalate. Risk of inmate suicides climb significantly after receiving the news of a family death.

Few inmates go home at a time of death. Even if their custody level allows it, finances usually don't. An inmate must pay in advance for the wages and travel expenses of two accompanying armed guards. He is not permitted to attend the funeral and is granted only a maximum of an hour to view the body of his beloved in the presence of only two family members. For most inmates, the expense and the lack of privacy are major deterrents. They grieve alone in their cells.

· · · · ·

To follow up on a death notification one day, I called a funeral home to verify that they held the body of a man named Trevor Wilson.

"No," the director said, "I don't have anyone here by that name."

I took a second look at my notes and named the Philadelphia street on which the murder had reportedly taken place. "My information tells me it occurred at three o'clock in the morning," I added.

"Oh, well, yes, I do have a body that fits that scenario exactly," he said. "Only thing is, the body has four aliases attached to it, and Trevor Wilson is not one of them."

Nevertheless, I was satisfied with the verification and called Trevor's father to my office to give him the news.

He looked at me in shock, and with tears welling in his eyes, he lamented, "My son was such a good boy! Why in the world would anyone want to kill him?"

I sympathized with the man. His father's heart was deeply grieved.

But I kept my thoughts to myself about his "good boy." I'm inclined to think that if a boy has a minimum of five aliases, he is probably not the good son that his father thought he was. And given the time and location of the murder, I'm guessing he probably wasn't going home from a church prayer meeting.

· · · · ·

His mother was dying, I told Jawan, and offered him a phone call.

She answered with a weak "hello" on the fifth ring.

"Mom!" he said harshly. "Why didn't you take better care of yourself?"

I couldn't believe my ears! No greeting. No words of comfort or of love. No questions about how she was doing. Just a harsh rebuke and an impatient pause as she began her response.

He cut her off and shouted into the phone, "But Mom! You gotta stay strong! It's tough enough for me in here! You gotta stay strong for me! You hear me, Mom? Stay strong for me!"

I picked my jaw off the floor and motioned for Jawan to end his tongue-lashing phone call. Then I sent him from my office and prayed for deeper love, more grace, and patience to deal with men like Jawan who were afflicted with Center of the Universe Syndrome.

• • • • •

Clay got permission to call his terminally-ill mother who lay in a hospital bed. They were several minutes into the conversation when Clay stiffened. His eyes widened with fear.

"Mom? Mom?!" he shouted into the phone. "Mom . . . are you there? Mom?!"

He held the receiver out to me. "Chaplain, I think she just took her last breath! My mom . . . she just died! I was talking to her, and now she's gone!"

Clayton was both shaken that death had snatched her mid-sentence and comforted by his siblings' belief that their mother had held on just until she heard her imprisoned son's voice. It was enough; she could pass in peace then.

• • • • •

I had to deliver bad news to Terrance, one of my most vocal critics at Mahanoy prison. My first run-in with him stemmed from my refusal to allow him to sing a solo at a church service. If I permitted him to sing, a line of men was sure to clamor for equal time in the limelight, and the worship service would be reduced to a competitive circus. In addition, Terrance's reputation as a musician wannabe was a joke among fellow inmates who described how he routinely carried his keyboard into the prison yard and attempted to cover a lack of musical ability with volume and theatrics.

"Please, please, if he ever asks, don't let him sing at church," they begged.

He asked.

I suggested he try out for the choir.

"Pshaw!" he snorted. "My talent outshines them by far, and I'm not wasting it on that sorry bunch!" He squared his shoulders and pointed a long accusatory finger at me. "You think you run this place but God does, and He wants me to sing! If you was a real man of God you'd let me sing! Chaplain, you ain't nuthin' but wickedness in high places!"

It would not have been so bad if he had stopped there, but he took pleasure in airing his opinion to others. "See that Chaplain Zeiset over there?" he would ask in a loud voice, obviously wanting me to hear. "He ain't nuthin' but wickedness in high places!"

Terrance had even brought his venom to my office area under the guise of meeting my new supervisory chaplain. He first poked his head into my open office, and satisfied that he had my attention, he turned his back and leaned against the doorframe between my office and the supervisor's.

At the outset, I was surprised by his polite conversation with her. I'd never heard him speak with such courtesy. But then his voice rose, and I knew he intended for me to hear every word. He began ripping me apart limb by limb, telling my new supervisor that I was a rotten chaplain who wouldn't let him bless the congregation with his songs, that I didn't know how to preach, that I was racist, and that I worked only for the money. "Pure and simple, Chaplain Zeiset is wickedness in high places!" he said.

I listened with a mix of annoyance and humor, and finally stepped to my door. "You know, Terrance, one thing I like about you is that you'll never talk behind my back."

His eyes shot me daggers.

My new supervisor sat in stunned speechlessness.

Now, with memories of that latest encounter with Terrance, I needed to tell him of his son's brutal murder. It was my chance to show him pastoral care and sympathy, in spite of his recurring malignment of my character. "God, give me a hefty dose of compassion," I prayed as he approached my office. "Let Terrance see Jesus in me."

He fixed a sullen glare on me and growled just one word. "What?"

I motioned for him to take a seat.

He plopped down. His neck muscles tightened, and his glare bored deep.

"I'm sorry to have to relate bad news to you, Terrance," I began, and told him of the details I had gathered—that his son had been shot in cold-blooded murder on a Philadelphia street the night before. It was horrible news to pass on to a father, and I offered my sympathies again.

His eyes narrowed to steely slits. "Hmph! The only thing I'm sorry about is that I didn't get to shoot him myself!" Terrance spat. Without a further word, he stalked from my office.

Okay then. So much for my intent to show the love of Jesus to Terrance.

•   •   •   •   •

Felix sent me a request slip, hoping for a free phone call, courtesy of my office. His girlfriend had been hospitalized after a serious accident, and it was impossible for him to make the mandatory reverse-charge call because, as he explained, "The hospital won't accept collect calls. Would you please give me a phone call from your office?"

I verified Felix's story, and discovered that only part of it was true. His fiancée had suffered an accident and been through several surgeries. But she was in rehab now, and had in fact been there for some time. I went by Felix's cell in the RHU to remind him of the criteria for getting a free phone call from the chapel. Because she was already stabilized, the situation did not warrant an emergency.

A week later, Felix sent a second request slip, scrawled in red ink to indicate its urgency. "I would like to get an update on her condition," he wrote.

I knew what that meant. He would launch another attempt to snag a free phone call. But there was nothing I could do for him. Inmates knew their options, and I could almost bet on their responses.

If I reminded them that they could buy a phone card, they were likely to look at me as if I were a kook. "What, and not have money to buy Honey Buns from the commissary?" They would rather keep up efforts to con a free call from staff.

If I suggested they call home by collect call, they would probably reply that their family didn't have the money to accept the calls. Sometimes that is the sad truth. But more often, the family refuses calls because they are sick and tired of the demands, manipulations, and guilt lobbed at them across telephone lines.

And if I suggested they write a letter, the responses were varied but predictable. "It takes too long."

"News is stale till they write back."

"I can't spell good."

"I ain't got no stamps left." (Never mind that inmates received ten free stamped envelopes every month.)

"It's too impersonal."

"No one writes back."

I empathize. It must be tough to be separated from family during traumatic times. But I was obligated to uphold policies. "If you do the crime, you do the time," goes the saying. They probably didn't think through these tough scenarios when they launched into crime. Indeed, as Scripture says, the way of the transgressor is hard.

• • • • •

I had to tell Jared that three of his cousins had been killed in a car accident. "Who would you like to call?" I asked.

He stared at the floor and muttered, "Don't know."

"Who's your closest family member?"

He shrugged. "I had a wife. Kids too. But they won't talk to me anymore." He leaned forward, holding his head in his hands, and still staring at the floor. I let him gather his thoughts.

His voice was husky when he spoke again. "I got nine brothers and two sisters. But none of them are full blood, and they don't want anything to do with me. It's pretty much just me." Jared swiped at the tears dribbling down his cheeks.

Another minute passed. He dug a paper from his pocket. "Maybe I could call a cousin."

I dialed her number, and they talked for a few minutes before he handed the phone back to me. "She wants to talk to you."

"I hardly know Jared," she told me. "We didn't spend time together as kids, and I haven't heard from him in years. It seems that he must be awful lonely though. Do you think I should write him a letter?"

"I think that would be a great idea," I said.

Jared had burned a lot of bridges in his lifetime. Maybe one of them could be rebuilt again.

· · · · ·

Occasionally an inmate was unmoved by the news of a close family member's death. "Is that it?" one asked after I relayed the bad news.

I nodded. "That's it."

"Okay," he said with a shrug. "Ain't no skin off my back."

As he walked away, I couldn't help but wonder what deep pain had seared his soul to render him so hard-hearted.

· · · · ·

Delivering bad news to inmates created opportunities to talk with them about spiritual matters. An inmate might tell me that his Mama was a Christian. That gave me a chance to talk with them about the glories that his Mama might now be experiencing in heaven.

Sometimes I asked, "And what about you? What will happen to you when you die?" Or I talked with them about God's comfort. "You know, there's Someone who loves you dearly and would love to carry you through this difficult time."

Some were receptive, and my connection with them over death was the beginning of their attendance at church where they heard the Gospel message of hope and redemption through Jesus.

• • • • •

At its peak, Mahanoy housed 2,500 men. I couldn't possibly know everyone I called to my office, but I did recognize Wade when he showed up at my door. In recent weeks he had been attending church services regularly, but I had not yet had the opportunity for more than a hurried handshake with him. Now I had to tell him that his twenty-three-year-old son had been shot.

Wade hunched over in his chair and sobbed. I gave him time to process the news and compose himself.

Two weeks earlier, he told me through tears, his nephew had been shot and killed. "And now my son! I got one other boy." Wade swallowed. "And he's in prison, just like his old man."

I gave Wade a phone call to his family. "Please don't seek revenge," he pleaded. "Let God handle this." Later in the conversation he said, "Things are different since I'm a Christian. I'm not gonna get revenge. And please, don't you go there either."

Obviously, God had begun a good work in Wade.

• • • • •

When bad news came in for RHU inmates I went onto the unit to talk with them, after first checking in with the lieutenant on duty. "Omar's grandmother died. Where do you want me to tell him?"

"Were they close? Did she raise him?" he asked.

Yes, and yes.

The lieutenant considered his options. The easiest choice was to go by Omar's cell and deliver the bad news through his cell door, above the racket on the block. But that was neither private nor pastorly. If there were any chance that he would act out by harming himself or trashing his cell, the choice was obvious but much more involved: two officers would escort him to an office where additional staff gathered and I would tell him of the tragedy.

The lieutenant sighed. "Omar's been in RHU for a year, and he's stacked up a lot of assaults and destructive behavior. I can't take a chance on him. We'd better bring him to the office. I'll get my men together."

While they prepared to get Omar from his cell, I recalled a previous conversation with him. He was Rastafarian, he had told me, and explained a bit about his faith that regarded Emperor Haile Selassie of Ethiopia as the Messiah. It taught that Blacks are the chosen people, and that they would eventually return to Africa. Omar had obtained a religious haircut exemption that permitted him to wear the dreadlocks of his religion. He made it clear he had little use for me or for my Christianity.

Now, two officers told Omar that the chaplain wished to speak with him. I can only imagine the dread that seizes men when they know that bad news is coming their way. A thousand scenarios must pass through their minds in the long minutes until they are told of the particulars.

Omar knew the customary procedure for leaving his cell. Under the watchful eyes of officers, he undressed and passed his clothing through the wicket in his cell door. The officers searched every piece, handed it back, and watched as he dressed again. That done, Omar backed up and extended his arms through the opening to get handcuffed behind his back. The steel door slid open and he backed to the doorway where the officers, one on either side, firmly grasped his arms and escorted him down the hallway to the office where a lieutenant and I sat behind the desk. The RHU sergeant joined us and took a seat on the corner of the desk. Omar's escorting officers stood close beside him.

Imagine four officers, a chaplain, and one handcuffed inmate in a small room. Omar was on high alert, his body tense. And then I told him that his grandmother—the woman who had raised him, and was likely the only person who ever showed him a lick of love—had died.

Omar fixed dark eyes on me in a penetrating glare.

The officers stood at the ready, watchful against Omar's tendency to violence.

I offered my sympathy.

Omar stiffened but didn't utter a word. His jaw tightened. He swallowed to choke back tears, but Omar would not cry. Not here, in front of the five of us.

He accepted my offer for a phone call to his mother and when it ended, he unleashed seething anger on me. He'd been worried because he hadn't gotten mail from his grandma for several weeks, he complained, but he hadn't been allowed to call home.

I knew what that meant. He wasn't given a *free* call home.

He spilled his frustrations and his anger and I tried to speak kindly, yet firmly.

When the officers led Omar away, handcuffed behind his back, I prayed for wisdom. For compassion. For faithfulness to shine light into deep darkness. And I thanked God that He never, ever tired of my desperate pleas for help.

• • • • •

"Hey, you guys got my uncle Allen locked up there at your jail. I need to tell him his mama died," the caller said.

"Was he aware that his mother was sick?" I asked.

"He knowed she was sick, but we ain't tell him she was *this* sick. He probably ain't gonna take the news too good. He's on meds and all."

I verified the death and then looked up Allen. He was in the RHU.

"He's going to act out," said the lieutenant, "and I'm short-staffed for the next shift. We'll have to wait until tomorrow to tell him."

I was just finishing up a prayer group the next morning when the psychologist from the RHU called. "Chaplain, the lieutenant wants to get this over with. Can we give Allen the news now?"

I told him I'd be there in fifteen minutes, and sent my prayer group off. The psychologist was waiting for me when I got to the RHU. "No one expects this will go well," he said, "so the lieutenant wants to bring him out handcuffed, and you can tell him in the hearing room."

"Okay, I need to know if the lieutenant will allow Allen a phone call. We can use that to motivate appropriate behavior," I said.

Yes, he replied, Allen could get a phone call on the promise of decent conduct.

The lieutenant, psychologist, and I gathered in the room. After a while they came—the inmate handcuffed behind his back and an officer on either side, each with a firm grip on his arms. Most men are pretty sober under such circumstances.

Not Allen. You would have thought he was off to a picnic. His face lit up when he saw me. "Hey, I've seen you before!"

"Yes, I was just by your cell last week," I returned in an upbeat tone. Maybe this would go better than anticipated.

The guards seated him, still holding onto his arms. I tried to gently break the news of his mother's death. A look of shock registered on his face. He gasped, as though fighting for his breath, and burst into tears. He jumped to his feet.

I quickly got up, too. I didn't want to be seated if fists started flying. The officers moved in to restrain and seat him again. He resisted. His crying grew uncontrollable and big tears dropped onto his brown shirt. Attempts to calm him only agitated him further. His eyes grew wild. "My mama didn't die!" he wailed. "My mama didn't die! It's all a lie! I know she didn't die!"

When he seemed to run out of steam, I asked him to sit down so we could talk. Surprisingly, he complied.

"Look," I said, "I can let you call your nephew, but you have to promise that you are going to act appropriately on the phone. Do I have your word on that?"

Tears still spilling down his face, he nodded in agreement.

"No craziness now, you hear me?"

He nodded again. The lieutenant handed me the phone. I dialed the number and held the phone to Allen's ear. Every time I did this for a hand-cuffed inmate, I was fully aware of how close my hand was to his mouth, and how quickly he could clamp it between his teeth.

Allen wasn't far into the conversation when he stiffened and resumed great gulping cries. The guards tightened their grip on him.

I put my free hand on his shoulder. "Relax, Allen. Calm down."

His tears dripped onto my hand that held the phone. He got himself under reasonable control and soon ended the call.

The officers needed to get on with other duties and I needed to wrap up this meeting. "Will you be okay?" I asked.

"Yes," he mumbled.

"Will you hurt yourself?"

"No, no, I won't do that," he assured me.

The officers escorted him back to his cell, and I returned to my office. It had been a long forty minutes of drama.

All in a day's work.

• • • • •

By far, the bulk of death notices were those that informed inmates of their loved ones' passing. Occasionally the reverse was true, and for a time, we chaplains had to notify family members when an inmate died. In later years, the prison superintendent took on the task, and the chaplaincy department was instead charged with holding memorial services for deceased inmates. The services were not open to family members, but were strictly for fellow inmates and staff who wished to pay their respects. I held about thirty services in my twenty-three years at Mahanoy.

In the spring of 1995, Jake lingered in the prison infirmary for weeks, wasting away from AIDS. The last time I went by to visit, his voice was barely a ragged whisper, and his sunken face wore the gray pallor of death. His eyes were closed, but he moaned with pain and picked at his bloody nose.

I tried not to gag, and read a Psalm to Jake. After a prayer, I turned to leave. He raised his hand a few inches as though with great effort and rasped, "God bless!" A few days later it fell to me to call his family to inform them of Jake's death.

The task went better than it did when Albert died in the prison infirmary. He had spent most of his adult life behind bars and his only known living relative was an aunt, whom I called to inform of his death.

"Whaddaya want me to do about it?" she growled.

Perhaps she wanted to make arrangements, I suggested.

She swore, and said she had never wanted to see Albert in all of his miserable life, sure didn't want to see him in pathetic death, and she didn't care diddly-squat what we did with his body.

Those weren't her exact words, of course. She laced her statements with a lot of profanity unfit for print.

Albert's aunt's sentiments reminded me of King Jehoram, the Old Testament ruler of Jerusalem who "passed away, to no one's regret." (2 Chronicles 21:20)

What a tragic postscript to a wasted life!

Wade was a new believer when he got news of the deaths of both a nephew and then a son. Already, the Spirit nudged him to a different response than what he may have had prior to his conversion. How do you view hardship differently than you might if you didn't know Jesus?

Jared had cut off a lot of family and friends because of his self-centered choices. Maybe you know someone like that. Can you be a bridge-builder and help to restore relationships?

CHAPTER TWENTY-FIVE

Speed Bump

*I*n 2004, Renee obtained her driver's license.

Emily earned her high school diploma.

Joel announced his engagement.

I benefited from a living room and bedroom remodel.

And Nelson received a troublesome diagnosis during an overnight hospital stay.

The year was filled with an odd mix of joys and heartaches.

2004 was also the summer when Leon Stauffer, the lead pastor at Green Terrace Church, was stricken with pancreatitis. By fall, when it became apparent that Leon's recovery would be a long time in coming, Nelson asked our bishop for assistance with the added responsibilities that had been thrust upon him at church. They planned to meet in the first week of December to discuss options.

Meanwhile, the Zeiset household was alive with excitement. In October, Joel proposed to Anita Burkholder, whom he'd met at Rosedale Bible College, and they began plans for a summer wedding. The next month, Emily, eighteen years old, left for a six-week term of study at Rosedale. And I, having just hung up my painter's brush after the remodeling project, began working a part-time seasonal job. Earlier in the year I had "retired" from seventeen years of babysitting.

I was in my second week on my new job when Chaplain Whalen, Mahanoy's head chaplain, called me at work to say that Nelson had been taken to Pottsville Hospital with shortness of breath and chest pains. It came upon him suddenly, as he unlocked his office *door at the start of his workday. Prison nurses came to Nelson's aid, and considering the possibility of a heart attack, summoned an ambulance.*

When I arrived at the hospital more than an hour later, Nelson looked washed out and was undergoing a battery of tests, with special attention given to his admission that he had nursed a persistent headache for two weeks. Nothing significant showed up, but doctors wanted to keep him overnight for observation. Twenty-four hours later, on Friday afternoon, I took him home. He was pale and exhausted.

On Sunday morning Nelson sat in his usual pew, second bench on the left side. Two women scurried front to greet us before the service began. "What's your doctor saying?" they asked.

We both shrugged. "Nothing definitive yet," said Nelson.

"I'll bet it's stress," said one, and the other nodded knowingly. I shook my head.

"No, listen," she said gently. "It's obvious that Nelson's carrying a heavy load in Leon's absence."

Her friend cut in. "If I didn't know better, I might think our church is hexed! First Leon gets sick, and now Nelson."

It took weeks for the apparent diagnosis—stress, anxiety, and depression—to seep into my mind. How could this be? How could a Christian be overcome with stress? Did this mean Nelson had taken on more responsibility than God planned for him? Did it indicate a lack of trust in Him? Was my husband operating on an empty tank?

"You've used up a lot of adrenaline on your job over the years, so this isn't really a surprise," explained our family doctor. "We'll get you stabilized with medication and you'll be feeling your upbeat self in no time. But . . ." he paused and looked Nelson in the eyes, "I can pretty much assure you, that if you continue your stressful job at the prison, and also pastor a church on the side, your struggle will be ongoing. You'll function as normal, but this will continue to sit on your shoulder."

Unlike our family doctor, a psychologist at the prison was sur-

prised. "What?! You've been working in corrections for twenty years, and this is the first time you've experienced stress and anxiety?" He laughed and slapped Nelson on the back. "You're lucky to have escaped it this long!"

I told myself that Nelson's health issue was just a little bump on the road.

I had always been a sound sleeper, but now sleep eluded me, and I was shocked to realize that Nelson stopped breathing for long seconds and multiple times during the night. And then, suddenly, his legs twitched and he gulped deep, desperate breaths.

His doctor ordered a sleep study. Without question, Nelson had sleep apnea and would need a CPAP machine.

The little bump on the road became more like a gigantic speed bump that had to be taken at a crawl. Of necessity, we worked harder at good self-care. More sleep. Deeper sleep. Exercise. An occasional Friday afternoon on the recliner with a book.

Nelson's health returned slowly. I wish I could say we did everything right and he never slumped again. Not so.

I still wonder if Nelson's health crisis at forty-three years old was connected to not taking a day of rest. Most Sundays, he preached either at the prison or at church. Sometimes both. He rarely had downtime.

Leon Stauffer never came back as Green Terrace's pastor. He died in 2005, leaving his wife, Dolores, and nine children, who ranged in age from two years to nineteen.

The church had a succession of interim and short-term pastors during the next years. Occasionally, discussion went toward Nelson's role. Would he take on the lead pastorate? But he declined each time. He would remain as assistant pastor; his primary calling was to prison ministry, and he would focus his energy there.

• • • • •

Joel and Anita were married on June 18, 2005, while they were both students at Millersville University, and they moved into a small apartment in Lancaster. Joel graduated the next spring, and we were disappointed to miss the ceremony because it was on the very day of Renee's high school graduation in Pensacola, Florida. As we had done for both Joel and Emily's graduations, we again took a two-week celebratory trip to Florida and included time for visiting friends in Atmore, Alabama.

On one of those occasions, we had dinner at Martin and Anna Weber's house. "You know," Martin said to Nelson in a slow drawl, a smile playing at the corner of his mouth, "when we first met, I wasn't too sure about you. I didn't know how well you would fit into the New Life Foundation." He grinned broadly. "But I was wrong. You proved yourself to work out very well in the prison setting. And now look at you, a Pennsylvania chaplain for all these years since."

We might have pressed Martin on the reason for his reservation but suddenly he grew introspective and spoke of his own missteps as a visionary who tended to plow over others on his way to the goal.

God is a good and a patient God. How humbling that He entrusts us—imperfect and inept sinners—with the message of the Gospel!

Remember that Facebook meme mentioned in the introduction? It says, "When God called you, He already factored in stupidity." Our stupidity spans a wide range of actions, or the lack thereof—things that we may not see in the moment. The consequences usually catch up with us in time. Health issues. Relational difficulties. Regret.

Even then, God is gracious. What a merciful, loving, and good God!

CHAPTER TWENTY-SIX

Request Slips and Lawsuits

R equest slips served as the official means of communication between
inmates and staff. On average, I processed probably one hundred
request slips every week. Some of them sought time slots for counseling (a
term used somewhat loosely, as I provided pastoral counseling but am not a
licensed professional counselor). Others requested religious literature. A few
had gripes to air and arguments to raise.

John's request slip was typical. He had just been sent to the RHU and
requested the whole gamut of resources—a Bible, daily devotional book,
Bible courses, Christian magazines, and prayer books. "Please try to make
them long and thick ones," he wrote. "I will be in here for a long time."

• • • • •

Arlin's request slip took issue with a point in my sermon. "I was in
church today, understandest thou what thou readest?" he asked.

I smiled at Arlin's quote of the question Philip asked of the Ethiopian
eunuch, as related in Acts 8. Arlin, it seemed, offered himself as a patient
expounder of truth. He referenced two dozen verses for my further correction and closed by quoting John 7:17: "If any man will do his will, he
shall know of the doctrine, whether it be of God, or whether I speak of
myself."

Earlier in my ministry I might have allowed myself to get pulled into
Arlin's habit of cherry-picking verses to shore up fruitless arguments. These
days, demands on my time necessitated better discernment. The best re-

sponse I could think of to give Arlin was simple. I wrote just two letters—
OK—and sent it back to him.

· · · · ·

Kirk, an ardent Jehovah's Witness, had often tried to ensnare me in our
doctrinal differences through rambling request slips. This time he attached
eight photocopied pages of notes, attempting to lure me into a debate about
the Crusades and his perception of the offensive nature of the cross as a
Christian symbol. Apparently, an article describing Wheaton College's decision to scuttle their Crusader mascot gave rise to Kirk's convoluted train of
thought. At his request slip's conclusion he thanked me for considering his
arguments, added a smiley face, and said he hoped for more than my "usual
one-word response."

I obliged. "I cannot follow your reasoning," I wrote, adding that the
subject had nothing to do with the cross of Jesus, that Kirk had taken a
quote out of context, and he would do well to read the article again. I ended
with, "By the way, what's your point?"

There. I gave Kirk forty-four words. I hoped he got my point—that
my Savior's cross is not to be trifled with.

· · · · ·

Landon wrote a four-page letter peppered with capital letters, under-
linings, and exclamation marks. "We [need] a *real* church—a *real* man of
God with a healing ministry to come to Mahanoy." He ranted that more
than half of the congregation suffered from physical disabilities, blood dis-
eases, mental illness, and drug addiction, and added, "Inmates' lives are in
ruins—under your ministry!"

He charged me with having a form of godliness but denying its power.
Proof, he said, lay in the fact that none of my sheep had been healed of
physical infirmities. He called me "Mr. Pretender," and a pawn and a pup-
pet to the Department of Corrections. "Do you know where to locate a rope

and a millstone?" he asked. In case I missed his insinuation, he added a final zinger. "A pile of horse manure is more beneficial to the farmer and his land than you are to your sheep!"

· · · · ·

Brad often decorated his request slips with smiley faces, even on those where he rambled about injustices suffered at the hands of staff.

In one request he chided me for not visiting him on my last round through the RHU unit. He had seen me walk past his door as though I were on a tight schedule, he said, but then I had talked with an officer for a full ten minutes. Did I bypass him just because he believed differently from me, Brad asked. His scolding tone abruptly changed to flattery. He wrote that I was one of the most beautiful Christian ministers he had ever met. He wished me blessings and signed off with a big smiley face. His request slips were more about venting than they were about asking for something.

In contrast, I could count on Larry's requests slips to be full of thanks and encouragement. He wrote in a back-slanted loopy style and addressed me as "Chappy." His typical sentiments were messages like, "Enjoyed your message today!" and "You're a great teacher and very important to us!"

· · · · ·

Stan wrote to tell me he decided to drop out of the Tuesday Bible Study. "I'm struggling with things, including my Christianity. As soon as I can stop back-sliding and get myself together, I'll start attending again. Please pray for me."

How tragic that Stan withdrew from fellowship and from instruction in the Word in his time of need. I put him on my call list at the next available slot, but he didn't come, and I learned he'd been transferred to another prison. I could only pray that the seeds planted in Stan would take root and grow.

· · · · ·

Jed's request slip confused me. "Dear Heavenly Father," it began. I read it again, wondering whether he was writing a prayer to God or a request to me. He said that he desperately needed to see me so he could make a confession and wrote, "Father, I want to be a born-again Christian. I wanna be saved. I want you, need you to bring light to my darkness."

I carried Jed's paper with me into the RHU and looked him up. "I came by to talk with you about your request slip," I said.

Jed backed up and scowled. "What request slip?"

I held it up for him to see through the window in his door. "You wrote that you'd like some spiritual help."

He squinted closer. "That ain't my handwriting, I didn't send it, and I don't need your help!"

"All right then," I said and moved along.

Obviously, someone wanted to mess with Jed. Or with me. The games abound in prison. Forging someone's request slip is only one of them.

Frivolous request slips plagued every prison department. Morris, an RHU inmate, made a nuisance of himself by requesting right-to-know information on a variety of subjects, and kept staff busy with printing out the data he demanded.

"Hey, Chap, look what I got!" Morris called out as I approached his door one day. He held up his latest trophy, a thick stack of papers.

"What now?" I asked.

"Man, this is about the food service company that makes my grub."

"Yeah? And how is that information important to you?"

He shrugged and grinned. "It's not. It's just fun to keep people busy."

"So it's all a game for you?"

"Guess you could say that." Morris shrugged again. "Gives me something to do. You can't hate me for that, can you?"

• • • • •

Policy mandated a response to request slips within five business days. Administration reminded employees to write succinct replies and cau-

tioned, "Never write a response on a request slip that you might not want
to see in court one day." The potential for responses to develop into a grievance or a lawsuit was very real.

I had been slapped with a lawsuit in 1997, over my refusal to allow
secular cassette tapes to pass off as religious materials. The judge ruled in my
favor. In the next decade I was named in two additional lawsuits.

Six major faith groups—Catholic, Jehovah Witness, Jewish, Muslim,
Native American, and Protestant—shared the use of the chapel. For years
there had been tensions among them, especially during the Christmas season. In an attempt to remedy that, Chaplain Whalen ordered that the chapel's twelve-foot Christmas tree be placed on a platform on wheels so it
could be moved out of the line of sight of worshippers who objected to it.
Six wreaths decorating the walls could also be removed for the duration of
the services. But every week following Muslim Jumah services, complaints
surfaced about broken ornaments and crushed wreaths.

Chaplain Whalen had heard enough. The tree must be wheeled *gently* to
the back of the chapel, he said, but the wreaths were to remain on the walls.

I was the only on-site chaplain on December 30, 2005, when the Muslim set-up crew arrived to prepare the chapel for Jumah. Their leader, Clint,
ordered his fellow inmates to take down the wreaths.

"Actually, they are to stay up," I said. "That's orders from Chaplain
Whalen, FCPD."

Clint argued that they represent Christianity and were offensive to a
true Muslim.

No, I replied, they are a cultural symbol, not religious in nature.

That was it. The Muslim crew quit working.

I decided the situation was beyond my pay grade and called for the
Inmate Program Manager, supervisor of the chaplaincy department. After
a brief discussion with the agitated Muslim inmates, he relented and gave
permission to remove the wreaths.

Whatever. I had only followed the dictates passed on to me.

But Clint, the Muslim leader, was not happy. He pursued the matter
through grievances, resolution meetings, and appeals, but rulings were not

to his satisfaction. In the summer of 2008, he filed a civil suit against me and six other defendants.

By then Chaplain Whalen had retired from Mahanoy, and I again reluctantly assumed the role of FCPD for five months until a replacement was found. During that time, Marvin, a Nation of Islam (NOI) inmate, filed a religious accommodation request for himself and other inmates of the movement. The NOI organization is led by Louis Farrakhan, and combines elements of traditional Islam with Black nationalist and race-based ideas.

I viewed NOI more as a racist and cultural movement than a religious group and felt safe in denying Marvin's request. My position was based, in part, on the fact that similar requests had been turned down in other institutions and the state held that it already provided for Muslim services but could not accommodate splinter groups.

Marvin filed further requests and grievances and was dissatisfied with the outcomes. In August 2009, he filed a civil suit claiming conspiracy, discrimination, prejudice, and racial bias. He contended that a denial of foods pertaining to his faith resulted in his constant hunger, headaches, listlessness, and a weight loss of almost twenty pounds.

Apparently, both Clint's and Marvin's lawsuits are still in litigation. I was quite annoyed in 2011, when Esther and I applied for a small short-term loan to purchase an investment property. It should have been a shoo-in. Esther took the call from the loan officer who informed us that the bank denied our loan because of an outstanding lien against our property.

Surely there's some mix-up, my wife thought, and she cast about for a delicate way to say as much to the banker. And then something stirred in the back of her mind. "Does this have anything to do with a pending lawsuit from a state prisoner?" she asked.

The loan officer seemed hesitant to divulge details, but indicated that this was the case.

We were shocked. We never gave thought to this tying up our personal finances. The officer was understanding, and in the end, a document of explanation from the Department of Corrections cleared the way for our loan.

How tragic that Stan withdrew from Christian fellowship at Mahanoy because he viewed himself as a spiritual failure. Is there a "Stan" whom you could walk alongside and help to restore to faith? And what of your own tendency to withdraw at those times when faith is fragile?

CHAPTER TWENTY-SEVEN
Zeiset Family Goes to Prison

Soon after Joel's eighteenth birthday, he asked to go to a Sunday service with me.

"That's great, but you've got to participate in some way," I said. "The prison is not a zoo where you just go to look around."

Joel led the opening prayer. It was the beginning of my family's visits to the prison, maybe once or twice a year. Prison rules did not allow minors inside the facility, but when our daughters turned eighteen, they too, visited. It allowed them a window into my work.

These visits also allowed the inmates a view into our family. They kept up with our kids' lives through college, dating, and weddings. They cheered each time a new grandchild was born and extended their sympathies when Esther's parents and my sister died. "Your family is the most-prayed-for family anywhere!" inmates told me.

I didn't doubt them.

Christmas 2008 was fast approaching, and I wasn't feeling it.

Neither was Renee. "It's not gonna be any fun this year," she grumped. "Emily's going on that mission trip to China, and Joel and Anita are spending Christmas with her family. It's just Dad and you and me. Stinks to be the youngest in the family!"

"I know," I sighed. "It's time to start new traditions."

"You could go to prison with me," Nelson said.

For some years now, he held services for the inmates on Christmas morning. Our children were okay with that. It gave them a chance to sleep in late after Christmas Eve festivities with Nelson's family. To stall for more time, I served them breakfast in bed. By the time they dragged themselves out near noon, Nelson was already driving home, just in time to begin our family celebration.

The arrangement had worked well for a few years. But now a new stage of life was upon us, and we needed to rethink our Christmas celebration. I balked at Nelson's idea. It was one thing for him to go to prison on Christmas morning, quite another for Renee and me.

Renee groaned. "What a thrill."

"No better way to cheer yourself up than to cheer someone else," Nelson said. "Think about it."

We did.

"I guess going to jail on Christmas morning wouldn't be any worse than staying home, just Mom and me," said Renee.

I nodded. "Okay then, count me in too."

More than a hundred inmates came out for the service. Renee played her violin, and the men rose to applaud. When she sang "Mary, Did You Know?" they dropped their heads to hide unbidden tears. After the service, they thanked us profusely for cheering up their otherwise lonely Christmas in prison.

Renee had been contemplating a career in music education, but lacked confidence. The extent of the inmates' emotions shook her. Maybe God had given her a musical gift that could bless others.

A new tradition was born for our half-family.

At some point Nelson switched to Christmas Eve services. One year, Renee introduced her boyfriend, Andrew Stauffer (eldest son of our former pastor, Leon Stauffer, and his wife, Dolores) and they played a guitar-violin duet.

After the service, Gary, an inmate serving a life sentence, rushed to greet Andrew. "Years ago you sent me a Christmas card and letter!" he said.

Andrew's face scrunched in bewilderment.

"Yeah, you did!" Gary insisted.

With Nelson's help we untangled the story of how, about twelve years earlier, the junior boys' Sunday School class at Green Terrace Mennonite Church sent Christmas cards and letters to several inmates. Andrew drew Gary's name, but he had long ago forgotten the project.

But not Gary. After all those years, he still remembered that a boy named Andrew Stauffer had taken the time to send a card to him, an unknown inmate forgotten behind bars.

Year after year, Renee's music drew inmates to the Christmas service. "My sermon is only a sideshow," Nelson teased. "They only endure it so they can hear you sing."

When Renee graduated from college, the men congratulated her. They cheered and clapped when she and Andrew announced wedding plans, and hurrahed when she landed a job as music teacher at Ephrata Mennonite School (EMS).

From there, an unlikely alliance developed between the school and the Resident's Betterment Association (RBO), an inmate organization that utilizes in-prison fundraisers to give back to community associations. The school's music department qualified and received a $300 check. For a Christian school teacher on a scant annual budget, the gift was a windfall.

At the next Christmas Eve service, Renee expressed her thanks to the inmates and described the students' excitement in using boomwhackers purchased with the gift.

Kory caught up with Nelson after the service. "I want to help your daughter's school out too. How can I give a personal donation?"

Nelson turned this over in his mind while Kory laid out the rationale behind his generosity. He collected substantial retirement and pension checks every month, far more money than he would ever be able to spend in prison, and more than he wanted to send to his only daughter who squandered it on a drug habit. "I've always loved music and could get some vicarious enjoyment from seeing it put to use in the school's music program."

Nelson was unwilling to get embroiled in anything smacking of a breach in ethics, but of course, nothing could prevent Kory from donating to any organization he wished. Over the course of a year or two, both he and the RBO continued sending donations to EMS. The school's music room accumulated a variety of instruments that had only been pipe dreams: xylophones, tone chimes, a bass guitar, djembe drum, and an assortment of percussion items.

In return, the school administration sought a tangible way to express their gratitude, and settled on adopting the prison for their annual Christmas project. They collaborated with Nelson to send chocolate bars to each of the 2,500 inmates. The plan was a major undertaking, without precedent, and one that required a detailed proposal to prison officials for distribution, and solid assurance that the candy was free of contraband.

Almost surprisingly, the proposal went through and the project drew much enthusiasm from EMS faculty and patrons. Students toted chocolate bars in their book bags, the kindergarteners staggering beneath the weight of their gifts. Grandmas and aunts dropped off boxes of candy. The sweet-smelling stack grew in the third-grade classroom where students enhanced their math skills in a regular tallying of donations. Junior high students designed and placed a label on each of the bars that read "From your friends at Ephrata Mennonite School."

A teacher went to a local grocery store to buy a contribution of thirty-six chocolate bars. The cashier eyed her curiously. "What is going on? We've sold more candy bars in the last few days than we have all year!"

The teacher described the school's Christmas project, and the cashier shook her head. "Candy bars? For a bunch of jailbirds? That's just dumb."

Nevertheless, distribution day came. Nelson and a fellow chaplain wheeled a cart stacked with chocolate bars onto cell blocks.

"For me?" inmates asked.

"From who?"

"What do they cost?"

"Why?"

For months afterwards, men got teary-eyed when they talked of the unexpected gift of a simple candy bar. That May, an inmate spoke to Nelson after a Sunday service. "I hear you're Mennonite," he said.

Nelson nodded.

The inmate looked around, leaned in closer, and whispered, "Do you know who I am?"

Nelson stepped back to view the name stamped above the man's shirt pocket. "No, I'm sorry. Have we met?"

"Nope, but I figured you knew." His embarrassment was obvious. "Remember those Mennonite women from Ephrata who got robbed and beaten two years ago?"

Nelson remembered it well. Three sisters, between the ages of eighty-four and ninety, allowed a man who posed as an insurance salesman into their rural home. In a two-hour drug-fueled frenzy, he beat the women, ransacked their home, and left them bound and gagged. A relative discovered them later that afternoon, and the assailant was arrested the next day.

"That was me," he said. "I'm so ashamed. And then I got that candy bar from the Mennonite kids . . ." Tears coursed down his cheeks.

Nelson placed his hand on the man's shoulder, waiting for him to go on.

"After what I did, I just can't believe they gave me a gift." He held his Bible out to Nelson with trembling hands and opened it to show an empty candy wrapper in its pages. "It's my bookmark." He inhaled deeply. "It smells so good."

More than the sweet fragrance of chocolate, it was the smell of love. Of grace. Of kindness.

The simple gift of a chocolate bar was not so simple after all.

And contrary to the grocery clerk's opinion, it was far from dumb.

• • • • •

Sometime around 2010, our entire family went to a Sunday afternoon service at Mahanoy. There were eight of us: Joel and his wife, Anita; Emily and her husband, Kenton; Renee and her boyfriend, Andrew; and Nelson and me. We sang a few songs together, and trust me, we most certainly did not deserve the inmates' standing ovation. One of us read the Scripture, and Joel preached the sermon.

The inmates couldn't stop thanking us for sharing in the service with them.

As we left the chapel that Sunday afternoon and walked toward the prison's main gate, Nelson told the kids, "This meant so much to the guys. Some of them have never seen a healthy family interact with each other."

Just then a mouse skittered across the walkway in front of us. Emily, who has long been given to hysterics concerning mice, stifled a scream and danced behind Kenton. Joel, who has an equally long history of teasing his sisters, lunged for the mouse. By God's providence it ran safely beneath a chain fence and out of Joel's reach. He bemoaned a missed opportunity to terrorize Emily with the mouse, and she hissed that he is absolutely the meanest brother of all times.

Healthy family, indeed!

· · · · ·

I think it was in 2015 when I went to Mahanoy for another Christmas Eve service. In the moments before call-out was announced, I stood in the quiet chapel and reminisced. After twenty-some years, Nelson was looking toward retirement. This could be one of the last Christmas services I would attend at the prison. What would become of the friendships Nelson had built with inmates over the years?

I thought of Jim, serving a life sentence for a grisly murder, who was always first to greet me, his face alive with the joy of the Lord.

Of Tony, whose gentle handshake always accompanied soft laughter and kind words about his chaplain.

Of Harry, a gentle giant who towered over me, who always smiled broadly and said how honored he felt by my presence.

Of the many others whose lives had intersected with ours over the years. Nelson had mentored and nurtured and poured his life into theirs.

The inmates' obvious respect for my husband eased my nervousness about visiting the prison. To some degree, I was always aware of the potential for danger. If a disturbance broke out, where would I run to for safety? Where could I hide?

My rambling thoughts were interrupted when a few officers entered the chapel. "Merry Christmas!" Nelson called to them and strode down the aisle to make small talk.

A female officer walked between the chairs, scanning every detail. She was trained to be watchful and to look for anything out of place.

"Merry Christmas!" I said as she neared.

Her face scrunched up in a grimace. "I can think of better places to be tonight." She turned questioning eyes on me. "Are you and the chaplain going out to party after the service tonight?"

The way she asked it, I knew she thought it weird that I had come into the prison on Christmas Eve, of all nights! "No, I just want to celebrate the reason for the season with the men," I said.

Nostalgia slipped out and I mentioned the friendships we'd developed over the years with some of the inmates. I should have quit with that, but blabbed on about my confidence that, should anything come down, I was sure they would look out for me and the chaplain.

"Hmmph!" She turned to face me head on and shook her head. Her blonde hair, pulled into a tight bun, bobbed back and forth. "Don't kid yourself! The only people they ever look out for are themselves."

My face grew hot with embarrassment. I meant no disrespect to her or to her job, which among many other things, included sniffing out fraternization between inmates and staff (and their naive visitors).

Inmates started filing in then, and she and I parted. Nothing further came of my encounter with her. Thank God, peace prevailed on earth, and in prison, that Christmas Eve.

Discovering God's purposes for our lives is not as complicated as we sometimes make them out to be. In most situations, it merely means doing what we know to be the right thing. The best choice. The selfless one.

When Renee and Esther reluctantly decided to go to the prison on Christmas morning, they could not have foreseen that it would be the first step in a series of God-happenings.

The godly actions you take today may very well set into motion a chain of events that only eternity will reveal.

CHAPTER TWENTY-EIGHT

Fraternization Fears

The fear of fraternization between inmates and staff makes a prison security department's blood run cold.

In 2013, more than a dozen Maryland correctional officers were charged with involvement in a smuggling scheme run by inmate gang members inside a Baltimore detention center. An investigation uncovered the fact that Tavon White, one of the gang's leaders, had fathered five children with four female guards while inside the prison.

Two years later in a New York prison, a three-week manhunt ensued after Richard Matt and David Sweat sawed and tunneled their way to freedom. They had sucked two prison employees into aiding their escape. A male officer who admired and encouraged Matt's painting skills provided the inmate with art supplies in exchange for a stash of paintings for resale; a female employee got sweet-talked into a sexual relationship with Sweat. Both employees became putty in the inmates' hands and caved to their manipulation.

Not all prisons make headlines, of course. But all prisons have their stories of drugs, weapons, cell phones, and other contraband being smuggled in by prison staff. All prisons have concerns about inmate-employee relations, which can easily spill over to bribery and blackmail.

Jethro grew up not far from my house and we had mutual acquaintances. When he committed double murder and ended up at Mahanoy, his mother called my house. "I'm so worried about my son," she cried.

She needed a listening ear and assurance that her son was okay. I hated having to tell her that I could not be the intermediary between her and her son because that violated state ethics.

"I understand," she said. But when long lapses occurred between his letters, she picked up the phone again.

"Jethro, you have to tell your mother to stop calling my house," I warned.

She was harmless, just a distraught mother who sought a connection with her son. But unfortunately, I could not provide that need for her.

One summer I came face-to-face with a paroled inmate on a hiking trail while on a family vacation to Pennsylvania's Grand Canyon. We were mutually surprised at the encounter and spent some minutes catching up. On my first day back to work, I had to report the meeting to my supervisor.

As a chaplain, I would have liked to be an exception to the state's mandates. While employed with Jubilee, I had been permitted to interact with released inmates. To visit them. To have them over to my house. To continue the discipling and mentoring relationship we had behind bars. That ended when I became a state employee.

* * * * *

Joe came to my office late in the 1990s, spooked and nearly jumping out of his skin. He told me the state police had come into the prison to interrogate him. He raised his right palm. "Honest to God, Chaplain, I done a lot of bad stuff in my life, but I ain't murdered two people!"

I let Joe talk. Bits and pieces of his story started to sound familiar—details that I had heard from another side!

The brutal murder of an Adams County couple had gone unsolved for four years. Their daughter-in-law, whom I will call Lori, drew the attention of investigators.

As teenagers, Lori and Esther ran in some of the same social circles, and we were invited to her wedding. She moved into her husband's area, and we had little contact with them for a decade or so. But rumors of their crumbling marriage and Lori's strong dislike for her in-laws filtered to us.

And then we heard of the brutal murders, the unfruitful search for the killer, and of suspicion directed at Lori.

Lori and her children moved back to our neighborhood. Esther sometimes saw her at the grocery store and lent a listening year. Lori spared no words in directing hot anger at her deceased in-laws and blamed them for her marriage woes, decimated now by the terror and stigma associated with being a suspect in their murders.

Four years dragged on.

And now the police were sniffing around Joe in this same case, and he was terrified. I told Esther about it that evening. "But please, please, you cannot whisper a word about this," I said.

"Of course not," she said. "But can you imagine how it would change things for Lori if the killer was arrested and she were finally exonerated?"

Pieces of the story continued to filter back to me through Joe and fellow inmates. A fascinating rumor said that a female friend of Joe's had been stopped by police in a routine traffic check. (I don't remember whether she was his girlfriend or his wife, current or long-ago tossed aside) but when the officer discovered a bag of marijuana in her possession, she got scared. Could she avoid arrest, she asked, in exchange for information about an unsolved double murder?

Of course the officer was all ears!

And she got off—by selling Joe out for a single bag of marijuana! He was convicted of double murder.

I guess friendship is cheap among criminals.

$$\bullet \quad \bullet \quad \bullet \quad \bullet \quad \bullet$$

In 2008, the murder of Jan Roseboro rocked Lancaster County. At first her death looked like a drowning in the couple's backyard swimming pool, but eleven days later, autopsy reports revealed evidence of strangulation. Michael Roseboro, her husband of nineteen years, was arrested. He was a wealthy and well-respected funeral director in Denver, and we had been to funerals that he held, so I recognized his photos plastered in the local newspapers.

Salacious details surfaced of Michael's obsessive affair with a girlfriend who was pregnant with his child. His three-week trial unearthed deep dark secrets of philandering that kept a media circus running for months.

In time, Michael arrived at Mahanoy prison where he exchanged his dark business suits for drab prison browns. He traded his societal position for a prison number, moved from a sprawling house to a cramped prison cell devoid of comfort, and fell from the pinnacle of success to a pit of shame.

Michael and I talked a few times. "I know some Zeisets from Lancaster County," he said one day.

I didn't tell him that I was among them, nor that I knew exactly where he lived and often drove by his house. I suspect he may have already known, but his own professionalism respected my need for the same.

I don't know whether Michael still maintains his innocence, and that was not my determination to make in anyone's case. Many men, of course, claimed wrongful convictions, but there were others like Ricardo, who said, "I'm innocent of the crime they charged me with, but, man, if they got me for everything I did, I'd be locked up the rest of my life!"

• • • • •

Something went terribly wrong in the lives of prison inmates. How did they get to the dead-end in a prison cell? There is no one definitive answer. Over the years I compiled a list of characteristics that I describe as criminal thinking (see appendix).

There is no justification or excuse for criminality. However, the unthinkable stories I heard from men helped me to better understand why they made choices that got them locked up.

Terry just wanted to survive. He never knew his father. His alcoholic mother entertained a constant stream of men and they exposed Terry to debauchery from a young age.

At seven years old, Terry's landlord began abusing him sexually. He worked up the courage to tell his mother. In a flash, she backhanded him and screamed, "Don't you ever lie to me like that again!" Vicious swats and kicks followed.

A few days later, Terry's mother sent him to the landlord's apartment on an errand. He was still suffering from his mother's beating, and now he feared her more than he feared the landlord. Terry hoped to deliver the message and make a quick escape, but it didn't work that way. He was just a scrawny little guy, and the landlord easily cornered him. The scenario repeated itself every time Terry's mom sent him to report a clogged drain, a non-working electrical outlet, or a squeaky floorboard.

One day Terry overheard his mother arguing with the landlord about a rent hike. "But I send Terry over every time you want him! You promised me a break!"

Terry was crushed by the realization that his mother had been selling him out. His landlord's abuse grew worse and more frequent until Terry could stand no more. He was only ten years old when he stole money from his mother and slipped off to the Scranton bus terminal to purchase a ticket to Harrisburg. Hungry, scared, and without a plan, he found himself on the steps of a church.

A kindly old man stopped by, talked with Terry for a while, and invited him to his house for a meal. He took advantage of the boy who just wanted food and a safe place to sleep. After a few more encounters, Terry ran away and drifted aimlessly through the unfamiliar city.

A policeman picked him up and pried Terry's story from him. "Show me where he lives," said the policeman.

They drove up and down Harrisburg's streets, but Terry couldn't locate the man's house or give a clear description of him. The police called Terry's mother, who hadn't even bothered to report him missing. She was in a nasty mood when she arrived at a Harrisburg police station in a friend's borrowed car to pick up her son. A few blocks away, she unleashed her fury on Terry. The trip home was a marathon of screaming, pinching, slapping, threatening—and only a foretaste of what was to come.

At sixteen years old, Terry was charged with armed robbery and landed six years in prison. "And that was just the beginning," he said. His voice was flat. "I've been in and out ever since, a few years here and there. I guess I'll end up doing life on the installment plan 'cause this is my fifth time in the Big House."

"What about your mom? Do you talk to her?" I asked.

His eyes burned with anger and he swore. "Nope. She's dead twelve years now. Could've happened a lot sooner, for all I care."

· · · · ·

Ezra's childhood was saner. He grew up going to church and accepted Christ as a young boy. But he neglected his spiritual life, got caught up in the wrong crowd, and did some county jail time for shoplifting. His family drifted apart, and when Ezra's older brother died, no one bothered to contact Ezra until a cousin called two days later. He was hurt so deeply that he refused to attend the funeral, and he nursed the insult to a slow-boiling rage.

A few years later, a business venture failed, and his anger intensified. "I'm gonna get what's coming to me," he vowed, and started buying and selling gold—honestly enough, at the outset. When his daughter's boyfriend began bringing him a steady supply, Ezra squashed an uneasy feeling that something might not be on the up and up. The boyfriend never admitted to it, but Ezra felt certain it was stolen property. He warned the younger man to be careful, but the steady stream of goods only increased.

When the boyfriend and two accomplices were arrested for burglary, they fingered Ezra as the mastermind and he got a twelve-to-twenty-four-year sentence. Sitting behind bars, Ezra brooded over the injustices thrown at him. Anger became a constant miserable companion.

"But one day a clear thought struck me," Ezra said. "I realized I was the big idiot. No one else. Just me. I couldn't blame a single person for my prison sentence but myself."

"But they made you out to be the mastermind," I said.

"Yup, they did. And that wasn't true. But I did coach my daughter's boyfriend in how to avoid suspicion. I guess he learned my lessons well," he said with a rueful smile. "But you know, the day I stopped blaming everyone else for my miserable life was the day I returned to the God of my childhood, and a heavy weight dropped from me."

Ezra's smile grew brighter as he spoke, and then it faded again as he recalled the pain he inflicted on his family. "I'm so embarrassed at what I've become. All because I let anger consume me."

He shook his head and uttered the words I've heard time and time again: "I never thought I'd ever land here. Never in a million years."

Ezra's final words are echoed by so many inmates. Never, in their wildest imagination, did they ever think their choices would land them in prison.

There's a lot of truth in the quote that says, "Sin will take you farther than you want to go, keep you longer than you want to stay, and cost you more than you can pay." Do you need to change your life's course? Do it now! Jesus offers forgiveness and direction and help in living a productive and joyful life.

CHAPTER TWENTY-NINE

Mental Health and Security
Threat Group Inmates

I n the mid-twentieth century, a social experiment got underway to empty
psychiatric hospitals of their patients. Critics say the movement resulted
only in moving great numbers from hospitals to jail cells.

Around 2014, Pennsylvania's prisons held an estimated 10,000 mental
health inmates, or about 21% of the inmate population. An investigation by the
U.S. Department of Justice looked at the length of time that such inmates were
housed in solitary confinement, and found that more than a thousand were held
for ninety or more days. Some were isolated for as long as a year.

Lawsuits for reform followed, and Mahanoy was designated as one of
several institutions to house a large number of mental health inmates. This
required additional staff and special training and added extra stress to the
workplace. When I left Mahanoy in 2017, mental health inmates were still
arriving, and as far as I know, there were no caps in place.

One morning a sergeant at the control center stopped me when I
picked up my keys. "Hey, Chaplain, there's a problem with an inmate in
RHU. Can you go down there and talk him off the cliff?"

"I'll see what I can do," I said and headed in that direction.

Psychologists or chaplains were sometimes called upon to attempt negotiations with inmates to avoid a forcible cell extraction. But usually the
situation was too far gone by the time I arrived, and my attempts at negotia-
tion were mostly ineffective—except for one notable time when I thought I
had accomplished the goal. "Okay," the inmate said. "I'll agree to cuff up if
you get me a peanut butter and jelly sandwich."

Simple enough, I thought.

But the lieutenant wasn't going for it. "I'm not giving him a single thing!" he said.

And that was that. I'd done my job but the lieutenant didn't like it. I didn't hang around any longer. For lack of a peanut butter sandwich, four guards had to suit up in riot gear, storm in on the inmate, and remove him from his cell. After all that, they had to file a bunch of incident reports. It seemed like getting the guy a sandwich would have been a lot easier, but maybe there was more to the story than met my eye.

That was the thing. I never knew what was going on, and usually there was little time to get briefed.

This time guards clustered in front of the inmate's cell and a psychologist was already on the scene, trying to speak calm through the steel door. And what a scene it was! The inmate had wrapped himself with toilet tissue so that only his face was exposed. He clumsily held a cigarette lighter in his wrapped hand and flicked the flame close to the shroud of toilet tissue. His threat to light himself on fire was credible; a week earlier he had burned his mattress.

RHU inmates are not permitted to have cigarette lighters, and staff was astounded that for the second week in a row, he had somehow acquired one. But for the moment, that was a secondary issue; we all just hoped he wouldn't carry through on his threat before our eyes.

After some tense minutes, the psychologist talked him into giving up the lighter and everyone took a deep breath, grateful that it had ended as well as it did.

But it hadn't ended, really. Now an incident report needed to be filed, and after that, an investigation would get underway to discover his source for lighters.

• • • • •

Lloyd wanted my help. "Can you contact NASA for me?" he asked.

Apparently, he'd been telling his psychologist that he had flown in a space shuttle, and when it passed the moon, Lloyd reached out to touch it.

"But he thinks I'm crazy! I'm not crazy, Chaplain! I'm not! And if you can get NASA to release the footage—they have it all on video—then he can see it for himself. He'll know then that I'm not crazy. You don't think I'm crazy, do you, Chaplain?"

Somehow, I extricated myself from Lloyd's incessant pleas. I never did contact NASA on his behalf.

• • • • •

I had just finished giving the benediction at a Sunday service when Lance came to me. "Chaplain, can I have a hug from you today?" He flashed a toothless smile and the purple burn scars on his cheeks stretched taut. His disfigured face and the musty smell he carried with him generally kept people at bay. But there he stood, in front of the congregation that I had just blessed with God's favor, asking me for a hug.

I gave him a big one.

He grunted. "Thank you, kind Chaplain, thank you, thank you!" He drew back and gripped my shoulders. "I love you, Chaplain, and Michael the archangel loves you, too!"

And then Lance was gone, leaving me to inhale a horribly musty smell, and to wonder what had just happened.

• • • • •

Galen's cell walls were plastered with pictures. "That's God there!" he said, pointing to a picture of outstretched arms. Three small raggedy magazine cutouts were glued haphazardly onto the arm. They were so small I couldn't determine what they were.

It didn't matter. He drew my attention to a photo of an Egyptian mummy. "That's my wife. She's a really good dancer."

Galen disliked showers, but when he imagined that guards told him he could be released early if he showered more often, he began doing so three times a day. Shortly thereafter he flagged me down on the walkway.

"Look!" he hiked up his pant leg to reveal a double layer of socks and peeled back the outer one. "Look at the one on the inside. It's clean ain't it?"

Before I had a chance to formulate a careful response, he flashed a bright smile. "I think it's clean enough that they'll soon let me go home."

In spite of Galen's frequent showers an early release wasn't forthcoming, so he tried another angle. He waited his turn in the medication distribution line one afternoon and suddenly announced to no one in particular, "I can't take it anymore. I'm going home today!" He stepped out of line and hightailed it toward the gate. At the push of a button the door opened for him. He went to the next one, and it, too, swung open. This was easier than he'd ever guessed!

What he didn't know was that the sergeant at the control desk saw Galen coming and let him inside so he could be intercepted. And now, as Galen stood in front of the control room window, he leaned in and waved at the officers behind it. "Bye! I'm going home now!" he called out as flippantly as if he were a child leaving a friend's birthday party.

It could hardly be called an escape attempt.

An officer took him by the arm and gently led him back to his cell. Galen was home again.

• • • • •

Chris had his eccentricities too. I don't remember whether his aversion was to making a right turn or a left, so let's say it was to the left. He never made left turns. Never. It wasn't like he ever began to do so, caught himself, and corrected course. He just did not do left hand turns, period. If he got to a juncture where a left turn was necessary, he simply made a wide right circle and came in from that direction.

His peculiar movements, of course, drew chuckles and occasional jokes, but I never heard anyone giving Chris a hard time for it. He kept to himself, head down, moving mechanically, and always to the right.

• • • • •

Mental health inmates like those described were the easy ones. Others were quite disruptive and violent. Perhaps not as much, however, as the

prison gangs, also known as Security Threat Groups (STG). At a Monday
night Spanish service, I noted a concerning interaction between two inmates and reported it to a security lieutenant.

He thanked me for the heads-up and invited me to attend monthly
STG meetings. "We need your eyes in the chaplaincy department, Chaplain. The meetings will keep you abreast of gang activity within the prison."

I got an education, for sure. I learned about specific inmates to look
out for and the gangs that they associated with, their operations behind
bars, their plots, their rivalries, their codes, and their identifying tattoos.

Not all tattoos are gang-related. One inmate had the numbers *666* tat-
tooed above one eye and *Satan* inscribed above the other. Another man had
a vulgar threat to police etched onto his cheek. I often wondered how his
arresting officer took to that!

· · · · ·

William Cramer, a self-avowed white supremist, began his criminal
career with robbery. At a county jail in 2012, he strangled his White cellmate when he learned his cellie had fathered a child with a Black woman.
Two years later, at Coal Township Prison in neighboring Northumberland
County, Cramer brutally attacked a Hispanic officer.

Immediately after that attack Cramer was transferred to Mahanoy, and
he arrived with a clear objective—to kill a guard so that he could go to
death row. He was only in his twenties, already had a life sentence, and was
convinced he had nothing to lose.

Mahanoy's staff took no chances with Cramer. Extra reinforcements were
brought in whenever he was taken from his RHU cell. Instead of two officers
(as is typical), four officers, a lieutenant, and a videographer were dispatched.

One day Cramer was taken outside to the "dog run" while officers
searched his cell for contraband. I went outside to talk with him. The dog
run sat about fifteen feet from the RHU unit, and as soon as I stepped
outside, I saw that Cramer wore only boxers. His orange jumpsuit was torn
in shreds and strewn about his cage. Some of it lay outside the chain-link

enclosure. He worked a larger piece through his hands, tugging and pulling it vigorously.

I called his name. He nodded and returned his attention to the orange fabric in his hand. "I'm gonna hang up today."

Was he serious, or was this just a game for his own amusement? One could never tell with Cramer.

"I don't think that's a good idea," I said.

He gave no response except to busy himself with wrapping the strip around his neck. He tied a knot and tugged on it to test its strength.

My heart hammered in my ears. "Let's talk about this. There's got to be another way."

"There's not," he said in a flat tone. He stretched on his tiptoes and attempted to thread the other end of the strip through the chain link fence.

"Hey, man, do you remember what we talked about before? God values your life and He has a plan for you. Taking your life isn't going to fix anything. God has good things in mind for you."

Cramer successfully looped the strip onto the fence and tied a knot. "Nah. I'm done. I'm gonna hang." He tugged the rope. It came undone. He tried again. Once more, the knot slipped. Was he faking it?

I kept talking and Cramer continued working with that orange strip of fabric in his hands, answering only in monosyllables and grunts.

Time seemed to stand still until finally officers emerged from the building. What a relief! Not wanting to witness the outcome, I hurried back inside and was chatting with another RHU inmate when the mass of officers came back inside. They carried Cramer among themselves.

For the duration of his two-year stay at Mahanoy, he continued making vicious threats against staff. In 2015, a jury found him guilty of the attempted homicide at Coal Township.

Less than forty-eight hours after the verdict, Cramer complained of severe chest pains. Medical staff went by his cell to check him, and the situation seemed to warrant taking him to the infirmary for tests. Obviously, he could not lie on an examination table while handcuffed behind his back, as was standard procedure. He would have to be cuffed in front.

Everyone was on high alert and took extra precautions. A huddle of officers and the videographer gathered to begin readying him to leave his cell. Handcuffs were fastened and his door opened. Officers moved in.

The violent movement happened in a flash. An officer staggered and dropped to the floor. Blood spurted from his arm and neck.

Seeing is believing, they say. Yet when I watched the video of the attack, I found it difficult to comprehend. Apparently, Cramer obtained the razor while at the county jail during his trial, swallowed it to smuggle it into Mahanoy, and passed it in his cell's bathroom. Then, faking a medical emergency, he deftly concealed the razor and utilized it with stunning speed and accuracy. His calculating scheme was absolutely bone-chilling. A trauma surgeon would later testify that the guard's wounds were just a few millimeters short of fatal.[28]

Within hours of the brutal attack, Cramer was shipped out of Mahanoy. He carried out a string of assaults on staff at other institutions, including a nurse at SCI Forest and a guard at SCI Somerset. State officials described him as "the most dangerous person in the Pennsylvania Department of Corrections."[29]

At the time, when I worked in the craziness every day, I counted it as all in a day's work. But it was starting to take its toll on me.

> **Inmates like William Cramer really tested Nelson's conviction that all people have value and are to be loved. There's a temptation to view such a person as being hopelessly incorrigible and beyond redemption. Yet the truth is that God's grace reaches even to the most depraved.**

---

[28] Haley Bianco, April 3, 2018, "Inmate Attacks Corrections Officer, Found Guilty in Schuylkill County," https://www.pahomepage.com/news/inmate-attacks-corrections-officer-found-guilty-in-Schuylkill-county/

[29] Patrick Buchnowski and Mark Pesto, *The Tribune-Democrat*, November 14, 2018, "Most Dangerous Person in the DOC': Prosecutors Want Extra Restraints on Razor Attack Suspect," https://www.tribdem.com/news/most-dangerous-person-in-the-doc-prosecutors-want-extra-restraints/article_6e979baa-e796-11e8-8f65-3bdf3b7c46cf.html

CHAPTER THIRTY

Changes, Changes

When Chaplain Whalen retired in 2008, I was in my fifteenth year of employment at the institution. Chaplain Menei, head over all state chaplains, had retired a few years earlier. Although we were on different pages doctrinally, both men were my allies in many ways. Neither stood in the way of my ministry at SCI Mahanoy.

Whalen's replacement was a female ordained minister in the Metropolitan Community Church, a denomination known for championing human rights issues, including gender and sexual orientation. She wore her liberal philosophies proudly but didn't interfere with the Protestant programs already in place at the prison. Her time at Mahanoy was relatively short—only two and a half years. After her departure the prison's Inmate Program Manager filled the role of FCPD for six months, until Chaplain C, a Russian Orthodox priest, was hired in December 2011. He also allowed me to continue as before. His biggest concern seemed to be filling time for a few years so he could get health insurance to see him to retirement age.

Early in 2010, Kevin Dobbs obtained a contract through Jubilee Ministries for twenty hours a week at Mahanoy. Like John Ritchey and Guy Giordano, Dobbs was a capable man of God. Giordano and Dobbs worked together at Mahanoy for four years, and both took on a Sunday service each month, giving me two quiet Sunday afternoons and evenings at home. How I relished those times of rest!

Joel and Anita gave us our first grandchild, Ariana Rose, in April 2008. The next summer, on June 27, 2009, we gained our first son-in-law, Kenton Bucher, whom Emily met through a home-school group. Their first wedding anniversary was already approaching when we drove them to the Newark airport to catch a flight to China, where they would visit Kenton's brother and his family.

"Take my cell phone, Mom," Emily said. "It will make meeting up on our return flight a little easier."

I smiled. Neither Nelson nor I had yet capitulated to buying cell phones. We're non-techy and a phone seemed like a bother. Nevertheless, I grabbed it up on a whim a week later when Nelson and I traveled to Asheville, North Carolina, with Guy and Barb Giordano to attend an Aurora Ministries conference. We were excited to introduce them to the ministry that had blessed us with support and resources for prison chaplaincy.

Not yet halfway into our trip, Emily's phone rang. It was my sister-in-law, with news that my father had suffered a major heart attack that morning. Guy offered to turn back, but I hated to abort our conference plans. Nor did I yet have enough information; Dad was still undergoing tests, but he made it clear—he would not stay at the hospital. He had made that decision while quietly suffering through severe chest pains in prior weeks. Undoubtedly, my mother's illness and her diminished quality of life through prolonged months of medical treatment factored into his choice.

When we arrived at the conference center, Nelson and I stashed our suitcases in a corner and waited for more news from home. It was late afternoon when my youngest brother, Jim, called. He doesn't get worked up quickly, but now his voice trembled with raw emotion. "I'm taking Dad home soon and I'll let you know when I get him settled. You can call then and tell him goodbye."

Tell my father goodbye over the phone?

Nelson and I made the quick decision to grab a rental car and head right home. We drove until midnight, snatched a few hours of restless sleep, and pushed on, hoping and praying to make it home in time. When we arrived the next afternoon, Dad looked terribly pale and weak. As it turned out, he faded slowly for two agonizing months until death mercifully claimed him on August 9, 2010.

In Nelson's family there were also major health concerns. About a year earlier, his younger sister, Elaine, was diagnosed with cancer while pregnant with her eighth child. She delivered a healthy dark-eyed baby girl, but Elaine's health was compromised.

Then Nelson's mother suffered a mini stroke. She escaped lasting significant damage, but increasingly, she and Dad Zeiset showed signs of aging.

In June 2011, Elaine passed away at forty-four years old, leaving her stricken husband, Bryan High, and a large family.

And then another change came. The Green Terrace Church leadership team had been in transition since Leon Stauffer's death, and was in frequent conversation with our bishop about long-term solutions. Prior to this, Nelson had declined suggestions that he take on the lead pastor role, but now he began reconsidering. "I'm starting to feel tired at the prison," he told me. "I'm not burned out yet but I can see the day coming, and I want to retire before that happens."

Maybe, we thought, the time was coming for him to assume more responsibility at church.

It was not to be. We were blindsided by our bishop's suggestion that Nelson step off the team, and mystified by the lack of explanation. In 2012, after twelve years of pastoring at the congregation, Nelson resigned and we moved on.

In 2013, the state's prison population across twenty-six facilities stood at 51,512. Mahanoy's census peaked that year, at just over 2,500 men.[30] The prison church had been growing steadily since the institution opened

---

[30] Pennsylvania Department of Corrections, *2013 Annual Statistical Report*, p. 14, https://www.cor.pa.gov/About%20Us/Statistics/Documents/Reports/2013%20Annual%20Statistical%20Report.pdf

twenty years earlier. Chaplain Giordano taught classes to new converts in preparation of baptism.

My reserved Mennonite friends might have been surprised at the celebratory mood at baptismal services. The prison audience clapped and cheered for those who shared their testimonies. Shouts of "Amen!" and "Praise God!" rang out repeatedly. As men stepped into the baptistry, inmates in the congregation stood and stretched on tiptoes, intent on watching every detail in a public declaration of faith in Jesus Christ.

Richard's newfound joy in his Savior was obvious in the request slip he sent me the week after his baptism. "I left alot [sic] behind in that water," he wrote, "and I hope this place has a good filtration unit because I don't want my sins, pains, and old worrys [sic] to come back through these pipes and polute [sic] any of our Christian brothers."

I loved his expression of wonder at God's grace and of his relief at sins forgiven. That, by far, trumped all his misspellings!

By 2013, we had five grandchildren, born within five years. Joel and Anita had three children; Kenton and Emily had two. It was a good start toward Nelson's order for eighteen grandchildren. Our children laughed him off, however, and said they weren't making any promises.

On November 16, 2013, Renee married Andrew Stauffer, and just like that, we became empty nesters.

By then, Nelson had been in prison ministry for almost thirty years and began exploring possibilities for the next decades. His love of teaching motivated him to lead several workshops on the nuts and bolts of prison ministry. He also taught a few non-accredited Bible classes at Lancaster Bible College.

We settled at Indiantown Mennonite Church, near Ephrata, and soon found ourselves teaching Sunday School and leading Bible Study groups for young adults and mentoring them. Nelson occasionally preached.

If I'd entertained thoughts of slowing down, those notions flew

out the window. "God," I often prayed, "if You insist on bringing
people to us, You need to give energy and wisdom!"

We'd felt displaced and unsettled since 2012, as though we were
on a detour and without a clue as to where God was taking us, or
why. We wouldn't have chosen this detour.

In 2014, Chaplain Giordano left Mahanoy to fill a chaplaincy contract at SCI Retreat. After thirteen years at Mahanoy, I was sad to see him leave, but without doubt, the men at Retreat would be blessed by his ministry. Shortly after Guy's departure, Kevin Dobbs was granted full-time hours. He took on three Sunday services each month, and finally I reduced my Sunday work to only once a month.

I couldn't quite put my finger on the problem of why Sunday services weighed me down. I enjoyed preaching and found refreshment in the fellowship at Mahanoy. But the long drive, especially in the winter months . . . the need to hurry from my church service, often even before it dismissed . . . the lack of downtime . . . the stress of needing to police the services . . . it was taking its toll on me. More and more, I felt that my time at Mahanoy was drawing to a close. But what would I do then? I was only in my mid-fifties.

In April 2016, an item for discussion at Indiantown's congregational meeting concerned the hiring of a pastor. At the time, the church had three bivocational pastors and two deacons to serve a congregation of about 130. Something stirred within me. But no, it didn't seem possible that God would call me to ministry at Indiantown, not with five men already on the leadership team.

In late summer of 2016, amid preparations for a public auc-
tion of Nelson's parents' house and their move to a retirement home,
nominations were taken at our church for the hiring of a full-time
pastor. We'd been down this road before—this soul-searching, heart-
thumping process of coming to terms with God's leading.

On a Sunday morning in August, the results of the nominations
were announced. Assistant pastor Lee Zimmerman and Nelson both

received the three required votes. A discernment process would get underway soon. "Pray for Lee and Lisa and for Nelson and Esther as we seek God's leading," the pastor urged the congregation.

I heard a stirring on the pew behind us, and then a little boy's loud whisper, "Daddy, who is Esther?"

I couldn't help grinning. For years I'd been telling Nelson, "I'm just in this for the ride, wherever you take me." He was the public figure, the outgoing one who hunkered down with the kids at church and talked with them about loose teeth and lost kittens. Me? I was content to remain in the background.

"Nuh, uh," he'd protest. "I couldn't possibly do what I do if it weren't for your support."

It was a high compliment, and I appreciated it.

No sooner was the announcement made that Sunday morning, and Nelson took a nervous glance at his watch. It was 11:12. In three minutes we would have to make a hasty exit so that Nelson could get to the prison in time for the afternoon service. Our congregation had come to know the reason for our routine of slipping out early. It was a bit awkward, however, to have to do so on that morning.

The timing seemed a bit unfortunate on another level. Our long-anticipated three-week trip to Utah and Colorado would hold up the discernment process that involved a series of meetings with the leadership team, congregational oversight leaders, and ourselves. However, the time away gave Nelson and me lots of time to talk and pray about our future.

By 2015, transgenderism began making inroads into prisons, just as it did across the face of America. Pennsylvania state prisons held about 150 transgender inmates that year, and the state implemented policy updates to comply with federal regulations. Prior to that, tax money was not used for inmate sex-reassignment hormone therapies and surgeries. Biological male prisoners were housed with biological males, and biological females with their counterparts. Now that was all being upended. Prison commissaries in male institutions were mandated to stock items like makeup, barrettes, and female underwear.[31]

Soon after the changes were implemented, a transgender inmate put in a request slip to see me. Kelly showed up in my office with a heavy application of eyeliner and red lipstick. His dark hair was curled at the ends. He settled into an office chair and blurted, "Chaplain, I'm really confused. I don't know if I'm male or female."

"Let's talk about it," I said, and thus began a forty-five-minute discussion.

Every two weeks or so, Kelly came back again, and we talked more about God's design for men and His specific purpose in creating Kelly as a biological male. He engaged in thoughtful discussion, and in time, his makeup and feminine mannerisms became less noticeable. And then he was paroled. I could only pray that he would come to embrace the truth about himself and experience the regeneration of heart and mind through Jesus.

In the fall of 2016, transgender issues dominated discussion at the state chaplain's conference. A top official stated in no uncertain terms that if we chaplains were unable to embrace the new policies, perhaps we were in the wrong profession.

I sucked in my breath when Nelson told me of the conference discussion. "It's time you get out of there," I said, and immediately regretted my cowardice. We'd often talked of courageous people like Baronelle Stutzman, the Washington florist, and Jack Phillips, the Colorado baker, whose stand for righteousness above political correctness took them before the U.S. Supreme Court. They were willing to risk their careers, their reputations, and every dollar they owned.

And, to my shame, I worried about Nelson's retirement fund.

---

[31] Samantha Malamed, *The Philadelphia Inquirer,* September 23, "PA Prisons Overhaul Policies for Transgender Inmates," https://www.inquirer.com/philly/living/20150923_Pa__prisons_overhaul_policies_for_transgender_inmates.html

In November, Indiantown's leadership team offered me the role at church, with an eye toward starting in late winter. After a unanimous January affirmation vote from the congregation, I turned in my resignation letter at the prison. I'd informed my supervisor of the possibility in previous weeks, but it caught many of the inmates by surprise.

"What? You're leaving us?" Tony asked. "I . . . I don't know what to say, Chaplain. I mean, I've known you since my days at Camp Hill, back when you had a shag on your head!"

All those years ago, he'd been imprisoned on a burglary charge. Tony was a happy-go-lucky kind of guy, unconcerned about his future, and just wanting to have a good time. After his release from Camp Hill, I lost touch with him for a few years, and then he arrived at Mahanoy to serve a life sentence for murder. At some point, I led Tony to Christ, baptized him, and watched him launch on a spiritual journey marked by irrepressible joy and easy laughter.

But Tony wasn't laughing now. His shoulders slumped and he hung his head. "Man, Chaplain, this hits hard."

Later that day he slipped me a scrap of paper that read, "Pastor Z, I went back and did some thinking plus prayed and I hope you stay here because so many will miss you. Your brother, Tony."

I swallowed at a lump caught in my throat.

Nelson's ministry at Mahanoy prison was coming to an end, and although we both felt God leading that way, there was a certain sadness to it. "Some of those guys might take it hard," I said.

"Why's that?" he asked.

"You're not just their chaplain. You're like a brother to them. Or the father they never had."

"You think so?"

"Don't underestimate the impact you've had on a lot of lives," I said. "It was hard on them when Chaplain Giordano left and now you're leaving, too. And there they sit in prison. No doubt, they feel abandoned."

The Men of Faith team told me to mark my calendar for January 26. "We're throwing a farewell service for you," they said. "This is the one time we can plan a service and you aren't gonna tell us who or how or what. Just be here. Your wife and kids, too."

"Hey now—"

"No worries!" one of the men laughed. "We're working with Chaplain Dobbs on this so he'll keep us in line. But just so you know, Chap, we're gonna roast you, real good."

The date worked for my entire family, minus our eight grandchildren, of course, but Esther, Joel and Anita, Kenton and Emily, and Andrew and Renee all met me at the prison that evening. The officer at the front desk called to notify me of their arrival, and while they made their way through the metal detector, I walked the length of the prison compound to greet them and escort them to the chapel, as I had done with all guests throughout the years.

To my surprise, Del Burkholder, Delmar Weaver, and Adam Hurst, three of the regular Monday night Bible study volunteers, stood among them. Guy Giordano also showed up. And then the inmates began arriving, about 130 men, to join in a service that alternated between somber reminiscing and good-humored jabs.

The choir hijacked the hymn, "There's Not a Friend Like the Lowly Jesus," to poke fun at me. They meant no disrespect to either the songwriter nor to me. Their lyrics covered all the inside jokes we'd shared over the years and the men sang with gusto.

There's not a pastor like Chaplain Zeiset,
No, not one, no, not one.
None else could preach while hardly moving,
No, not one, no, not one.
Zeiset knows all about your spinnin',
He will expose you while still grinnin';
There's not a buggy he's not driven,
No, not one, no, not one.

Laughter rang out across the chapel. The choir faltered a bit beneath their merriment but regained their composure. No doubt, the men intended to roast me, and roast me good. I was enjoying the song's lyrics as much as they were.

No Mennonite can eat like he does,
No, not one, no, not one.
And poor Esther will get no days off,
No, not one, no, not one.
Zeiset knows all about your cussin',
He doesn't want to hear you fussin';
There's none like him who exposed your lustin',
No, not one, no, not one.

There's not a Sunday song that we dare miss,
No, not one, no, not one.
No dusty hymn is off his song list,
No, not one, no, not one.
Zeiset knows all about your tickets,
He will preach on your evil tablets;
There's none of you who will ever fool him,
No, not one, no, not one.

The audience erupted with applause. When the laughter died down, the men moved into a more somber segment in which they expressed their appreciation for my ministry among them. Many of the guests and the five Men of Faith spoke such kind words about me that I hardly recognized myself.

Tony recounted that I'd led him to faith and mentored him like a big brother.

Jim thanked me for shaping his weakness into strength.

Harry blessed me to continue touching lives at my church as I had in the prison.

"Chaplain treated us, not as inmates," Lou said, "but as God's precious creation."

Gary, a clerk who worked outside my office door, recalled how he sometimes overheard my conversations with other inmates. "It wasn't pretty stuff that Chaplain gave ear to," he said, "but then I'd see him give the guys hugs and I'd think . . ." Gary's voice grew husky. He paused and swallowed. "I'd think, 'I wanna be like that.'" He dropped his head, unable to continue.

I heard sniffles among the congregation. An inmate in the front row swiped his palm across his face.

"C'mon now," someone in the audience called out. It was a common phrase voiced during services and meant as encouragement to the speaker.

Gary straightened and rubbed his eyes. A weak smile surfaced. "Man! How 'bout that Cowboys game the other night? Real sad, wasn't it?"

Laughter broke out at Gary's attempt to cover his emotions with humor.

Our family was invited to say a few words. Joel went to the podium, and murmured approval followed him. No doubt, many of the men remembered a Sunday when Nelson had invited our son to preach the sermon. Knowing the inmates' pleasure in lovingly grinding up his father, Joel had draped his arm around Nelson's shoulder. "A lot of people say I'm just like my father." He eyed Nelson, half a head shorter, and made exaggerated hand movements to measure their height difference. "But I ask you, do I look like my dad?"

Chuckles floated around the chapel.

Encouraged by their response, Joel rubbed Nelson's head. "There's not much hair on that head. But look at mine. Really, do you think we look alike?"

Outright laughter. "Yeah, c'mon," and "Uh huh," rang out.

"And this," Joel said, pointing to his father's stomach. Nelson obliged by pushing it out over his belt and Joel exaggeratedly sucked in his own abdomen. "Do you still think I look just like my dad?"

The men clapped and cheered. And at the end of the service they said, "Joel, you preach just like your dad!"

Now, as Joel stood before these men for the final time, he took on a more subdued tone. "As a young kid, I didn't realize how unusual it was to have my dad work in prison," he said. Their stories and experiences, he told the men, had contributed to our family life in remarkably unique ways.

Renee reflected on nearly a decade of participation in prison Christmas services, and I left them with a blessing from 1 Corinthians 15:58: "Therefore, my beloved brothers, be steadfast, immovable, always abounding in the work of the Lord, knowing that in the Lord your labor is not in vain."

It was March 2, 2017, the day that I had anticipated for quite some time. After twenty-three years, I would leave SCI Mahanoy and the many staff and inmates with whom I had interacted. My oft-repeated prayer in past years was that God would enable me to finish well; that I would neither overstay and burn out, nor that I would leave before my work at the institution was done.

At the end of my workday, I locked my chapel office for the last time, turned in my keys, said my last goodbyes, and drove away. The onslaught of conflicting emotions that I had braced for never came. In their place came the realization that, although I loved my job through to the very end, I had not one inclination to stay. God had called me to prison ministry and now He was calling me away.

Such sweet peace!

EPILOGUE

On March 5, 2017—thirty-two years and one day after starting with Jubilee Ministries, I took on the pastoral role at Indiantown Mennonite Church. Back in 1985, at the outset of my prison ministry at Camp Hill, I was intrigued with a play on words. It was March fourth, and I determined that, with God's grace, I would march forth wherever He would lead.

I don't think I ever anticipated that the march would go on for thirty-three years. I was twenty-one years old when I entered Fountain Prison in Atmore, Alabama, and had advanced to only a mere twenty-three and a half years when hired by Jubilee. I could not have comprehended the thought of a career stretching longer than my then-known years.

The march grew wearisome at times, particularly at those times when I caved in to discouragement and impatience. At those times, God carried me on the march, strengthened me to continue, and if that weren't enough, He gave me much joy along the way!

Now, more than three decades later, a new phase of life loomed before me. I had every confidence that my Lord would again catch me when I stumbled, strengthen me when I grew weary, and carry me when I could not walk. He has proven, over and over, to be just that kind of a faithful God!

Several months into pastoring, a friend remarked that my new role must seem stressful. I wanted to laugh because, although pastoring a congregation has its challenges, my stress load had been reduced after leaving the prison. None of my parishioners had yet cussed me out, I had not yet needed to kick anyone out of a church service, and not one single person had yet threatened to kill me!

One of my disappointments since leaving the prison is the fact that I am not permitted contact with inmates. I had hoped to keep in touch with my Christian brothers behind bars through letters, and for a short time I did so—until I got a letter of reprimand from prison officials. Security staff get nervous about such contact. As they see it, I potentially have information about the inside workings of the prison that could pose a security risk.

So the letter-writing ceased, and I feel badly about that. I can only entrust my inmate friends to a loving Father who began a good work in them, and it is He who will bring it to completion (Phil. 1:6). Our family has been blessed abundantly by the faithful prayers of my friends behind bars.

To date, Esther and I have eleven grandchildren, and our three adult children and their spouses are walking with Jesus. We are blessed beyond measure!

APPENDIX

GLOSSARY OF TERMS

Browns – an inmate's brown colored state-issued shirt and pants

Cell restriction – disciplinary measure that confines an inmate to his cell except for meals in the cafeteria. Restriction is for thirty days or less.

Cellie – cellmate

Count (or count times) – a census of all inmates, taken periodically throughout a day

CPE (Clinical Pastoral Education)

DOC (Department of Corrections)

Dog run – a grouping of small outdoor enclosures surrounded by chain-link fencing in which RHU inmates are taken for "exercise." Only one man is placed in each enclosure.

FCPD (Facility Chaplaincy Program Director) – the title given to a supervising chaplain at a prison

LCP (Lebanon County Prison)

Lifer – an inmate serving a life sentence

Max out – to serve out a prison sentence in its entirety, to the last day of the maximum sentence

Minimum/Maximum Sentence – the range of a prison sentence (e.g., seven to twenty years). The exact length of time served is dependent on various factors, including the nature of the crime, behavior while imprisoned, and compliance with programming.

RHU (Restricted Housing Unit) – a unit within a prison where inmates are held, usually for behavioral reasons and for a specified time (generally for a minimum of thirty days, but up to several years). Prisoners leave their cells only for an hour-long time of exercise five days and for showers twice a week; also known as The Hole.

SCI (State Correctional Institution)

Shank – a homemade knife used for protection in prison

The Hole – see RHU

VS (Voluntary Service) – missions programs established by the Mennonite
    church

Yard – the outdoor exercise/recreational area on prison grounds

RANK OF PRISON OFFICERS (PENNSYLVANIA)

Superintendent

Deputy Superintendent

Major of the Guards

Captain (Shift Commander)

Lieutenant

Sergeant

Officer

Characteristics
of a Criminal Mind

In thirty-three years of prison ministry, I heard dark stories from hundreds of prisoners from a spectrum of ages, ethnicities, and social backgrounds. Many shared common deeply-entrenched thought patterns that contributed to their criminality.

No doubt about it, all of mankind is sinful. A criminal mind, however, thinks in the extreme. For example, a conscientious person feels guilty when he tells a lie, but the criminal mind views lying as a huge score and takes great pride in his deceit.

I offer the following lists as generalities and a sobering reminder for each of us to purge our minds of tendencies toward sinful and selfish thinking that may ultimately lead us further into Satan's territory than we ever intend to go.

COMMON PERSONALITY TRAITS:

Rationalization. He offers excuses for his behavior and shifts blame onto others.

Minimization. He downplays the severity of his crimes.

Denial of Responsibility. Feels no responsibility for his crimes or to provide for himself.

HOW A CRIMINAL VIEWS HIMSELF:

He is infinitely superior to others.

He is a decent person at heart (in spite of what his rap sheet says).

If he has any faults, they are compensated for with his good deeds.

He is an exemption to all the rules.

He had good reason to commit any and all of his crimes.

Whatever it takes, he will always come out on top of the pile.

He is a victim; fails to comprehend that he victimized others.

He is a failure only if he gets caught for his crimes.

He has a need to maintain fearlessness; gets a thrill from high-risk situations.

HOW A CRIMINAL VIEWS RELATIONSHIPS:

He controls through anger; it establishes his place in the world.

He demands respect, yet seems indifferent to the rights and feelings of others.

He concedes to having hurt someone only if blood was drawn.

He is a ruthless critic of others but rarely applies those criticisms to himself. He builds himself up by tearing others down.

He takes but rarely gives; demands that his needs and wishes are tended to first. Only then will he attend to others—if he feels like it, and in his own time.

He reacts against advice and accountability.

He values others only to the extent that they play his game.

His desire for conquest is never satisfied.

WHAT A CRIMINAL THINKS OF THE WORLD AROUND HIM:

The world is a chessboard and he is king. All others are pawns and easily disposed of.

What is his is his, but what is yours is, of course, his also.

He is threatened by anyone whom he cannot control.

HOW A CRIMINAL PRESENTS HIMSELF:

He is almost always angry, yet thinks he hides it well.

He has little interest in improving himself but is more intent on conquest and remaking his world to be as he wants it to be.

He wishes to reach the summit of achievement without taking the necessary steps to get there.

Secrecy is its own achievement. He takes great pride in being slick.

Getting into trouble is a boost to his self-image.

He sets his own standards of acceptability.

Trust, love, loyalty, and teamwork are incompatible with his lifestyle.

He has no regard for the law—until he is locked up. Then he fights tooth and nail for all that is due him.

HOW A CRIMINAL VIEWS RESPONSIBILITY:

His own convenience and pleasure trump obligation and responsibility.

He scorns others' pursuit of responsibility and deems them too stupid to have found an easy way around it.

He defines responsibility as being a big wheel and acquiring fame and fortune in any illegitimate way possible.

He views his status and authority as being far more important than the quality of work he does.

HOW A CRIMINAL VIEWS GOD:

He blames God when life goes sour and rants that He should have done better.

He bargains with God when he gets caught.

What Does It Take
to Be a Prison Chaplain?

1. A clear call from God. Prison ministry is tough work and the burnout rate is high. There is no glamor in mingling with a prison full of inmates who have committed every crime in the books, and there are not nearly enough success stories to keep you going in the work. But if God has called, be assured He will equip you to proclaim a message of hope and redemption through Jesus Christ.

2. A test of the call. Contact Bible-based prison ministries in your area and see where you can fit in as a volunteer. Give it time; a call from God does not fade with time.

3. Teachability. Prisons are a culture to themselves so listen to the advice of seasoned prison ministry workers and prison staff. They have tips that can make your entry smoother.

4. Thick skin. Inmates will size you up from the minute you step behind bars. Certainly, there are prisoners who are hungry for the Gospel and eager for spiritual nurture, but there are more who will delight in picking you apart. It might be something as insignificant as criticizing your clothing, or as devastating as framing you for criminal charges. Remember, inmates are not locked up for singing too loud in Sunday School.

5. Ability to say no. Some inmates are masters of manipulation and will play you for everything they can get. They may work on your sympathies. For example, they may complain about a lack of personal hygiene items. I've rarely seen the legitimacy of such gripes. If inmates learn to be frugal, the distribution of toilet tissue and shampoo will likely last until the next restock. More significantly, they may attempt to draw you in on their legal case. Listening to their pain is an important aspect of ministry but you are there for their spiritual needs, not their legal action.

6. Faithfulness. God does not need your success stories. He only expects faithfulness in the task He has given. So plant and water the seed of the Word, but trust God for the increase.

Dos and Don'ts
of Prison Ministry

1. Do respect prison administration and their rules. Administration will not tolerate anything other than strict adherence to the rules in place. Obey them even if it doesn't make sense to you.

2. Do relinquish your desire to be the Holy Spirit to inmates. You can teach and preach and counsel righteousness, but you can't hammer it into his heart and mind. Only the Spirit can bring conviction and transformation through Jesus.

3. Do protect your mind and spirit through regular study in the Word. Prison workers are subjected to unbelievable stories of abuse and violence and are utterly dependent upon the Scripture's cleansing power.

4. Do pray, pray, pray. Seek God for wisdom and discernment to cut through to heart issues. For energy. For compassion, grace, and love. To view the unlovable through the eyes of Jesus.

5. Do not write to an inmate of the opposite sex. This is simply a common-sense protective measure. If a male inmate refuses a male pen pal and insists he needs a woman's perspective, you can be pretty sure he is up to no good.

6. Do not give an inmate money. Never, ever, ever give cash to an inmate. Cash is contraband in prison.